THE CHANGING AMERICAN ECONOMY

THE CHANGING AMERICAN ECONOMY

Edited by *JOHN R. COLEMAN*

BASIC BOOKS, INC., PUBLISHERS

New York *London*

Library of Congress Catalog Card Number: 67–15951
Manufactured in the United States of America

The Authors

Morris A. Adelman, Professor of Economics at the Massachusetts Institute of Technology, is a specialist in the economics of market structures.

G. L. Bach, formerly Professor of Economics and first Dean of the Graduate School of Industrial Administration at Carnegie Institute of Technology, is currently on the faculty at Stanford University and a key spokesman in the field of economic education.

Gary S. Becker is on the staff of the National Bureau of Economic Research and is a Professor of Economics at Columbia University.

Adolf A. Berle, a New York lawyer who has had prominent careers in domestic and international affairs, has been a student of corporate behavior for more than three decades.

Wilbur J. Cohen, a long-time contributor to thinking on economic security, is currently Under Secretary of Health, Education and Welfare in Washington, D.C.

John R. Coleman, former Professor of Economics and Dean of Humanities and Social Sciences at the Carnegie Institute of Technology, is currently on the staff of the Ford Foundation in New York.

Myron L. Joseph is Professor of Economics and Chairman of the Department of Industrial Management at Carnegie Institute of Technology.

Charles P. Kindleberger, Professor of Economics at the Massachusetts Institute of Technology, is a specialist in international economic issues.

Richard A. Lester is Professor of Economics at Princeton University and a past Director of that university's Industrial Relations Section, a pioneer research organization in the human resources field.

BEN W. LEWIS is Professor of Economics at Oberlin College and a long-time leader in American economic education.

MAX F. MILLIKAN is Professor of Economics at Massachusetts Institute of Technology. He has been Director of the Center for International Studies there since that center was set up as a major American intellectual resource for studying the United States in a turbulent world.

JAMES N. MORGAN is Professor of Economics at the University of Michigan and a member of that university's interdisciplinary staff engaged in applying survey research techniques to the study of consumer and voter behavior.

EDMUND S. PHELPS is Professor of Economics at the University of Pennsylvania.

VERNON W. RUTTAN is Professor and Chairman of the Department of Agricultural Economics at the University of Minnesota.

LEONARD S. SILK is economics editor for *Business Week* magazine.

GERALD G. SOMERS, Professor of Economics at the University of Wisconsin, was one of the earliest of the new entrants into the field of economic inquiry and action on problems of poverty in the midst of affluence.

JAMES TOBIN is Sterling Professor of Economics at Yale University. He was a member of President Kennedy's Council of Economic Advisers 1961–1962.

LLOYD ULMAN is Professor of Economics and Director of the Institute of Industrial Relations at the Berkeley campus of the University of California.

MURRAY L. WEIDENBAUM, Associate Professor and Chairman of the Department of Economics at Washington University in St. Louis, has written extensively on the subject of the economics of disarmament.

HAROLD F. WILLIAMSON, an economic historian on the faculty of Northwestern University, is Secretary-Treasurer of The American Economic Association.

Preface

When men have realized that time has upset many fighting faiths, they may come to believe even more than they believe the very foundations of their own conduct that the ultimate good desired is better reached by free trade in ideas—that the best test of truth is the power of the thought to get itself accepted in the competition of the market, and that truth is the only ground upon which their wishes safely can be carried out. That at any rate is the theme of our Constitution. It is an experiment, as all life is an experiment.

—Oliver Wendell Holmes, Jr. (1919)

This book of essays deals with another of the Americans' experiments, their economy. The theme of each essay is change in the ways that Americans are doing business with one another, privately and collectively. Those who look here for pleas to return to an older, perhaps simpler, day will be disappointed. But those who look for blueprints for an entirely new America, embarked upon fundamentally different paths from those we now know, will be equally disappointed. For these are not lectures on why America is going to the dogs or how it is going to the stars. They are attempts by twenty economists, linking the past and present with what they believe to be the future, to say what is interesting about their fields today.

I make no claim that these economists are "representative" of the profession today. That would be presumptuous. I claim only that I asked lively and responsible men to write about the changes with which they were familiar. Most of the writers are academic economists—from the great universities of the Midwest and Far West, from the Ivy League, from the institutes of science and technology, and from private institutions in mid-America. A few are from other fields—government, private research, private practice, and publishing. They have one thing, other than their professional qualifications, in common: they tackled their assignments with gusto. For that, an editor can only be grateful.

PREFACE

The major portion of the royalties from this book go to the American Economic Association, with an expectation that its leadership in economic education will continue to bear fruit.

Beyond my debt to the contributors to this volume lie my obligations to Theodore A. Wertime and Joy MacFadyen of the United States Information Agency for counsel, trust, and patience, and to my secretaries, Anne Ramey and Rose Marie Rosso, for orderliness and good humor when I needed them both.

JOHN R. COLEMAN

New York
September 1966

Contents

CONTENTS

THE CHANGING AMERICAN ECONOMY

1 AN ECONOMY IN FLUX

John R. Coleman

The stage is set for the essays which follow in a series of questions on the American economy in the 1960's. To understand why these questions present problems in a wealthy land, it is important to see the American economy in pursuit of multiple goals, with some possible conflicts among those goals. Hence there is discussion here of what we are trying to accomplish and of why we cannot have everything.

Maybe Edmund Burke was right. He felt that "the age of chivalry is gone; that of sophisters, economists, and calculators has succeeded." Certainly economic forces play an ever bigger role in an American society that becomes more complex and more impatient each year. And the economist, in turn, plays a more central role in outlining the nature of the choices open to his countrymen.

The story of the American economy in the 1960's is a story of achievement and of unfinished business too. It is a story of a past that contained successes and excesses alike, of a present marked by both progress and problems, and of a future that will bring its own blend of challenge and change.

At the core of all study of economics there is one key problem: scarce resources in relation to the demands made upon them. Strip away all the frills and the increasingly elaborate structures of analysis in economic thought, and this problem stands in sharp outline. There is simply never enough to go around. Thus choices have to be made. And economics is little more than the study of man's choices under changing sets of conditions.

This definition of economics will be familiar enough to economists everywhere. But it will strike the layman as strange when applied to the United States of America. How can one speak of scarce resources when talking of the wealthiest society the world has yet seen? The answer is that American resources are scarce relative to American expectations of what is desirable here and now. Wealthy beyond the dreams of most other men on earth, the American still sees himself with unfulfilled desires, and hence with the necessity of choices. He might like to see a fellow countryman be first on the moon; but by now he should know that the price of putting massive resources into that contest will be a little less progress made on other things which he also wants—a better highway system, more beautiful cities, or more understanding of the mysteries on the ocean's floor.

No one feature of the American economy is more important than that most decisions are made in highly decentralized ways. In contrast with some of the tightly planned and autocratic societies, present and past, and with those societies where forces of tradition dictate what choices will be made, the American society makes millions of its citizens into "economists" who decide by their own actions what goods and services shall be produced, how they shall be produced, and for whom they shall be produced. True, some economic decisions are highly centralized (e.g., how much to spend on the race to the moon), but even those decisions involve large numbers of decision-makers (the United States Congress, for example). For the rest, the individual and the family are left largely alone to make decisions as best they can. The key assumption in this process is that the best judge of what is best for any one American is that American himself. His behavior in marketplaces, i.e., in buying or selling this rather than buying or selling that, reflects his personal preferences. He votes those preferences for himself and then accepts the consequences of his actions.

But giving men a substantial role in making the economic decisions affecting their lives carries no guarantee that their decisions will be wise for themselves or for the society as a whole. Today's concern of many Americans for more widespread economic understanding is a response to the fact that the choices ahead demand more wisdom than we have yet shown. There are more things than ever before that may be done with America's resources. This economy is now more intertwined with all of the other economies of the world. At home and abroad alike, there are more chances to make wise choices and, equally, more chances to make mistakes.

PERSISTENT PROBLEMS IN A DYNAMIC ECONOMY

No one has yet prepared a list of priorities on which the American people might be expected to agree for the years ahead. Yet certain exciting and baffling questions keep pushing themselves to the fore in public and private discussions, as they will too in this series of essays. Just to list ten of the most persistent questions is to show some part of the mood of an economy adjusting to a world of change:

1. What patterns of competition can be sustained in those industries where new technology and new marketing arrangements seem to dictate that old patterns of many small firms making identical products and meeting in fierce day-to-day competition will no longer survive?

2. What can be done to make labor markets work more effectively (i.e., with better information, less discrimination on artificial grounds, and more mobility) in the face of rapidly changing job structures?

3. What is the public responsibility for seeing to it that technological change proceeds swiftly enough to give more progress to Americans and their friends throughout the world and yet not so swiftly that the dislocations caused by this change put too heavy burdens on some men?

4. How can the economy promote those individual incentives and rewards underlying much of the progress made in the past and still manage to provide enough security so that everyone, regardless of his contribution to the society, may have at least a minimally decent standard of living?

5. What part of the nation's resources shall be devoted to col-

lective needs shared with one another (highways, schools, parks) and what part to individual needs, where each consumer decides for himself what is important to him?

6. What policies will most effectively promote a steady, high level of employment while preserving a maximum of freedom and decentralized decision-making?

7. How can a free economy live comfortably with private price and wage decisions under conditions of employment so full as to threaten excessive spending and, hence, inflation?

8. What steps can and should this economy take to plan its adjustments to a world in which expenditures for armaments no longer loom so large?

9. What role is the United States to play, through its policies of foreign trade and foreign aid, in helping the world's underdeveloped nations achieve their own economic aspirations?

10. To what extent will this nation offer one example of how men may organize themselves for economic activity, believe deeply in the merits of that one way, and still respect the choices of other nations to pursue quite different paths?

To each of these questions, professional economists and laymen alike will offer responses that change with new conditions and with new knowledge. Some of the current responses are discussed in later chapters in this book. At the moment, all that they can do is to convey part of the flavor of current discussion and controversy in American economic circles.

IN PURSUIT OF MULTIPLE GOALS

Just as the discipline of economics takes its problems from the necessity of making choices, among competing ends, so too the fascination of the American economy—or any other economy perhaps—lies in the unending pursuit of a new and better balance among goals that are sometimes complementary and sometimes conflicting.

Well, what then are the goals of the American economy? What are the yardsticks against which we can evaluate the American's success in using his available means to fulfill his wants? Answers to those questions must be difficult to give, a characteristic shared by every interesting question in economics. Moreover, the answers must be highly subjective. But some such checklist is necessary here so that the chapters which follow can be fitted into the whole for, whereas each chapter looks at a separate part of the contemporary scene, one condition for approaching each area is that proposed courses of action must not exact too high a cost in terms of adverse impacts in other equally important areas.

What follows here then is one man's attempt to set down what he thinks the American economy is trying to accomplish in the 1960's. The point of the list is simple, even if the list itself be presumptuous: the goals are discussed to make the central point that an evaluation of any specific American policy or institution can be made only by seeing it against a backdrop, not of one or two goals, but of many. Like other economies, the American economy is pursuing multiple goals. Sometimes the most accurate answer to any such question as "Why don't the Americans do so-and-so?" is "Because they're also trying to do such-and-such at the same time."

What then does the American expect of his nation's economy? My own answer has these five points to it:

1. *A competitive, consumer-oriented economy.* The tenet which lies at the center of most economic thinking in the United States is that the consumer is king, or, more accurately, since women may make more of the consumer decisions, queen. The measure of what is good is most often the measure of how the individual fares: Does he or she have a free and wide choice in the goods to be bought, the labor markets to be entered, and the allocation of personal resources as between present and future spending?

This orientation to the individual is obviously not a complete one; there have always been and there will always be important qualifications to it. But it is pervasive enough that no one can pretend to understand this society without giving heavy weight to individualism as a guiding force. It underlies much of the emotionalism in American discussions of the proper role of governments at home and abroad. And it occasionally leads to what must strike the non-American as some strange and roundabout devices to achieve economic ends.

The consumer orientation of this economy gives a special urgency to the question of how that consumer is protected in marketplaces. Suspicious of many types of government interferences, how then is the American saved from constant exploitation by particular producers or groups of producers? The safety device on which we rely is competition. Let one producer try to exploit a consumer through high prices or low quality and the consumer will take his business elsewhere in retaliation. Thus it takes no ruler or police force to check the abuse, or so the theory goes.

But does the theory work? The fairest answer for the American economy is that it works to a very large extent, but not always. The evidence that competition usually works is widespread; it is in the large numbers of competing firms in many industries, in the turnover among such firms, in the constant improvements in technology, and in the pricing behavior of most firms. But there are trouble spots. There are places where competition either is impossible, as in such natural monopolies as telephone and water services, or is made ineffective, as in cases of collusion among sellers. Competition has not proved self-policing; it has required a strong and enforceable antitrust law to keep it operative. These laws, by and large, have done the job of keeping the competitive game going. And the American's standard of living has been improved thereby.

Perhaps nowhere else on earth is competition believed in so strongly as a regulating force in economic life. Yet one may accept the truth of that statement and still insist that the belief is far from an absolute one. To look closely at the economy is to see that there are ambivalences here: public policy both supports competition, as in the antitrust laws, and restrains it, as in agricultural-aid policies and minimum-wage laws. So here, within the context of a single goal, there is some attempt to have things both ways at once: i.e., to foster competition and yet to protect people against the harshest results that might stem from it.

2. *Stability in employment and prices.* The great depression of the 1930's opened a new era in American economic thinking. Where the principal concern of economists in the years before

then had been the functioning of individual product and factor markets, the enormous waste of human resources in a depressed economy awakened a burning interest in the working of the economy as a whole. The consumer remained at the center of the system, but now the additional question was posed, "How can the total spending of consumers, and of businesses too, be stabilized so as to avoid leaving massive resources unemployed?"

Once there may have been a widespread belief that there was not too much that could be done about fluctuations in overall economic activity between periods of too little and too much economic activity. But the 1930's changed all that. From the bitter experience of seeing as many as one in four workers out of work in 1933 came a resolve, now beyond major political contention as a goal, that such a waste must not recur. Today, it does not take anything like a 25 per cent unemployment figure to cause grave concern. The biggest domestic economic issue of the 1960's has been an unemployment problem which for four years running left from 5 to 7 per cent, out of a labor force of over 70 million workers, without jobs. Here was persistent unemployment in the midst of general prosperity, and what might once have been looked upon as a natural consequence and a minor irritation of the free society became urgent public business. It was not that the physical hardship of unemployment had worsened over the years, for financial aid to the unemployed made that an unlikely result; it was rather that expectations as to what was tolerable had risen sharply.

Economists will differ on just how much we know about the ways in which a 5 per cent unemployment figure can safely be cut to 4 or possibly even 3 per cent (which most men see as a minimum figure in a society with old firms dying, new ones coming into being, and some inevitable turnover in the labor force). They will differ too on whether we are politically ready to use all of the economic know-how now at hand to keep unemployment at the lowest possible level. But there will be little quarrel among them with the judgment that no major depression is likely to recur in the United States. Minor recessions, yes, for many years to come; but major depressions, no.

Between the 1930's and the 1960's were two decades when the

problem which bulked larger than unemployment in public discussions was inflation—i.e., a general rise in the price level. The American experience since World War II was not that of runaway inflation, which has plagued some other countries; consumer prices increased 9 per cent in one postwar year, and 6 per cent in three others, but the more common pattern was 3 and 4 per cent annual increases. Still these were enough to cause real hardship to those on fixed incomes and loud cries from whichever political leaders were out of power at any moment. The result again has been that expectations of economic performance have risen. In the early 1960's, when prices rose less than 2 per cent each year, there remained a potent pressure to restrain more rapid price increases. That pressure increased in 1965 and 1966 when prices began to go up by almost 3 per cent. And those who advocate some special solutions to the lingering unemployment are likely to run headlong into insistent demands that we consider only those solutions which are unlikely to result in any greater inflation.

The net result is the mid-1960's find the American economy, through both public and private channels, pursuing the twin goals of high-level employment and reasonably stable prices with considerable vigor—and always with the uncomfortable feeling that the goals may not be fully compatible with one another. Here too is an arena of tradeoffs. Some amount of unemployment may be the cost to be paid for price stability, or some amount of price increases may be the cost of maintaining full employment.

3. *A high rate of economic growth.* For all of the fluctuations just mentioned, the American economy has continued its general upward climb, measured in terms of real increases in total product, at an average rate of about 3 per cent over the past century.

With so many people already living so well and so much progress already evident, why is it that economic growth has become a subject of great interest? Why was so much thought and energy put into replacing the lagging growth rate of the early 1960's with the more respectable figure (over 4 per cent) in 1964 and 1965?

The answer is clearly more complex than a simple desire for bigger stocks of goods. And it is much more basic than any desire, however strongly held in some circles, to match or at least approach the growth rate of any of the planned economies in the world. Instead, the answer must be found in those domestic issues which are most baffling to Americans today and which seem to demand greater economic growth as part of their solution.

Those domestic issues include problems of automation, of imports from abroad, and of economic opportunities for minority groups. The elimination of some jobs through new technology, at the same time that the labor force was swelling rapidly as a result of much higher birth rates in the late 1940's, has generated demands for new jobs to be created—and that means a higher growth rate. Increased imports into the United States have led American workers to insist upon new job opportunities to replace the ones lost to foreign competitors—and that means a higher growth rate. Even the most zealous members of the civil rights movements perceive that equal job opportunities for Negroes and other nonwhites are likely to become a full reality only when there are sufficient jobs to go around—and that means a higher growth rate.

The issue then is not whether the healthier growth performance of 1964–1966 as compared to the years just before that should be sustained. The issue is how it is to be done. Public and private policies alike will surely come in for new examination in the years ahead. The American people will try to have both an unplanned society and one geared to mesh decentralized decisions into a healthy whole.

4. *An equitable income distribution.* The American economy distributes most of its goods and services on the basis of the sales of productive factors in markets: the man who gets the most for selling his labor, his land, or the use of his capital can command the most goods. In an economy that has expanded steadily and that has seen relatively free movement of resources, this rewards system has produced an income distribution pattern with less of a gap between top and bottom than is true of many other nations. Most Americans do in fact live rather well, even if not quite so well as some Hollywood movies might suggest.

Yet the economy today is deeply concerned about a still fairer pattern of distribution. No significant group cries out for *equal* distribution in this incentive-oriented society, but many ask for more equitable distribution. The problem of lingering pockets of poverty in the midst of such widespread comfort in the nation has lurked in the background for many years. Today it is front-page news. Sometimes hesitatingly, sometimes confusingly, a crusade against some of the worst aspects of poverty is under way. The crusade is a difficult one to launch, not because there is a shortage of good will, but because there is too little know-how to apply. Labor markets are changing so rapidly in the skills demanded to earn a good income that anyone starting today as an unskilled adult faces an almost insurmountable task just to catch up with the others. Indeed a man must now run fast just to stand still.

The resolve to attack this problem is evident on many sides in the United States. But no one is sanguine that it will be conquered in any short period of time. American ingenuity now faces one of its most baffling—and humane—challenges.

5. *An environment of freedom.* This brings us full circle, for we are now back to the individual. In varying degrees, Americans want all of the goals just described—and freedom too.

The argument here is as much philosophic or political as it is economic. It is an argument which speaks for unfettered man, put on his own, reaping the rewards for what he accomplishes, and suffering for his own shortcomings. The human being, checked only by the competition of others similarly motivated, can aspire to the stars. The United States economy in the 1960's clings to this ideal with the same emotional commitment—and the same practical reservations—as it does to the political ideals of its Declaration of Independence.

We cannot at the outset of this book attempt a balance sheet showing how the individual fares in this ever-evolving economic system. All we can do is pose so that it may be kept in mind throughout the rest of the chapters. Then, toward the end, perhaps, we can make a balance sheet, aware that most Americans, whatever their differences on other issues, would find little comfort in achieving all of their other goals—competitive society, high level of employment with reasonably stable prices, higher rate of growth, and equitable distribution of income—at the expense of freedom.

2 THE MARKET ECONOMY TODAY

Ben W. Lewis

No feature of the American economy is more distinctive than its heavy reliance upon market mechanisms to allocate resources among competing desires. This remains true even with the increasing role of government in the economy. But few non-Americans—and too few Americans—understand what markets do and what they do not do in today's economy. This chapter looks at the changing and the unchanging character of the market economy, with an emphasis on both the "invisible hand" of which Adam Smith wrote in *The Wealth of Nations* in 1776 and the "visible hand" of government in 1966.

The American economy has undergone widespread and profound changes during this century, and the change continues. Many moderate changes have been made; several have struck deeply into the system; a few have been spectacular. The basic elements, however, have persisted. Throughout the decades the central economizing apparatus of the economy—the market—has maintained its essential character and its vitality. We are aware of its continuing imperfections and inadequacies. With some of these we are willing to live; others we move sporadically to eliminate or ameliorate. In some areas we have supplanted the market. Yet the market remains today as the very core—the distinguishing core—of the American economic system. Its throbbing processes are still the most powerful forces guiding and determining the use of resources and the division of the product in the American economy.

THE CORE FUNCTIONS OF AN ECONOMY

Certain functions are common to all economies or economic systems; every economy, whether it be market, Marxist, or mixed, has certain economizing jobs to perform. These tasks spring naturally from two elemental facts of economic life: (1) human beings in the aggregate have vast wants and desires, while (2) the aggregate resources available directly and indirectly to satisfy these wants and desires are limited. We could argue for hours on end over the extent to which human wants are inherent or are the creatures of artificial stimulation (and what difference it makes!), and we all know of situations in which there are oversupplies or gluts of particular resources or products in particular locations (usually at particular prices). We are told that the American economy is so affluent that we deliberately create wants for frivolous gadgets just to keep the economy working. But we all know of distressing pockets of poverty in America, and even the least perceptive among us is aware of great unsatisfied needs for public goods such as education, housing, highways, and public health. The sheer fact is that mankind, constituted as it is, has always been, and always will be, faced by the presence of economic scarcity. Some men and some societies have more to work with and to enjoy than others. No societies have ever had so much that in the aggregate and over time everyone had more than he wanted of everything, without thought and without effort. Even in America we cannot have everything for everyone.

When men live and make their living together, they are forced to organize themselves more or less systematically to deal with the problems which arise from the fact of economic scarcity. These, essentially, are problems of choice. When resources are limited and all wants and desires cannot be satisfied, choices must be made: how are the resources (the land, the labor, the capital and the capital goods, and the management) to be used? What goods and services are to be produced, and, perforce, not produced? How are the resources to be combined to achieve the utmost in productivity? How much is to be consumed to satisfy present wants, and how much is to be "saved" and held for future consumption or made into factories, tools, and machinery for further production? Who among all the members of society are to receive and enjoy the products and in what respective amounts? In short, men in society must *economize;* they must *manage* their resources to produce what they want, in the amounts they want, as they want, and *for whom* they want—just as each man, in his own "personal economy" must manage his own limited money resources. "What?," "How?," and "For Whom" must be answered continuously and endlessly in all societies of men. An economic system, or economy, is a man-made (and constantly remade) set of arrangements, institutions, and processes which continuously and endlessly provide answers acceptable to society.

We have said that the essence of economizing, and hence the essence of the work of an economic system or economy, is *choice,* and the point has emerged that choice is, by its very nature, costly. Resources used in one direction and to satisfy a given want or desire cannot be used in another direction to satisfy other wants or desires. In a world of scarcity, thus, the cost of economic satisfactions is satisfactions forgone. When we select one opportunity from an array of competing opportunities, we deprive ourselves of the satisfactions which the rejected opportunities might have afforded. Hence, the term familiar to all economists, "opportunity cost." Economic decisions or choices make a difference, and as members of society we are all concerned about the way—both the processes and the results—in which, in the societies in which we live, economic decisions or choices are made.

All of us have a tendency to discuss economic systems in terms of extremes: we talk about "free" economies and "authoritarian" or "command" economies. These expressions are intended to distinguish between economies where the answers to society's economizing questions flow "automatically" from the complex of free choices made by individuals in carrying out their personal economic affairs, and at the other pole, economies where the economizing answers are imposed upon men, as individuals and in society, by the government or state, however constituted and supported. This approach helps to set out the issues; it also confuses them, because no economy is wholly "free" or wholly "authoritarian," and no economy is fixed and unchanging in its economizing mix. All economies, in varying degrees, are made up of individual decision-making and collective or state decision-making; and all economies, in varying degrees, change their mixes from time to time. It is nonetheless true that the mixtures in different economies at any time are significantly different, and that the differences persist over periods sufficiently long to enable us realistically to characterize certain economies as "freer" or "more authoritanian" than others.

ESSENCE OF THE AMERICAN ECONOMY

It is realistic to characterize the American economy as a "free enterprise" or "market" economy. Government (that is, all of us acting collectively through the machinery of democratic government) has come increasingly to play an important part in economic decision-making and economic enterprise, but it is still the case that the use of scarce resources and the division of product in the American economy is determined overwhelmingly by the meshing together of freely made individual economic choices in the market.

Except in the case of military draftees or in the event of national emergencies, government does not force individuals into lines of economic activity, and it does not tell individuals what or how much to consume. Each person, in his capacity as a producer and earner of money income, is free—within the limits of his abilities and opportunities—to go into any line of work or business he chooses. As a consumer (spender of money income) he is free, within the limits of his purchasing power and opportunities, to buy in the market any goods and services he chooses to satisfy his wants. Both as producer and consumer, each person is expected, in his own self-interest, to seek maximum self-satisfaction. In making his individual economic choices, the interest of *society* is not his concern; he has no responsibility to society other than to keep within the broad boundaries of the law and to behave decently.

The market provides a test both for productive skill and efficiency, and for individual performance in anticipating and meeting the economic wishes and demands of society; it provides, as well, a mechanism for directing production and for rationing or distributing the results of production. "The market" is made up of many markets—for consumer goods and services and for intermediate and basic factors of production (such as natural resources, labor, capital goods, etc.). These markets, even though they may be remote functionally and physically, are interrelated. Together, they make up a total economic complex or mechanism which grinds out society's decisions on who shall produce how much of what, and who shall have how much of what to enjoy. In the process, each individual plays his part in society's decisions and receives his reward as society decides.

The market we are talking about is an *economic* concept: it is made up of buyers competing with each other for a good or service, and sellers competing with each other to dispose of the good or service. The activity may take place in a single structure in a given location; it may involve no structure or many structures in many locations. The essential features are simply that the price bids of competing buyers and the price offers of competing sellers shall be known to all self-seeking participants and shall come to focus in a price that "clears the market." Goods will be bid for and offered at such prices as each of the participating buyers and sellers shall determine, but at any time they will be sold—actually change hands—only at *the price* at which all buyers who are willing to purchase and all sellers who are willing to sell are satisfied. Buyers who are unwilling or unable to buy at the "market price," and sellers who are unwilling to sell at this price, will be unsatisfied. In this fashion, goods and services are rationed in consumer markets; and goods, services, and factors of production are rationed in intermediate and factor markets.

Money incomes, which enable individuals to participate as buyers in consumer markets, are determined, in the form of factor prices, in the markets for factors—labor (wages), capital (interest), natural resources (economic rent), and business enterprise (profits). The money incomes which individuals earn from the sale of their services in the free markets for services reflect the economic value that society places upon their services.

When we combine our markets and interweave their activities, the process by which the market in a free-enterprise economy performs its economizing function—the allocation of resources and division of the product—comes into play. An enterpriser bids in the free market against competing enterprisers for labor, capital and natural resources in their original or intermediate forms. Competing suppliers of these factors offer them for sale. In his bidding, each producer anticipates that he will be able to buy and combine the necessary factors at a total cost which will bring him a satisfactory *profit* when he offers the resulting product for sale. The prices that he actually pays for the factors (his costs) are determined in the markets where the offers and bids of competing sellers and competing buyers come together and are cleared. The prices, both as incomes and as costs, reflect market evaluations of the factors. If it costs an enterpriser five dollars to make a product, he is using resources which society values at five dollars.

As we have seen, society, by the same demand-and-supply process, places a firm value upon the enterpriser's product when he offers it for sale in the product market. If the best price he can obtain—in competition with others who offer the same or similar products—is, say, four dollars, he loses money, and his prospects are grim. But, of greater importance for our consideration of the role of the market, society, too, suffers a loss. Resources which society values at five dollars are being converted by the unwise or inefficient action of this enterpriser into a product which society values at only four dollars—a sheer waste of resources. And society reacts, firmly and decisively: it says quite forthrightly to the enterpriser and all such enterprisers, "Stop! Mend your ways or go bankrupt!"

For the wiser or more efficient enterpriser, society has a happier message: "You have transformed resources which we value at five dollars into a product which we value at six dollars; we want you to continue along these lines, and we want other enterprisers to do likewise. As an indication of our approval, and as an incentive to you and to others, take this profit and enjoy it, and earn more if you can."

Here, then, is the market system at work: consumers bidding

against other consumers for the things they want and are prepared to pay for; enterprisers seeking profits vying against each other, in the selection of goods for production, and in the efficient purchase and use of factors, for the favor of consumers. Innovation, progress, and efficiency in the production of goods that consumers want are rewarded and encouraged; lethargy, inefficiency, and stupidity are penalized. The rise and fall of prices at all levels reflect changing demands and supplies, and induce corrective consumer and producer responses. The desires of consumers are felt directly in the markets for consumer goods and prospectively, through the eyes of eager and perceptive enterprisers, in the markets for the factors of production. As enterprisers, bidding against each other, buy factor services, money incomes which reflect the market's evaluation of the services are paid into the pockets of those who furnish the services. These, the consumers with which this paragraph began, are thus equipped to enter consumer markets and bid for the things they want, and the process goes on and on. And society gets what it wants from its human and natural resources even though it resorts to no governmental directing agencies or governmental coercion, and even though each individual in society, both as a producer and a consumer, is free and expected to follow solely the dictates and suggestions of his own economic self-interest. Self-interest is the driving force; profit is the lodestar; competition is the spur and the whip—the market's built-in regulator.

To keep the record straight, we should emphasize at this point that while the individual in a free-enterprise system is free to make his economic choices without government coercion, he is not free from economic penalties or punishments if his choices are not in line with the desires of the society in which he lives. Remember, by its very nature, an economic *system* is a set of arrangements for imposing, systematically, the economic will of society on the economic activities of its members. There could be no survival of society without some such set of arrangements. A free-enterprise economy eschews imposition of its will by government, but the coercion of the competitive market which it employs, with its penalties of bankruptcy, poverty, and economic degradation, administered impersonally, ruthlessly, and without compassion, leaves the individual producer really free to perform as he pleases only so long as society, speaking through the market, also is pleased.

MODIFYING THE MARKET SYSTEM

In the foregoing we have frequently used the terms "market evaluation" and "society's evaluation" interchangeably. It is fair to ask whether it makes sense to speak of the wishes of "society" as guiding the use of resources when it is evident that different individual members of society speak in the market with quite unequal force. In the market poll, some voters cast more ballots than others—the demand of the rich man with his great purchasing power influences the market's disposition of resources more than the demands of many men whose incomes and purchasing power are low. The rich man's whims are attended to; the needs of the poor may be sacrificed. Is this "society" speaking? The cold logic of the market economy supplies an affirmative answer. Incomes, it says, are the *prices* of services, and, determined in free markets, they are society's measure of the contributions made by income-receivers to society's product. Individuals receive their respective money incomes in such amounts as the market determines, as an essential part of the process by which society induces and coerces individuals "freely" to carry out its will. When the individual, as a consumer, spends his money income, whatever the amount, he is making his claim on the economy's product in line with society's calculated will. Thus the individual's demand is society's demand.

But this logic is cold and forbidding, and American society has long since tempered the results of the stark processes of market income-determination by conscious collective governmental action. Redistribution (or redivision) of income, and hence of product, through taxes levied on the principle of "ability to pay," and provision of an array of public services available without prices to everyone, are accepted features of the total American political economy. Real incomes, as remade by taxation and public goods to express society's considered will, are significantly different from the pattern of money incomes woven by market forces alone.

The market lies at the core of the American economy, but we have never been happy solely with the core, and our unhappiness has led us over the years, and increasingly in recent years, to embark on a wide range of government programs designed to affect the operation of the market as our economizing apparatus. Our market is, indeed, a changing market. Redistribution of income through taxes and expenditures on public goods is one program through which change is wrought. There are many others—to improve and support the market, to supplement the market (to modify both its processes and its results), and to supplant the market. Economic systems or economies are, inherently, *political* economies. The government—that is, all of us acting consciously and collectively through government—is in the business of economizing society's resources in a big way.

There would be little point in trying to catalogue and classify the many, many instances in which, today, the American people, through government, undertake consciously to perform the function of social economizing. Illustrations of such activity may be illuminating, however, and will give some indication of the character and extent of the change to which the American market has been, and is constantly being, subjected. Concerning the "principles" that have determined when and what kind of social economizing should be undertaken, it is probably more realistic to see the "principles" as emerging after the event rather than before it, and more as boxes for academic classification than as propositions which have actually determined action.

A major group of government activities is pointed directly at strengthening and supporting the market as an economizing instrument. This includes, for example, the maintenance of national defense, law and order, the development of the law of private property and contracts, the establishment of a monetary system, labor exchanges, labor retraining programs, programs to assist business firms in domestic and foreign markets, activities of the Bureau of Standards, pure-food-and-drug and "truth in advertising" legislation and the like. More dramatically, the antitrust activities engaged in by the federal government since 1890 fall into this category of market support. Competition (to vary our figure of speech) is the market's policeman. Without competition, individuals pursuing their own self-interest in the market could produce nothing but chaos; with some competition but not enough, the economy would be characterized by misallocation of resources (too much of this and too little of that) and maldistribution of income (too much going to those who contribute too little to the economy's output). Only in markets where individual self-interest is disciplined by really effective competition is it possible for the market to guide resources and to divide income systematically and in line with acceptable social-market evaluations.

Effective competition is an absolute pre-condition for a workable free-enterprise economy. American antitrust laws seek to prevent agreements between independent firms to restrain competition; they also seek to prevent combinations of firms undertaken for whatever purpose, if the effect of the combination may be unreasonably to restrain competition. We know, of course, that some degree of monopoly is bound to be present in all markets, even if it is no more than that afforded by location, individual personality, or distinctive trademarks or slogans. We are prepared to settle for "workable" competition. But even workable competition is not easy to ensure. A nice problem of public economic policy which is still far from resolution is posed by our attempt to deal with mergers of erstwhile competing industrial firms: how much productive efficiency that may flow from large-scale combinations are we willing to sacrifice in order to maintain a more competitive industrial structure—or, conversely, what are we willing to pay in lesser competition for any benefits of larger-scale production? And what should be our attitude toward a giant firm that has simply grown to dominate its market? In the process of answering these questions the American people are, perforce, shaping the arrangements that perform for them the social-economizing function—their economy.

Within the past quarter century an even more significant problem area has been opened up by the identification of a serious shortcoming in the market system. For many decades the American economy has suffered from "booms and busts"—chronic instability which has manifested itself in recurrent periods of feverish industrial activity and prosperity followed by industrial decline, depression, and widespread unemployment. Instability has been aggravated by more unemployment of resources even in "good" times than seems tolerable in a society concerned to economize because of resource scarcity. Recent diagnosis has spotted the difficulty within the market system, and even more recent prescription has taken the form of massive remedial fiscal and monetary action by the government to supplement the processes of the market. The remedy is not easy to apply "scientifically," and it carries its own peculiar dangers. Application threatens the economy in some measure with inflation if unemployment is to be eradicated. We are facing up to the threat, however, and the remedy is gaining acceptance in principle, and at least tentatively in action. This represents another major addition to the market system. It promises to bolster the system and so to permit it to perform its allocative and distributive functions more satisfactorily. A system designed to allocate resources and divide the product is a happier system if there are always places for all of its resources to go, and if the product for division is always and regularly plentiful.

On many occasions, particular producer groups in the economy have found market processes to be too rough for their liking. This is not unnatural: good stiff competition for the other fellow and a little "reasonable" protection for myself is not an unprofitable working doctrine, if you can get the rest of society to agree; and in a considerable number of instances society has been convinced. Several groups, from time to time, have persuaded the electorate in democratic America that in the economic areas served by these groups the interests of society would best be satisfied by public action designed to soften the pressures of the market. Protective tariffs, resale price maintenance, fair trade and quality control laws, oil pro-rates, farm aid programs, are examples. Labor unions which exercise substantial control over the supply side of the market for labor services are afforded distinctive protections by law and practice from market forces, as are many professional groups. In many of these instances it can be shown that the unfettered market is quite unsuited to work out socially acceptable answers to the "what," "how," and "for whom" problems with which these groups, together with the rest of society, are involved. Overriding national political considerations, diffused incentives, immobilities, inequalities in bargaining power, and the like are cited. In some instances, however, the evidence of the incapacity of the market seems to lie largely in the fact that its processes are uncomfortable to the persons affected. In the final analysis, however, the decision lies within the realm of public political-economic policy and, in *all* cases where the market mechanism is being modified by public action, we find ourselves in the presence of the free American people remaking their economizing arrangements—their economy—to match their current convictions.

Notable examples of situations in which we are dissatisfied with the possibilities under the rule of the market for the provision of sufficient supplies by enterprisers or for sufficient demand by paying consumers are to be found in the whole vast array of public goods and services: national defense, public health and sanitation, public highways, public housing, social security, unemployment benefits, medicare, public education, law and order, fire protection, and others. In the case of some of these, the market furnishes alternatives; in all cases the market furnishes many of the constituent parts of the public services. Economists are prone to talk learnedly about "collective goods," "external consumption effects," and the "exclusion principle"—and we all realize that some goods can be supplied only to groups (they cannot be withheld from individuals who refuse to pay), and that divergences may occur between private and social benefits and costs in the case of certain goods which make public provision much more feasible than production for sale in the market by individuals. Sometimes, technical reasons for supplanting or supplementing the market are quite apparent. In other cases the public takes over by collective decision just because enough people "feel that way." Again, this is the way economic systems or economics are made—the way in which, at any moment, they are what they are. A clear technical case for supplanting the market is present in the so-called local public-utility industries—gas, electric power, telephones, water—where a combination of economic peculiarities added to peculiar physical circumstances results in the complete inability of market competition to perform acceptably its economizing role. Here, public regulation or public ownership and operation, in place of the market, is the almost universal answer. In a related field, public transportation, the once universally accepted answer—regulation—is now being challenged in the public forum by the free market, and even in the case of the "recognized" public utilities there is still strong advocacy for reliance on consciously strengthened market competition, *as a supplement,* if you please, to public regulation.

Political economies are always on their way; they never arrive. The market in our economy is bound to change, and to move on. It is very probable that in the years ahead the market will experience further inroads by public action. It is certain, however, that, modified, the market will remain as the distinctive, distinguishing characteristic of the American economy. It will always change; essentially, it will always be the same.

3 KEEPING COMPETITION ALIVE

Morris A. Adelman

Most Americans would subscribe to the belief that all power needs checking and policing lest it be abused. The policeman of the American market system is supposed to be the force of competition. But there turn out to be big differences as to what this policeman should look like when he's on duty and big problems in keeping him on his beat. This chapter discusses the policy issues associated with preserving a competitive economy today and outlines the perils in adopting too narrow a view of what degree of competition is required to make markets work for progress and freedom.

Competition means different things to different people. Opinions generally fall into one or the other of two groups. First, there is the idea that competition means having a great many businesses in any given industry, preferably small concerns. We may want this because it is supposed to have good political or social effects, or for any other reason. If we do want it, then we may try to keep the many small producers alive by warding off the competition from larger or more efficient companies and from foreign concerns, by imposing tariffs, import quotas, and the like. Since domestic products cannot be kept out, the state may resort to other methods. Particularly in Western Europe today there is a great deal of concern over the threat, real or fancied, of American companies in European markets.

The other concept of competition is very different. It is the idea that prices and production ought to be determined by business concerns seeking their own profit and acting in complete independence of their rivals, so that they cannot get together to decide what is best for their particular group, which would almost always be higher prices and lower production. The ultimate in group control is, of course, a single monopolist who is the industry as a whole. To the extent that groups of business concerns can get together to do what is best for the industry as a whole they are acting like a monopolist. The basic idea here is that competition will force or coerce the independent concerns to put forth their best efforts and offer the most product for the least money. Those who are not efficient enough to keep up with their fellows are eliminated. Furthermore, since the price is always being pushed down toward cost, the only way for businessmen to make higher profits is to devise newer and better ways of producing and distributing goods. A business concern which develops such innovations will make abnormally high profits until the rest of the industry catches up whereupon the whole process must be repeated.

In theory it can be shown that if competition works perfectly, we get the best possible use of our limited resources of manpower and capital at any given time. Of course, no process run by human beings will run perfectly or even very smoothly, but this applies as much to monopoly as to competition, so that on balance there is little doubt that competition does give society greater output at lower cost. The basic reason is that a monopoly raises prices by restricting output and leaving some kinds of resources idle or working inefficiently. Furthermore, a monopoly lacks the incentive to keep improving methods and bringing down costs.

In theory, a socialist economy could produce much the same result as the best kind of competition simply by calculating all possible costs and all possible demands and feeding them into a big enough computer. So far, at least, such a job is practically impossible, even though one must admit that it is theoretically possible. However, one problem for socialist or planned economies is not theoretical at all but is becoming extremely important for them. Up to now, most of the socialist planned economies have set up in advance the program for the amount of goods they wanted produced and where and by whom. It is obvious that they have become rather dissatisfied with the results. They are in process of setting up markets in important areas of their economies. Within these areas and still subject to general direction, production will be determined by how much profit the enterprises can make. The managements of these enterprises will have discretion, and therefore they will be acting just like the managements in a capitalist society and will have the same kind of problems. But wherever there is a market there is a problem of whether it will be run for the benefit of the producers as a group or whether each individual entrepreneur will be forced to run his own business and seek his own advantage and thereby exert a harsh kind of discipline on all the rest.

In other words, the socialist economies, by carrying out the various kinds of reforms in which they are now engaged, are creating for themselves a monopoly problem very much like those with which capitalist countries have been concerned for a hundred years and more. Whether they can cope effectively with it we shall see. A few years ago the economic planning agency in Yugoslavia was sufficiently disturbed over monopolies there to try to use the importation of foreign goods as a weapon against them. Unfortunately this did not work, because in order to save foreign exchange, imports had to be curtailed. But of course the problem does not disappear because it cannot be solved, and it remains in Yugoslavia today. I cannot tell whether the other socialist economies have caught up with Yugoslavia in this respect, but if they are not aware of the problem now, they soon will be.

At any rate, here we have the two general concepts of competition: (1) having a lot of small businesses, and (2) having more efficient and lower-cost production. An economist cannot say which of these goals is better any more than he can give a professional opinion on whether beer is better than wine or wine is better than water. He can, however—and should—point out that we cannot have both.

SIZE AND EFFICIENCY

There is no escape from the pain of choice, but an economist can lend comfort by pointing out that *some* difficult choices are unnecessary and are based on a mistake. At a time when people thought that babies would be affected by anything the mother saw, they went to a great deal of trouble to protect expectant mothers from seeing anything that would "mark" their children. But gradually it was learned that babies were not affected by prenatal experiences, and everyone was spared a lot of unnecessary work. Similarly there is a false dilemma about competition. Some argue that if competition is left alone, it will destroy itself. This idea rests on the notion that the bigger the better, always and everywhere. The bigger any business is, the more efficient it is and the lower its costs; eventually it will run all its rivals out of existence. Once this happens, of course, we have monopoly. Therefore, to save ourselves from monopoly we must put limits on competition.

This would be a hard choice, but fortunately it is a false one. There is no automatic connection between the size of a business and its efficiency. In some lines of industry companies need to be very large in order to be efficient; in other lines the smallest are as efficient as the biggest. Moreover, even when a concern must be large to be efficient, after a point the advantage of larger size diminishes. Even where a business concern must be very large, if the market in which it operates is also very large, the two offset each other. A business with a billion dollars in assets is a giant, but in the United States' petroleum industry, for example, a business of that size accounts for less than 5 per cent of the domestic market, to say nothing of the international one, and therefore has no particular influence on prices and production.

And a little reflection on this fact explains what might otherwise be thought rather strange. Business corporations in the United States are much larger than anywhere else in the world. This is the home of big business. Yet there seems to be general agreement that competition is also stronger and more effective here. Once we realize that the market is so much bigger because the economy is so much bigger, there is no further difficulty. And we are also brought to realize that competition is a matter of degree, of being more or less rather than yes or no. It is, in other words, a waste of time to ask whether there is any competition in a given line of business or whether there is any monopoly. Nearly always there is some of both; the important question is how much. (This is a conclusion of great practical importance in Europe and Latin America and every other place where we see regional groupings, common markets, and free-trade areas. In these places, national markets are generally too small to support companies that are big enough to be efficient. By removing trade barriers and thereby enlarging the market to include several countries, they are able to make room for big enough companies, and indeed for enough of them so that they will compete with one another.)

But even if the fear that competition destroys itself is an unreal fear nine-tenths of the time, there are some lines of industry where it is true. In such activities as local gas and electricity, telephones, and some kinds of transportation, the costs of having more than one company are so great that even if by accident two or more were started it would be only a question of time before they merged into one, or all but one disappeared some other way. These are sometimes called "natural monopolies," and plainly competition cannot be preserved here.

COMPETITION AND THE LAW

There are any number of ways in which competition can be maintained or increased. The experience in the United States is, after all, only that of one country following one particular method for about seventy-five years. Other countries have different legal and social traditions, and will not aim at quite the same mix of objectives, and they may choose very different methods and accomplish more or less. But American experience is interesting because this is the country where the policy of maintaining competition has had the longest trial. The first national law, the Sherman Act, was passed in 1890, with two provisions. Section (1) prohibited conspiracies in restraint of trade and Section (2) prohibited monopolizing or even attempting to monopolize any line of business. It is interesting that when the European Economic Community drew up its code, it enacted Article 84 to prohibit agreements and Article 85 to prohibit what it called the abuse of a dominant market position. In Great Britain also the law is divided between restrictive practices and what the British call monopolies, following more or less the same theory.

In the United States, Section (1) of the Sherman Act has been strengthened by later legislation to only a minor degree. The law itself stands pretty much as it did in 1890, but over the years the courts have interpreted it more and more strictly. Today all communication among competitors is prohibited if it has any connection with prices, the limiting of production, or the sharing of production among rivals.

Undoubtedly much of this kind of activity is still going on, but when there is no way to prevent conspirators from agreeing to cut prices to get more business, and when their illegal agreement is kept secret, enforcement of the conspiracy is difficult. A few years ago such an agreement was discovered in the electrical manufacturing industries, despite the precautions which had been taken to keep it secret, such as never keeping notes or minutes of a meeting and always making telephone calls from public pay stations. The exposure of the agreement caused a scandal, and a number of the people found guilty of breaking the law were sent to jail. Public disapproval was sharp and unanimous. So anyone engaging in such practices knows that he is running the risk of losing his job and his liberty. In some other countries, prices are set by trade associations or even with the approval of the government, and this is considered the normal and right way to do things.

The history of Section (2) of the Sherman Act, a prohibition on monopoly, has been very different. From time to time corporations have been prosecuted under it, and sometimes they have even been broken up. The most famous cases came in 1911, when the old Standard Oil trust and the American Tobacco trust were ordered to dissolve. Perhaps the best-known recent instance came in 1950, when the Aluminum Company of America had to split off its Canadian affiliate, which was and is the world's biggest aluminum producer. But these cases have been few and far between, and nobody would contend that this section of the Sherman Act plays a large role in the daily life of business.

However, in the last ten years American business management

has had to take account of a 1950 amendment to the Clayton Act which restricted mergers among business concerns and the buying up of one company by another. In the American legal system, as in the British, the effect of legislation can be seen only after it has been enforced for a few years and the courts have translated its broad and often vague language into more specific guidelines. The 1950 amendment has become a stringent prohibition against most mergers or acquisitions by big companies. Even when small companies are involved, if after the merger the new or remaining company were to retain as much as 15 or 20 per cent of the market, there is very little chance that the merger will be permitted. The courts will probably order the company to be split up again into its original divisions. Even when the case is not so clear, as when the two companies did not compete directly before merger, but had business dealings with one another, the courts have been very strict, and, if indeed there seemed to be a chance that the new company would be much more efficient than its rivals, it was not permitted to exist. Indeed, it may be, as some claim and others deny, that the law has gone so far that it has become not a protection against mergers but a protection of the less efficient competitor against the more efficient. But since a company which is not permitted to buy up another one is still permitted to build the facilities and hire the people it wants, the only obstacle to corporate growth is the prohibition against buying up other companies.

There are other minor sections of the antitrust laws (the common term for laws against monopoly) which are somewhat controversial, although there is no controversy at all about the Sherman Act and the general policy it embodies. The most important of these controverted areas is probably the Robinson-Patman Act against price discrimination, which was passed thirty years ago during the Great Depression. Although its purpose was to protect small grocery and other stores against the big chains which were supposed to be buying more cheaply, it applies to all kinds of business concerns. Many favor it as necessary to protect smaller buyers and sellers from the buying power of big companies, and also from the danger of big companies cutting prices in some lines of business or in certain localities in order to drive out competitors and gain a monopoly there. The opponents of the law deny that there is any need for it, and they also claim that, even when it is cheaper to sell to certain buyers because they buy a simpler product or require less service, the law prevents these savings from being passed on to customers. Therefore, they argue, there is really discrimination against the lower-cost buyers. They also contend that it helps sellers maintain the same price without talking to each other. The controversy still goes on, but Congress shows no disposition to repeal or change the Robinson-Patman Act.

HAVE THE LAWS WORKED?

Whether American legislation against monopoly is a success or a failure depends on what you think it should accomplish. If competition means having many small business concerns, the law is probably a failure, because since 1890 small business has not crowded in on big business. There is some dispute over whether big business' share of the national income is greater today than it was thirty or fifty years ago, but nobody has suggested that it is less. Therefore it is clear that the Sherman Act can have done little to break down the structure of United States business.

However, if this law was intended only to keep business concerns independent of each other, making their own decisions and putting pressure on each other to achieve lower prices and greater output, then the law must be considered a success. As I mentioned earlier, as compared with the rest of the world, American business does act much more competitively. But the many who consider the law a success think it would accomplish even more by taking action against industries where the sellers are very few and are therefore able to follow a common policy that results in higher prices and lower and less efficient production. The steel industry is a good example, since it repeatedly raised prices during the 1950's even when it was operating below capacity, which could not have happened if real competition existed. However, most steel prices have risen little since 1958, though there is no agreement over whether this was caused by the disapproval of the government or by the threat of imports from Europe and Japan; steel imports are today nearly 10 per cent of domestic production, while ten years ago they were only about 1 per cent. Steel prices in the United States are well above European and Japanese prices, a rather unusual situation. It is hard to say whether other industries are acting in the same manner as steel. Until we have some idea of the nature and importance of this problem of a few sellers who are able to do much industry planning without actually getting together, we cannot say whether this is a piece of unfinished business in United States antitrust legislation.

THE LAW'S EXCEPTIONS

I come now to the exceptions to the law, which fall into two groups. One includes such industries as telephone, electric light and power, gas, etc., which outside the United States are usually owned and operated by the government. Here they are called public utilities and for the most part they are regulated within each of the fifty states. There are also the Interstate Commerce Commission and the Federal Communication Commission which regulate railroads, telephones, etc., wherever they cross state boundaries. Whether federal or state, a commission generally fixes a maximum price for the service which ensures the regulated company earnings on its invested capital roughly equal to those of an unregulated company. This so-called "fair return" has nothing to do with fairness or justice; it is a technical question of the rate of interest which must be paid if the utility is to raise enough money to keep growing and provide the services needed. How effective this method of regulation has been is not easy to say. There seems to be general agreement that it has prevented the exploitation of consumers by public utility corporations' being allowed to earn too high profits, although there might be a difference of opinion as to what constitutes too high profits. There is some question whether such corporations have sufficient incentive to provide the highest quality and amount of service at all times; however, by comparison with the rest of the world, the quality of these services in the United States is very good. The biggest exception is probably in railroad passenger transportation, both long-distance and local commuter service, which has almost disappeared in many areas. Airplane transportation, on the other hand, compares favorably with that in the rest of the world and is considerably cheaper. One reason is undoubtedly the encouragement of competition among airlines, within a big market for passenger service. But the government agency has been able to look at the welfare of the American public together with the airline industry. In Europe, for example, each government has acted as the agent of its national airline in bargaining for landing rights and schedules, and the one ground upon which all governments agree is to keep fares high.

The other area outside the antitrust laws is agriculture, plus a few raw material producing industries like crude oil. Here government policy has been to discourage competition. In effect the government has set up a huge cartel to fix prices directly or indirectly and to share markets among all the producers. In agriculture, total output has not been successfully controlled and the large surpluses which accumulated have had to be dumped abroad. But the biggest surplus has been in farmers and farms, many of which could be abandoned and their production made up by expanding the more efficient farms. Many thousands of people are being kept on the farms scratching out a bare living instead of being helped to move into town where they could get useful jobs. This makes sense if the object is to preserve the small farm, but it makes no sense if the object is to obtain the efficient low-cost production which competition brings about. So this must be called a clear though minor contradiction.

4 CORPORATIONS BIG AND SMALL

Adolf A. Berle

The corporate enterprise is the subject of much discussion inside the country and outside, too. At once admired and feared, extolled and blamed, set free and regulated, it has changed as much as any other economic institution in the twentieth century. But the changes have a hard time catching up with the myths about corporations. Here is a survey of some of those changes and of the power issues that continue to be raised by organizations with enviable, but uneven, records of productive efficiency.

The changes in the American economy since the Great Depression of 1932 are enormous. Actual production has increased fivefold—allowing for changes in value of money. Real wages have more than doubled, although the population has greatly increased. Current estimates indicate a rise in the Gross National Product from a rate of $504 billion in 1960 to a rate of over $700 billion in 1966. Meanwhile, people's incomes—their personal receipts—have grown from about $401 billion in 1960 to $555 billion in 1965. They are expected to reach $700 billion in 1970. No major interruption of growth is in sight.

On the social side, the American record is historically impressive, although not nearly so good. The unemployed labor force, as we reckon it, has dropped from nearly 3.9 million in 1960 to about 3.5 in 1966. We hope to lower it still further. The "Poor"—about 15 per cent of Americans—have been diminishing. Yet we ought, in so rich a country, to have no involuntary poverty, and no involuntary unemployment.

Measures are being taken to steer a considerable part of the

American personal income into the pockets of the poorer, lowest-paid sectors of our population. President Lyndon Johnson's campaign to abolish poverty is more than a pious aspiration. Never until now has any large country had production and resources adequate for such a project; the United States now has both. If successful—and it should succeed—a new era will have opened in world history. The social and economic revolution begun by President Franklin D. Roosevelt will have been fulfilled—so far as mere economics can do it.

This did not happen by accident. Some of its elements have been discussed in the three preceding chapters. In this, the fourth, I focus discussion on one of the major American economic instruments—its system of production by corporations. Corporations have come to be a key tool in organizing and increasing production, distributing goods more widely to consumers, and redistributing property and income throughout the United States. They have solved some problems and created others; they are worth examining.

THE ROLE OF THE CORPORATIONS

The business of America, aside from farming, is almost entirely carried on by corporations. There are more than a million of these in existence—as well as nine million or more individually-owned enterprises. Yet between 75 and 80 per cent of all manufacturing, mining, transport, public works, and commerce generally is carried on by fewer than a thousand large companies. The remaining 20 to 25 per cent is divided among the several million small concerns. Most of these are owned by individuals or families. These are the remaining "capitalists" denounced by Karl Marx a century ago. Their number is considerable, but their economic power is gone.

American corporations, with rare exceptions, are not socialist; they are not owned or administered by government. They are not statist. Yet many of them are so large that they cannot be called "private." They do not correspond to, or behave like, the personally-owned or family-owned businesses and enterprises of a generation ago. Their owners or stockholders may be numbered in the millions—the case, for example, of the American Telephone & Telegraph Company—or, more often, by tens and hundreds of thousands. In law, they are private; in fact, they lie halfway between the state and the individual. Their initiatives are their own. Theoretically they are free to do as they choose. Actually they are compelled by written or unwritten law to keep in reasonable balance with the American economic system as a whole. In effect they work within various types of state planning. But this planning is not rigid—as it is in the Soviet Union—nor as detailed as the planning in France. There, managements have extremely wide liberty to choose what they will produce, charge what prices they wish, and invest capital in new development and new construction where and as they choose. In certain aspects, nevertheless, they are carefully controlled.

This is why our main interest centers in the few hundred big corporations.

These are not operated by their owners—that is to say, by their stockholders. Obviously a thousand stockholders, still less a million, cannot manage or operate anything. Power must be and has been delegated in each concern to a few men. They are the directors of this corporation, and they in turn choose its executive head, usually the corporation President. He dominates the hierarchic pyramid of each corporate organization. Below him comes a staff of management personnel and, below them, are the workmen and laborers. Most of these workmen are organized into independent labor unions. Under American law, the union representatives have the right to bargain, collectively, with the employers for wage rates, working conditions, old-age pensions, vacations, and other benefits. For practical purposes wage level rates are set, in most parts of the United States, by contracts worked out between the unions and the corporations and others who employ the workers.

The largest corporations attain enormous size. A recent calculation, for example, showed that only four nations in the world—the United States, Russia, Britain and France—had gross revenues greater than the gross revenue of General Motors Corporation alone. Many, perhaps most, of the two hundred largest

American corporations take in more money from sales than do most of the smaller independent countries on earth. Many corporations have more stockholders than they have workers.

More remarkable still, they are able—after paying nearly half their profits as taxes to the American government and after paying part of the remaining half as dividends to their shareholders—to save from the price of the goods or the services they sell each year about 90 per cent of all the new capital they need to improve their plants or to undertake new projects. This means that they are no longer dependent on banks or bankers, or financiers, or on the savings of individuals for the new capital they constantly need. To this is due the fact that the Marxian "capitalist" is quietly disappearing.

SOCIAL CHANGES IN THE MAKING

From this combination of developments two social facts have emerged—perhaps new in economic history. The American corporation has split the old capitalist structure down the middle. There is no longer an owner of wealth who applies his money as capital to construct a mill, a forge, a chemical plant, or an automobile industry. He is not needed for that. He can buy stock, of course, from some other owner who wishes to sell. But his wealth does not go into the business; it pays off the previous owner. And there is no longer (in the large corporation) an owner who manages.

Consequently, two groups have grown up, side by side but increasingly independent of each other. One is the group of wealth holders—stockholders. They are outside the processes of production and management; they merely own shares. There are about 20 million direct shareholders in American enterprises—that is, about 10 per cent of the population of the United States. But in addition there are about 40 million or more "indirect" shareholders. These are chiefly workers whose old-age pension and welfare funds hold, as investment, stock of these corporations. The value of that stock and the dividends received from it are used to pay to these workers old-age retirement allowances—in addition to the government-paid old-age pensions which they also receive at a certain age. The total value of all this stock is approaching one-third of all the "personally-owned" wealth in the United States if direct and indirect stockholdings are lumped together.

Gradually—too gradually for my liking—ownership of American industry is thus being diffused among the whole population of the United States through this direct or indirect ownership. Two million Americans still own 20 per cent, or more, of all this. All the same, gradually ownership of American industry is increasingly coming to lie in the hands of the American people. Not, let us note, of the American state—government has nothing to do with it. Wealth, in the form of securities of corporations, can be, and is being, distributed widely without affecting the management or the effectiveness of the enterprise—and without throwing management power into political hands.

On the other side, as a second social fact, there are the managements of corporations. These, now, are coming to be chiefly professional administrators. Increasingly they are men trained in universities, in schools of business administration, in economics or in law. They form the executive staffs of the large corporations. They are well paid. They do not "own" the corporations—their stockholdings are relatively tiny. Sociologically, they are really second cousins of the bureaucratic executives who would manage the enterprises if they were operated by government. The difference between them and the bureaucrats is that the initiative is primarily theirs, not that of the government. As noted, this relatively small group of 40,000 or 50,000 directors and managers is responsible for operating the large corporate enterprises. Actually, far fewer have the real power. They contrast with the unorganized million or so of proprietors of tiny enterprises which among them divide between one-fourth and one-fifth of American manufacture and production.

Most corporate managers are astonished—even shocked—when they are compared to the managers and executives of, let us say, the state commissariats in the Soviet Union and other Communist countries. Yet essentially they are similar. True, their business is to make profits for their corporation—no corporation can run for long at a loss. But they are responsible, and know they are responsible, for more than merely profitable operation. They are responsible for the production of the goods and services on which America and its communities have come to rely. They must plan ahead. If they do not produce enough steel, enough oil, enough electricity, enough motor cars, enough shirts, enough machine tools, or enough cigarettes (as the case may be), their companies and they will be in trouble, and they know it.

And they must produce these goods and these services at prices considered reasonable or just by the American public who buys them. In some sectors the government fixes that price. It fixes, for example, the fares charged by railroads and airlines, charges for electricity and gas, tolls paid on the pipelines that take oil and natural gas from the fields of production to the cities consuming them. But even where the government does not fix the price, and where—theoretically—the corporation has the right to charge any price it pleases, corporate managers know that they will be in trouble if the public comes to believe that they are abusing the economic power inherent in these huge organizations.

THE CONTROL OF CORPORATE POWER

How is this outside control of these immensely powerful organizations made effective? There are a number of answers.

First, the United States does not permit monopoly. As long ago as 1890, the Sherman Antitrust Act was passed forbidding conspiracies in restraint of trade which tend to form a monopoly. It has been strengthened by later legislation designed to maintain a degree of competition. As our law has developed, any corporation achieving a monopoly in any substantial line may be attacked by the Department of Justice of the United States. The federal courts may decree that it be "dissolved" into a number of component elements. As of today, a monopoly is illegal—except where the government specifically permits it, as it does in the case of railroads, electric light companies and other public utilities. But in those cases the government usually fixes the price the corporation may charge. For the others, the result has been that in most industries, from three to five or six very large corporations carry on a majority of the industry, while perhaps 20, 30, or 50 smaller, economically powerless corporations operate the rest. An extreme case is the American motor car industry. There, three companies, General Motors, Ford, and Chrysler Corporation, manufacture and sell 80 per cent and more of all automobiles sold in the American market. We call this "oligopoly." Even so, the large corporations compete against each other up to a point—and this keeps the prices they charge within more or less reasonable limits. The government enforces competition on industry. Competition is not a natural state of affairs; rather it exists where the state requires it.

Second, the United States has its own peculiar and very loose form of economic planning. It is embodied in a little known law—the so-called "Employment Act of 1946." That act requires the United States government to use all of its resources to assure, under a competitive system, "maximum employment, maximum production, and maximum purchasing power." It constitutes a Council of Economic Advisers appointed by the President of the United States. These men advise him. They also work out statistically the situation of the United States. Where they see tendencies emerging which reduce employment, purchasing power, or production, they must recommend remedial measures. Since the administration of President John F. Kennedy, they have worked out "guidelines" covering the essential American industries. These guidelines indicate what the level of prices should be in each of these industries—what the rates of interest on borrowed money should be, and what should be the acceptable rate of wage increases. (As a rule, they recommend that wages can be increased in each year in an amount corresponding to the increase in productivity per man.) Factually, the real wage of American workmen goes up about 3 per cent a year. They can look forward to having over 30 per cent more purchasing power ten years from today. Prices charged by each corporation may or may not increase. The assumption is that the greater the volume of goods produced, the lower the cost. The resulting profit should be divided partly by increasing wages, partly by adding to the company's profits, for use either for dividends or for forming of capital.

When a labor union demands a higher wage increase than is justified, or when a powerful corporation raises prices beyond the guidelines, the federal government feels free to intervene. It tries to persuade and, if need be, applies pressure, so that the labor union and the corporate manufacturer, or both, shall keep wages and prices within these guidelines.

We are only part way along in development of this sort of control. President Kennedy made history by intervening to ask the steelworkers to moderate their demand for wage increases—as they did—and thereafter by attacking the steel companies which promptly raised prices all along the line. The corporations retreated; the price increase was cancelled. A similar discussion took place over the price of aluminum. Compliance has thus far been voluntary. Yet few corporations and, in general, few labor unions, despite their vast economic power, have challenged the power of the United States government. The guidelines have been in general, though not in all cases, respected.

So the corporation world which the managers control works always in the presence of three outside elements. Labor unions can and do demand wage increases; this gives them a continuing share in the greater profits of the corporations. Competitors are always anxious to take a greater part of the market; this means that prices are held down by competition. Finally, there is always the government, which follows the general thinking of the Council of Economic Advisers and is prepared to move in if the charges to the public become too great.

WHAT NEXT FOR THE CORPORATIONS?

So much for the present. The future is more exciting—more productive, possibly more dangerous. For, increasingly, science and mechanics are learning to make machines do the work which in the past was done by men. This is called automation. It is even learning to make machines which perhaps will make decisions formerly made by men. This is called cybernetics, and it has already led to the advent of the great computers. No one yet knows whether these applications of science, mathematics, and mechanics will displace great numbers of workers from their jobs. Yet everyone knows that the men displaced will not allow themselves to be thrown on a human scrap heap. What is the proper method of handling men who are displaced by machines? But what should be done if it develops that far less work is needed? I have no answer myself nor will I try here to summarize the answers of others. One thing can be said. The new industrial revolution can, readily, provide all goods and services needed to take care of everyone in comfort. The problem will not be how to support displaced men. It will be how their time shall be occupied.

Since corporations are the very organizations engaged in this new industrial revolution—they buy computers, their research supplies cybernetics, and theirs are the automated factories—they are crucial in the new era. A half-century ago, they would, after installing the machine, discharge the men and leave the problem to the community. No responsible corporate manager would take that position today, if only because it would lead to an immediate strike. He knows that the problem must be solved in conjunction with his production. He is calling in the best talent he can find from universities, engineering schools, and economic institutes. This is as far away from Karl Marx as one can readily imagine.

Both now and in the future another fact is important. The large corporations service a mass market. The larger and more prosperous the population, the larger these markets and presumably the larger the profits. It is in the interest of the large corporations to have purchasing power as widely distributed as possible. If, for example, every American family had a purchasing power of $15,000 a year, corporations could sell vastly more than they do today. If purchasing power is concentrated only in half of American families, they cannot possibly do as well. It has become literally advantageous for large corporations that poverty be abolished and that social problems be solved. Not often in history have the interests of the holders of economic power coincided with those of the masses; yet such is beginning to be the case.

This is a new element in American history—a far cry from the days when corporations fought social security, unemployment insurance, and old-age pensions; and fought Franklin Roosevelt when he inaugurated the program in 1933. Today they do not.

Not because they have become philanthropist or idealist—they haven't. They are merely discovering that, when social problems are solved, the size of their markets increases. Henry Ford prophesied this in 1917; now, his forecast is coming to be fact.

Resistance to solving social problems—evidenced by the conservatives who backed Senator Goldwater in the 1964 election—comes chiefly from the minority of small proprietors. Numerically, they are considerable. Taken together, there are several million individual entrepreneurs, still operating as small owners did in the days of Karl Marx and well into the twentieth century. But the total volume of their operations (farms aside) probably accounts for less than one-fifth of the total production of goods and services of the country. The powerful corporations are otherwise interested. Their managements and (to the extent that they have an opinion) many of the millions of shareholders of stock are more interested in the welfare state. Education of corporate managements along this line has proceeded, albeit slowly. They were massively against Franklin Roosevelt's New Deal in 1933. A majority of them (not all) nevertheless support President Lyndon Johnson's Great Society and his war on poverty. Controversy is more likely to turn on methods, on the speed with which social programs are enacted, and on the handling of money and credit. Policies which, as they understand them, may create inflation will be opposed; corporations in general want a stable price level—though each, of course, would like to see prices rise in its own field. While each corporation will fight for its own particular interest—this is the nature of corporations—they will be balanced by others with contrary interests. Steel companies will, of course, want higher prices for their product. On the other hand, General Motors and its associates, as principal steel buyers, will want the price kept down. They must all rely on the government to maintain a balance.

THE MODERN CORPORATION PUT IN PERSPECTIVE

The financial editor of the London *Economist,* Mr. Fred Hirsch, made a tour of the United States in October 1965. British commentators in general have been critical of the United

States. To everyone's surprise, his report was favorable. Everything, he said, "seems to be going right":

> It is not just that America now leads the western world in the duration and scale of its economic growth. . . . There seems to be an equal rejuvenation in the vigour and purpose of society as a whole, in pursuit not merely of economic enrichment but of social balance. More astounding than the belated acceptance by the American business community of the economics of J. M. Keynes has been its surprisingly early bowing before the politics of J. K. Galbraith

—who teaches liberal economics at Harvard.

Mr. Hirsch found no real business opposition to the "welfare program"—it was rather seen as a "defense of American values." The capacity of the corporate system to increase production indicated that the welfare job could be done without inflicting too much sacrifice on any group of Americans.

This is the managerial contribution provided by the American corporations. Their directors are not altruists. They are probably as grasping and ambitious as most. But they know how to organize, and to produce, and to increase production. They manufacture their own capital through the existing price system. So, they do not need to go to the big bankers who dominated them almost completely a generation ago. Only a vestigial remainder of "finance capitalism" or "Wall Street domination" now is left. The money brokers do not dictate to large corporations. If anything, it is the other way around.

Over the entire system, as we noted, there is a typically American and typically nebulous form of governmental control. It is political rather than legal. The government is relied on to keep the whole system in balance. It must curb rapacious price policies on the part of the corporation. It must keep the demands of labor moderate and reasonable. It must prevent monopoly and it must keep money, credit and interest rates in reasonable stability. It can use any tools it has at its command. A major question in American corporation law is whether our unorganized method of control through the guidelines of the Council of Economic Advisers can be kept in its present form or whether it must be crystallized into more conventional administrative regulation. For the moment, neither the American government nor the American corporations want bureaucratic regulation—probably both prefer the present procedure. The more intelligent members of the corporation community realize that government must keep a balance among the desires of the corporations to make more money, of bankers to collect higher interest, of labor to have higher pay, and of the public to buy cheaply the products it wants. On the whole, the system jogs along without too much strain.

It is not perfect. Among intellectuals here and abroad there is a good deal of criticism. Oddly, the criticism is philosophical and esthetic rather than economic. Advertising, it is truly said, is placed chiefly by the big corporations. So they dominate the billboards, plaster their stuff over newspapers and magazines, stimulate fears and emotions, and make American civilization unesthetic and unbeautiful. This is true, and it represents a set of problems with which the government, the corporations and the public generally will have to wrestle in the coming years. President Johnson had a brief skirmish with them when he caused the enactment of the first federal act designed to maintain the beauty of highways by outlawing some of the hideous billboards that defaced them. Eventually cities will have to tackle the problem for themselves—as the Governor of Puerto Rico, Luis Muñoz Marin, outlawed the uglier screaming electric signs that defaced his capital city of San Juan. A steady tattoo of criticism beats on the great corporations that handle television broadcasting, demanding that the Federal Communications Commission do something about it. In the not too distant future, problems like these will rank equally with the problems of abolishing poverty and of bringing the 20 million or so Negroes out of their present economic despair and into reasonable economic comfort. These lie ahead, and the corporate system as well as government will have to wrestle with them.

Of importance is the fact that without the development of the large corporation, control of any kind would probably have been impossible. I do not see that the present economic and social progress could have been attained had American production been wholly divided among many millions of small enterprises.

We do not have to thank the corporate system for producing results. We can say it has been an essential and increasingly cooperative part of the machinery—kept in bounds by a government which fundamentally reflects the value system of America.

5 THE CONSUMER IN AN AFFLUENT SOCIETY

James N. Morgan

If the corporation is the most discussed institution of the American economy at home and abroad, the consumer is still the one for whom that economy is assumed to operate. "The consumer is king" is a widely repeated statement–but this chapter makes it clear that it is hard to be a wise king in the face of such a flood of goods and services as the American consumer faces today. This king, like others, turns out to benefit from some outside help.

I have noticed that books make a splash with their titles, often without reference to what is said inside. People who haven't read the book *The Ugly American* don't realize that The Ugly American is a kind of hero or good guy in the book, though the general notion of bad Americans is in the book too. Similarly, Galbraith's book *The Affluent Society* got everybody talking about affluence, even though his main point was not a critique of sinful indulgence but a call for a larger allocation of resources to the public sector—more socialism, to use a loaded word.

The term affluent society has remained, partly because it is the only term we have to mean high income as distinct from large wealth. The average American consumer is not rich. He may own a home and a few assets and a growing right to a pension, but he is not wealthy. He does, however, have a high and growing current income.

WORK

Some have wondered why Americans work so hard to buy things they don't need. They argue that it is too bad that Americans in spite of all their productivity have less real leisure than they had half a century ago. Dr. Grazia's book *Of Time, Work and Leisure* represents a massive writing effort by one man urging others not to work so hard.

But apparently one of the reasons why our national income keeps rising is that most Americans would rather have the things money will buy than more free time. Many men have second jobs or work overtime; the average middle-aged married man claims he works 2,200 hours a year, more than 40 hours a week. Most women work even after they are married until the first child is born, and the number of older married women in the labor force has increased dramatically. The average wife who works, however, works only about 1,400 hours a year, even if she has no children. The average family with children also spends nearly 2,500 hours a year on regular housework.

Of course, having more money but not more leisure, we have developed ways to use our leisure more intensively, which usually means more expensively. Vacation travel by car or plane takes not only time but money.

All this has been possible because the United States has had good times, with only minor setbacks, for twenty years now—for at least a majority of the people.

DISTRIBUTION OF INCOME

This increasing affluence of those who had jobs has made the plight of those with little or no income seem relatively more serious and unacceptable. When it also became clear that cutting income taxes couldn't help those with no income, the war on poverty was started. Many of us think it moves too slowly and concentrates too much on getting people back into the labor market when what they need is income maintenance (some of them are unemployable), but at least a start is being made.

One problem of an affluent society, then, is the distribution of that affluence. In the United States it has been widely distributed over four-fifths of the population, and we need to do something for the rest. More recently, the demand for scientists for the space race, industrial research, government-sponsored research, and teaching has started an increasing spread of incomes as between the college trained and those with somewhat less education. This means increased inequality at the upper end of the income scale.

As an economist I'm concerned with the distribution of income not just because I want to see no one deprived unduly, but also because part of the justification, and the requirements, for effective working of a market economy is that the money demands for commodities and services should reflect real needs and wants being satisfied. This is true only if the needs of all the people can be expressed in money, and this will be true only if everyone has at least the income necessary for a minimum standard of decency.

PRIVATE VERSUS PUBLIC CONSUMPTION

A second problem that has become more obvious with affluence is the one Galbraith's *Affluent Society* focused on, the problem of the relative size of the public sector, or the proportion of the national output consumed socially, in the form of public parks, roads, schools, and other "social goods." It is relatively easy for people's earnings to increase over time and to be spent on a wider and wider array of things for their personal use. But expansion of social functions often requires votes of elected bodies to increase expenditures and taxes, and sometimes even means that people must vote for increases in the taxes they will have to pay. These changes take time and planning and farsighted wisdom. Indeed, as the new social wants become more elaborate, it becomes more difficult to be sure that they are really desired by the people. And, since any one project may benefit only a fraction of the people, it may be necessary to work out packages of projects in order to obtain a majority vote for the package. It may take some ingenuity to expand the public sector so that it remains true that everyone pays taxes and everyone benefits in one way or another.

COMPETITION

A third requirement for a well-organized market economy with maximum freedom is enough competition among the producers so that the consumer is offered a choice and, if he is really willing to pay for something, someone is likely to produce it for him. Perhaps more important, we need competition so that if a product can be made better or less expensively every producer will be forced to make it better or less expensively because he knows that at least one of his competitors will do so and he wants his share of the business, or more.

Some say it is easier to have competition in a growing economy with wide markets, but others argue that consumers then get careless and profits lead to mergers. We have antitrust laws, and they help. Sometimes, however, critical writers are needed to spot the exorbitant prices and profits or the slowness to respond to the consumer that go with collusion, and raise a hue and cry. But we always prefer it if the forces of competition lead to lower prices, or more for our money, or new and better things, without lawsuits or public hearings.

There is a fourth and final requirement before we can be satisfied with the way our economic system works, and this is that consumers must know what they want, and what they are getting when they buy.

CONSUMER: SOVEREIGN OR SUCKER?

It is easy to make a case for the thesis that consumers are merely buying what some clever advertiser tells them to, and then convincing themselves that they cannot get along without it. It may even be damaging their health, as cigarettes do. In the case of some products they may not even know which of the many brands is better or worse than others. Once again, it is not just the individual consumer but the whole society that has a stake in the matter. We must see to it that the consumer has information, and somehow gets what he wants but not what is harmful to him, or inferior.

CONSUMER INFORMATION—GENERAL INSIGHTS AND PRINCIPLES

How can we be sure that consumers are informed but still not tell them what to do? And if the government tries to inform consumers, how can it avoid the delicate problems that would come with ruining one man's business by reporting that his competitor's products were better?

What has happened in the United States, for better or worse, is that the task of providing consumers with information about the relative merits of individual products has been left to private groups, who by circulating printed test results and other information have obtained sufficient funds to be able to provide a continuous small stream of information over the years. The government has for the most part furnished only general information, and mostly in the food and household operation areas where brand names were not important. You can find many interesting pamphlets put out by the U.S. Department of Agriculture, by the various State Agricultural Experiment Stations, and by a variety of other government agencies, on how to select a cut of meat, or take care of a man's suit, or grow your own vegetables, or decide whether a smaller size egg is really more economical at six cents less per dozen.

There are all sorts of technical information in the libraries, of course, but it takes training to know how to use them. It is difficult to say just how much consumer education takes place in the public schools as a whole. It certainly varies, since the public school systems are run by locally elected school boards in the many school districts in the United States. Most of it is in an elective course which not every student takes. Children are taught something about nutrition, and if they take driver education, something about the costs and problems of owning a car. If they take the right course they may even learn something about credit and interest rates, or even a little about how insurance works. But it is probably a fair generalization to say that their courses in public school stay away from controversial areas, and particularly from comparison of the merits of competing commodities.

On the other hand, the kind of general training a consumer needs in budgeting, insurance, credit, decision-making, and the like has never been successfully conducted by voluntary groups either. Over the years many consumer associations and societies have been started, but only those survived which provided some more explicit service, such as the merchandising of commodities by the cooperatives or the specific brand and product information of such consumer testing groups as Consumers Union. People are just not willing to pay voluntarily for *general* information and education not connected with the specific problems they currently face.

There remain the general articles which appear in the various publications of cooperatives and credit unions, and even in some of the hobby and homemaking magazines. But the circulation of most of the former is small, and one must always be a little suspicious of the potential biases in magazines which carry advertising from producers. The bias generally seems to take the form of omitting discussion of problems rather than in any lack of honesty. Homemaking magazines continually sing the praises of new products but almost never mention their disadvantages or difficulties.

CONSUMER INFORMATION ON BRANDS AND PRICES

What about the more specific information about individual branded products? Here the various governments have mostly been afraid to do anything. Even if a state agricultural experiment station has a home economist who tests various washing machines, the results will be given without identifying the brand names of the machines. On the other hand, we have one successful and one moderately successful consumer organization devoted to product testing and rating.

The world's largest consumer organization is Consumers Union of the United States; it publishes *Consumer Reports,* which has a circulation that keeps edging up to a million. Consumers Union uses the money from subscriptions and sales of *Consumer Reports* to purchase samples of products at retail and test them in its laboratories. It also gets information from its own member-subscribers about their experiences with new products, and summarizes that in the *Reports.* Consumers Union was formed in the 1930's as a splinter group which broke off from Consumers Research, but has long since surpassed its parent. The arguments that caused the split were over whether such an organization should report on the labor conditions under which the products tested were made—this was before the Fair Labor Standards Act was passed, and there were some products made in sweatshops—and, secondly, over the question whether the employees in the testing organization itself could have a union. The new Consumers Union group believed that both answers were yes. Partly because of this, and partly because independent judging of the merits of products was seen as threatening (particularly to the advertising profession), Consumers Union was for years subjected to continued charges of subversion and Communist influence. It was never on the Attorney General's list of subversive organizations, but it was for some years on the much less reputable list of the House Un-American Activities Committee. Consumers Union fought the charges so effectively that it has the distinction of being the only living organization ever officially removed from that list of subversive organizations. And this was not because Consumers Union changed, but because it finally convinced HUAC that the charges were false. This was the period when individuals could make unsupported accusations before the committee and the charges became "evidence" without any of the usual legal safeguards.

So *Consumer Reports* has a circulation of less than a million copies, and the *Consumer Research Bulletin* of a few hundred thousand. Their readership is much larger of course. They are in many public libraries, and people borrow them from friends. And as any economist knows, if even part of the consumers are informed, they can make quite a difference in competitive markets and be a powerful force to which manufacturers respond. It is the few consumers at the margin threatening to shift to his competitor who worry the producer and motivate him to improve his product or lower his price.

The limitations on the supply of information for consumers remain serious, however. Limited funds restrict the *range* and *frequency* of the testing programs. Even where there seem to be only a few national brands of a product, rapid changes in models and details make it difficult for the consumer to be sure he is getting the same model that was tested. And there are wide variations in the prices at which the products are actually sold, so that the "best buy" may vary from place to place depending on which of several brands is actually cheaper.

Much of the opposition to Consumers Union by producers and distributors, and by the advertising and publishing business, has disappeared, though some suspicion and fear remain. Interestingly enough, the residual hostility comes from the advertising and publishing industry rather than from the manufacturers. This is easy to understand: if consumers bought brands on the basis of independent tests and ratings, advertising would be less necessary and less profitable. It is for the same reasons that resale price maintenance laws, cleverly called Fair Trade Laws, are supported by *Printers' Ink,* a magazine for advertisers and publishers, but not by *Business Week,* a magazine largely read by manufacturers.

Thus the general situation in the United States is that there are some private groups which on a limited basis provide both specific brand quality and price information and general consumer information, and some general consumer information and education are furnished by the public schools and by the publications of some government bureaus. But the total supply of information is limited, and depends on the interest and capacity of the consumers to read and use it. As in all kinds of adult education, the best-educated and upper-income people make the greatest use of the information. In spite of continued efforts by Consumers Union to reach lower-income people, the readers of *Consumer Reports* tend to be those who need it least.

There is some hope that under the Anti-Poverty Program of the

Johnson administration some projects may be set up to provide consumer education for low-income people. Such projects would probably concentrate less on brands and prices than on more general types of consumer education, such as how to plan and budget family expenditures, how insurance and installment credit work, and how to handle some of the legal problems faced by low-income groups such as garnishment of their wages for uncollected debts, eviction from their dwellings, and their rights when victimized by sellers.

CONSUMER PROTECTION FROM FRAUD, DECEPTION, AND EXPLOITATION BY MONOPOLIES

Even for the more educated, better-off majority, however, information and intelligence are not enough to deal with the possibility of outright fraud, deception, dangerous products, or exploitation by monopolies. So there are a variety of devices to *protect* the consumer, as distinct from merely informing him. The most important of these are government programs, and this is the area where there has been the most general agreement that the government has a legitimate function. (The budgets for these activities have been relatively small, and it has often taken a crisis or mass protests from consumers before the necessary laws were passed.)

At the national (federal) level, the Food and Drug Administration is concerned with keeping dangerous drugs and spoiled foods off the market. Its policing task is a mammoth one, and until recently was hampered both by limited budgets and by inadequate legal powers. It took the thalidomide scandal, with the births of deformed babies, to dramatize the problems; then the law was strengthened in 1962. But even at that, the FDA had done a better job of keeping down the use of thalidomide before the scandal than many other countries, including some in Western Europe.

The Food and Drug Administration is concerned with the safety, effectiveness, and purity of drugs and foods, and with unjustified claims, but not with the extent of competition. In the rapidly developing pharmaceutical field, particularly antibiotics, new and effective drugs have led to very high profits and what many charge is unusual slowness in the way competition drives down the prices of the new drugs.

To deal with misleading advertising we have the Federal Trade Commission, which had its concern with unfair competition broadened in 1938 to include deceptive labels and advertisements. The FTC can only stop statements which are demonstrably false, and advertisers can still brag vaguely that their product is "better" without saying what it is better than, or "new, improved" without proving it is any different from what it was before. The major frauds that can be stopped are fictitious "regular prices," used only to make the product seem more valuable, and "bait advertising," to get people into stores where they are steered away from the cheap item advertised—or even refused it—and sold something at a higher price.

The remaining government agencies deal with monopolies or potential monopolies and help the consumer either by preserving the competition that provides a wide choice and drives down prices or by regulating the rates charged by such natural monopolies as the utilities, railroads, and airlines. The Antitrust Division of the Department of Justice tries to preserve competition where it is feasible. The Interstate Commerce Commission, the Civil Aeronautics Board, and the Federal Communications Commission regulate those industries where there is natural monopoly. Most regulatory bodies have some limited representation of consumer interests. There is, however, a tendency for regulatory bodies in constant contact with an industry to become spokesmen for that industry and defenders of its interests rather than representatives of the broader consuming public.

There has been extensive opposition from business to recently proposed legislation calling for better information about the true interest rate on installment loans and for elimination of deceptive packaging.

STATE AND LOCAL GOVERNMENT PROTECTION FOR THE CONSUMER

The regulation of many utility rates is done by the individual states. The states and some localities also set standards for housing, medical care, sanitation, and weights and measures. Most Americans are completely unaware of these regulations, but occasionally standards slip, a furor erupts, and something is done about it. The problem of proper weights and measures has shifted with the coming of so much prepackaged and prepared food. And attempts are being made—at the federal level, since so many of the packages are shipped across state lines—to set up standards for letting the consumer know the actual contents of a package and for reducing the variation in content weights. Competition to provide more for the money is fine, but most people concerned with the consumer do not think it is desirable to have competition in the size and design of the package, even if it misleads the purchaser.

A few states have actually set up offices of consumer affairs, others have fraud bureaus in the state attorney general's office. But in general, the state administration of standards has been only passable, and its attention to other consumer problems minimal.

PRIVATE GROUPS THAT AID THE CONSUMER

Groups such as Consumers Union provide consumers not only with facts about brands and prices but with information on frauds and on the general techniques of deception. In addition there are some professional and "industry groups." The American Medical Association and the American Dental Association have committees concerned with frauds and quackery and the effectiveness of medicines and toothpastes, but they seldom attempt to rate branded products.

The American Standards Association and the Underwriters

Laboratories help set standards and thus help industry police itself. There are also trade association activities concerned with self-policing in many industries, but they are subject to the obvious limitations of any self-regulatory body.

Private consumer associations have never been very successful in this area, partly because the frauds and deceptions are sporadic and transitory practices, partly because they are employed mostly on the less well educated, who are hard to reach and help (or even to find to testify against a fraudulent promoter).

SUMMARY ON CONSUMER INFORMATION AND PROTECTION

All this adds up to a rather wide variety of activities dedicated to informing or protecting the consumer. How they compare with the measures adopted elsewhere is hard to say, though they are probably more extensive in the United States than in most other countries. Certainly the private consumer associations have until recently done better here, although in relation to its population England has surpassed us in the circulation of its magazine *Which?*

The consumer is still required to exercise his own intelligence and caution in the United States. Higher incomes make a little inefficiency less worrisome, but they also make it more possible for inefficiency to creep in if the consumer feels he can afford to be careless.

My guess would be that the problems of fraud and ignorance are minimal among the upper two-thirds of the population ranked by income. Thus the lack of consumer information and protection compounds the problem of poverty in the United States, because the people with the lowest incomes have neither the wisdom nor the time to shop around nor the training to figure out interest rates or the tricks in guarantees. Their struggle to earn enough to live on is made more difficult because they get less for each dollar they do have.

CONSUMER MOVEMENTS AS AN AMERICAN EXPORT

The consumers of the United States, then, are on the whole better informed than some, not so well off as they might be. The so-called consumer movement consists of Consumers Union, some professional educators, a few consumer cooperatives, and some help from the larger labor unions.

There has been no prosperous movement that could help start similar movements abroad. Consumers Union has provided small funds and large encouragement to other groups abroad. And there has been a dramatic increase in the number and strength of the consumer product testing organizations around the world. The president of Consumers Union, Colston Warne, has done much to stimulate this, but the major reasons were probably the growing income in many countries, the wider range of choices consumers could make, and their desire to have better information with which to make these choices. There is an International Office of Consumers Unions at The Hague which in 1964 issued a "Consumers Directory" of more than fifty consumer associations. Some are small; some are suspect, since they accept advertising or government subsidy; but their numbers and strength are growing.

There are problems, even for an organization which concentrates on factual information: lawsuits, competing groups, apathy, and the difficulty of merchandising something which should be a free good—information.

IS INFORMATION A SALABLE COMMODITY?

This is indeed the consumer's problem around the world. He is badly in need of information. But it is expensive to collect and process and distribute information. What is worse, information, unlike the commodities it may be about, is not salable. All a consumer group really sells is convenience. Anyone who wants the information can read the reports at the library or borrow them from a friend. Economists refer to such a commodity as a "social good," the output of which is usually decided upon by a political process with prior agreement on the distribution of cost (by taxes).

So consumers tend to be unwilling to pay for very general information because it is not of much interest to them. And they are unwilling to pay for specific information either because someone else has already paid for it or because it is not available at any price.

Perhaps, then, the government really should be in the business of providing consumer information. In Sweden and now in Germany the trend is in this direction. But how does one assure freedom from political control? And if trade associations or other groups of producers try to police their own industry by providing consumers with information, how can one be sure that this device is not misused to the advantage of a few large producers?

One possibility is the development of mass-media (television) programs for general consumer education (what to do when they threaten to garnishee your wages), paid for by the government and disguised as soap operas. Combined with the continued growth and effectiveness of private product testing organizations such as Consumers Union, and continued government protection against fraud and dangerous products, this might be sufficient. But it might also be necessary for the government at least to subsidize an independent agency, run by consumer representatives, devoted to the general interests of consumers. Perhaps there is even a need for a Federal Department of the Consumer.

Some fascinating and widely selling books about the motivation researchers and their techniques of mass persuasion certainly exaggerate the gullibility of consumers. What evidence we have indicates that the consumer doesn't believe everything he reads and is generally rather sensible in the major decisions he makes. He doesn't know how to calculate an interest rate, but he does shop around for the best terms, which include the interest charges. A great deal of advertising promotes competing products which are practically indistinguishable so far as the consumer is concerned. It may cancel itself out and lead to some wasted resources, but the consumer is not harmed.

During this period of rising incomes Americans have spent a great deal of their new money on homes, cars, television sets, and other appliances. Nearly one-fourth of the families in the United States now own two or more cars. Nearly two-thirds own their own homes, and there have been vast improvements in the quality of housing appliances. Basic necessities such as washers, clothes dryers, stoves, and the like still account for the bulk of the appliance expenditures. All these things satisfy obvious needs.

There is still the uncomfortable possibility that by making use of a person's unconscious drives he can be persuaded to buy something and then convinced that he cannot get along without it. But that unanswerable charge can be made about almost everything we do, and I'd prefer to worry about more immediate and obvious problems, such as how to get more information and economic insight to the ordinary consumer.

INFLUENCING AND PREDICTING THE CONSUMER'S BEHAVIOR

There is one more way the consumer is of concern in an affluent society. Where consumers are so important, and have so much money to spend and so much freedom to change their spending patterns, it is important whether they spend or save.

Consumers can shift from spending to not spending, with great inpact on the total economy. Hence it becomes increasingly important to assess and predict consumers' willingness to spend money. There is no fixed relation of aggregate consumption to aggregate income. Consumers not only change their levels of consumption but they may speed up or postpone investments in houses, cars, and appliances. To the consumer these expenditures are an investment, leading to only a small change in current consumption, but to the economy they may mean a major demand for labor and materials to produce the larger house or the new car. Even the crude national income statistics show greater year-to-year changes in consumer investments than in business investment in the United States, so it becomes important to forecast these changes.

My colleague George Katona has for many years now been measuring consumer confidence and optimism, and sorting out the events that change them and the changing spending patterns that result from them. Control over mortgage credit terms is being used to some extent to influence changes in consumer spending, and during times of emergency controls over installment credit were used in the same way.

CONCLUSION

Thus the consumer in the United States finds himself with an affluence and a freedom to choose his spending unparalleled in history. He also finds himself frequently without the information, knowledge, and sophistication necessary to make the decisions as well as he might like. Yet he is no pawn, and for the most part knows what he wants and resists being defrauded. He is willing to provide through government and private means a level of help for the poor in the United States and abroad which is insufficient and not in keeping with his own affluence, yet is unmatched in the history of philanthropy. In addition to foreign aid and the domestic poverty program, Americans give away between $15 and $20 billion a year in private charity. Some of it they get back in tax reductions, but only part. With his new economic power the consumer finds himself in danger of being expected to change his spending not only to fit his own needs but to help keep the economy in balance. So far, happily for the economy, he has shown himself willing to spend enough to keep the economy humming, particularly if well-designed tax cuts and other stimulants come along at the appropriate times.

came from President Grover Cleveland; they accompanied an 1887 veto of a Congressional appropriation of $25,000 for seed corn to aid Texas farmers who had been ruined by a drought.

There may be no economy anywhere else in the world that has seen so much controversy surround the gradual—some would say rapid—expansion of the government into new fields of activity. Even those who have been the architects of parts of the expansion have felt called upon to apologize for their handiwork while they still worked upon it. Many have defended their own favorite form of federal expansion and then turned the next moment to criticize the swollen bureaucracies of Washington. Thus, for example, those newspapers that call for a reversal of the trend toward bigger government are often equally vigorous defenders of the current federal subsidies on the mailing costs of their own newspapers. The issue is "the right of the people to know" when it concerns the newspaper subsidy; it is "rampant federal bureaucracy" when it concerns someone else's subsidy. There is no planned sweep of events in the growth of government; there is only a succession of pragmatic responses to new needs as defined by one group or another. A response here begets a new demand there perhaps, but this is a far cry from a planned march by one political party or another into bigger government.

Let me, at this early point, anticipate the two closing themes of this chapter. One is that the United States is paying a high price today for the emotionalism and name-calling—"socialism" has been the favorite epithet of generations of critics—which have long surrounded the issue of the public economy. Since the 1930's this price has only in part been one of slowing down new activities of government until the cost of intervention has become excessively high. To a greater extent the price has been one of lack of much rigorous attention to the question of how we might get the most for whatever public dollars we spend. The government has been painted as so much of a devil for so long that it has not been fashionable to ask about the efficiency with which it undertook its work; "government" and "efficiency" were assumed to be mutually exclusive terms. But the second closing theme of the chapter will be that the times are changing. The late 1960's, when government's new activities are manifest on all sides, may prove to be the years when this economy at long last developed some useful yardsticks to apply to its public endeavors.

AN OVERVIEW OF PUBLIC SPENDING

How much public spending is there in the American economy? At the present time, government's total spending on goods and services accounts for about 20 per cent of the Gross National Product. At the turn of this century, the figure was under 10 per cent; at the height of World War II, it was over 45 per cent. The current figure is thus a long way from either the 1900 extreme of minimum government or the 1944 extreme of an economy where half of all production was commandeered by government. Another comment on the statistics of public spending; for all of the persistent concern about the federal government's encroachment on more and more areas of economic activity, its spending as a percentage of a rapidly rising gross national product is actually falling in the 1960's. The marked growth is in state and local government purchases; 1965 was the first year in four decades when these state and local units together spent more on goods and services than did Washington.

By looking at a couple of examples of what is public and what is private in the American economy we may find a way to highlight some of the current issues and confusions in the perpetual public-private debate. The post office is a public enterprise here, as in all other countries. But, judged by the standards of a few other nations, it is not a model of efficiency or innovation. What is characteristically American is that it is easier to hear the conclusion, "What else would you expect from a government-run business?" or "It would be better to turn the whole mail-carrying service over to private firms," than it is to hear solid proposals to create conditions within government which would permit a better postal system. The problem is less one of technological know-how or of economic will-do than it is of political can-do, for the post office has long been locked into the political system in ways that impede rapid improvement in its operations.

Or consider an example of a private enterprise. The railroads, like the airlines and the telephone industry, are operated by private companies which seek profits—unsuccessfully in some cases—for their many stockholders. But all are so heavily regulated by law on most of their rates and many of their services that the distinction between them and their publicly-owned counterparts abroad is somewhat confusing. Then, too, the sicker among the railroads, particularly those with high losses on local commuter traffic, are increasingly looking to Washington to help them out with subsidies or even outright purchase. Some metropolitan areas have tried to make a dent in their mounting problems of traffic congestion by buying up the private and uncoordinated local transportation companies in their areas and operating them as a coordinated public enterprise. It is no panacea, but it sometimes offers a fighting chance. Indeed, the whole field of local transportation offers one striking lesson about public or private ownership: there are efficient public systems and private ones, and there are inefficient public systems and private ones. Mayor Fiorello LaGuardia of New York City used to say that there is no Democratic or Republican way to collect garbage; he might have added that there is no uniquely public or private way to run a railroad.

A MATTER OF ATTITUDES

Before we turn to considering how it happens that government's role in the economy has expanded, it is well to ask another question, not about facts but about attitudes: Why is it that Americans have agreed so strongly (if inconsistently) that whatever can be done privately should be done that way? No doubt some of the case is fabricated of emotion alone; this is where phrases such as "the heritage of our forefathers was private initiative" and "the business of America is business" come in. But, whatever merit these emotions may have, there is much more to the case than that. One additional basis for the argument is the firm conviction that no one knows better what the individual wants than that individual himself. To leave the maximum possible number of dollars in a man's hands to spend as he will, it is argued, is to leave him both the chance to maximize his personal well-being and the opportunity to grow in the process of making choices and living with the consequences. This way the goods that are produced will be those that individuals vote for by putting up their own individual dollars and not those that some government officers feel to be worthwhile for the people.

That argument, on first hearing, may seem to be the argument of the classical conservative. But it has more friends than that in the United States—and, I suspect, elsewhere. There is scarcely a man or woman, however vigorous his general defense of government's growing role, who does not object strongly to at least one particular form of public spending. The target of the wrath varies with the individual; it may be public funds for baseball or football stadia, or for transporting children to private schools operated by church groups, or for helping farmers to grow still bigger crops even while we try to figure out what to do with the last ones they grew, or even for defense itself. The point is that public spending must interfere with private spending, for no one has yet figured out a workable way by which each of us may pay taxes for those public activities in which he believes while passing up paying for those to which he objects. And the healthy by-product of what sometimes seems an obsessive American concern with government's growth may be that here more than elsewhere the costs of public spending have been forever in the limelight. "There's no such thing as a free lunch" is, originally, I believe, an American expression.

A second basis for the argument on behalf of privately produced goods and services is that, wherever there is competition among producers, there is a yardstick to measure the efficiency of producers. Survival is itself proof of efficiency if there is genuine competition. But let a public monopoly—or a private one, for that matter—produce a good and there is no way to tell whether it is being produced at the lowest possible cost. For a nation that has prided itself on being concerned about efficiency in production, this has long been a disadvantage in some public enterprises. And the argument has a corollary: when competition can be made to work, the government's role as regulator and prodder becomes less important. The Antitrust Division of the federal Department of Justice must still police the competition to guard against collusion; but, beyond that, Washington's activities can be severely restricted and men may be left to pursue their self-interests in relative freedom.

WHY HAS GOVERNMENT GROWN?

Now against the background of these arguments for keeping government's role to a minimum, how is it that this role grows in absolute terms if not in relative terms?

The first answer—and it is perhaps the cruelest commentary on our times—is that national security has pushed us in that direction. In the current fiscal year, forty cents in each of Washington's budget dollars will go directly to defense expenditures. Still other funds go to closely related items: the space program, payments to war veterans, and interest on a national debt which grew to its present size of over $300 billion primarily because of past wars. The merits of these heavy expenditures are of course open to debate in a free society. But three short points need to be made here. One is that, while they have all been approved by the elected representatives of the people, these expenditures involve tremendously complex issues on which it is harder and harder for the average citizen to comment intelligently. A second is that there are non-military by-products which flow into the civilian sector from these nominally military dollars; examples are the peaceful uses of atomic energy, improved aircraft design and performance, and even better educational facilities. A third point is that, as Professor Weidenbaum observes in Chapter 15, these expenditures are not essential just to keep the economy prosperous; there are few Americans who would not welcome enough easing of world tensions to permit diversion of defense dollars into a multitude of public and private channels.

The second explanation for bigger government today is to be found in new definitions of what public goods the nation must have in order to enjoy private goods. More and better automobiles create needs for more and better public highways. Rapidly changing technology and, at the same time, more leisure create demands for a better educational system. New medical knowledge creates expectations that it shall be made available to the public at large, sometimes without regard to individual ability to pay. The spreading decay in the central city cores of some of the largest metropolitan areas creates hopes that public enterprise, in league with private enterprise, may yet arrest the decay and rebuild cities of beauty and efficiency alike. And in time polluted rivers and polluted air will create an awareness that these things need not be, that men can improve their environment if they wish to devote resources to that end rather than to a competing one. Each of these areas is illustrative of democratic responses to new pressures in the society. Does government lead in building these demands (and hence confirm those who say the politicians live by creating new needs that men never knew they felt before) or does it follow the public (and hence confirm those who say, with Great Britain's F. M. Cornford, that nothing is ever done until everyone has been convinced about it for so long that it is now time to do something else instead)? The answer is probably both. It has taken both effective political articulation and widely based yearnings to produce today's public economy.

This present point, it must be admitted, embraces a broad range of degrees of urgency for public services. It speaks of needs, demands, expectations, hopes, and mere awarenesses. There is legitimate and inevitable debate about how far government should go along that range. Some needs are so obvious as to be beyond serious discussion. Water, which men agree should be plentiful, pure, and cheap, is such an example. But even this least controversial area illustrates why government has had to grow: new population, new communities, and new technology combine in some parts of the nation to make the adequacy of the water supply a matter of urgent concern. The problem reaches far beyond community lines and state lines for nature's watersheds and rivers show magnificent disregard for the lines man has scratched on his maps. The issue is not *whether* the federal government shall do more and more to ensure an adequate supply of water for tomorrow and the next day: the issue is only *when* that government will act with sufficient boldness and resources.

But over at the other end of the scale are areas where government programs deal with more controversial issues. Some programs, for example, are clearly designed as redistribution measures, and the goal of redistribution is itself in dispute. The most dramatic aspect of the American economy in the 1960's is surely the so-called war on poverty. Affluence elsewhere, the grip that poverty holds on particular, fast-growing groups in the population (the very old, the very young, and the racial minorities), and the access of the poor to new sources of power combined to make the issue one of widespread concern. But that concern has not yet produced unanimity about the rightness of large-scale government action to overcome poverty. If few men today are willing to use the Biblical injunction that "the poor ye always have with you" as an excuse to do nothing, still many men believe that private action, not public action, is the salvation of the poor. They can point to a few impressive private citizens' programs to bolster their case. And they can point to confusions, mistakes, inefficiencies, and even occasional corruption in the early years of the public war on poverty. But what they prove thereby to some, perhaps most, of their fellow Americans is that these are not "either-or" matters, that both public and private actions are necessary to lick an age-old problem suddenly moved to center stage.

This "either-or" point is critical for the American economy. It would be a bad day for that economy if we ever fell into the trap of believing that there is one and only one appropriate channel to deal with most of our challenges. Consider education, or health services, or housing, or employment services, or old-age security, or recreation: in each of these, we have a richer, more diverse society because there are both private and public mechanisms available to us. The economist has little to offer that will support an argument that any one area, except national defense, should be the exclusive terrain of either public or private spending. (The point cuts both ways; just as there may be good reasons why electric power should be generated publicly under some circumstances, so too there are good reasons why private enterprises should be permitted to be in the mail delivery business if they wish to do so.)

An extension of the point: the public and private spheres of economic activity do not operate under fundamentally different economic rules. In the United States, and elsewhere too, there is a tendency to forget in some public activities how much the price system can do to achieve particular ends. Prices do allocate and direct resource flows, be they public or private prices. And the public policy-makers must recognize the implications of any prices which they set. For example, water is now made available under government rate-setting at a considerably lower price for agricultural irrigation in Southern California than it is for the neighboring industrial-urban areas. The priorities may seem to some of us to be all wrong here, but the point remains that the prices have become instruments of a particular social policy. We cannot avoid the discriminating function built into all prices, but we can at least hold our governmental policy-makers accountable for the types of discrimination which they choose to make through their pricing policies.

THE SEARCH FOR A WORKABLE BALANCE

This then is an economy in search of a balance between its public and private sectors. In the balance, competition and complementarity alike play their parts, and the same economic rules govern both sectors. The optimum balance seems forever to be shifting as times and issues change, but the shifts when viewed in the aggregate are not dramatic ones. Nothing in the record to date justifies any conclusion of a headlong rush by this nation either toward an all-embracing government sphere or an all-private economy. And so as long as the balance continues, the stakes of public and private leaders alike in one another's affairs run high. Public leaders depend upon a healthy private economy for their revenues and for much of their ability to act effectively. Private leaders depend increasingly upon government for a wide range of essential services and for economic stabilization. This interdependence makes any mutual suspicions or misunderstandings rather perilous for both sides.

THE PRICE FOR MISTRUST OF GOVERNMENT

And so to the closing themes that were anticipated early in this chapter. One theme is the price which we have paid in America for the past record of widespread mistrust of government's activities in a predominantly private enterprise economy. Maybe we have not been alone among the world's peoples in having some skepticism about government's activities. And some such skepticism is healthy; as a nation we see no case to be made for the proposition that government anywhere can afford to be beyond criticism. But our degree of skepticism has been carried further than elsewhere in the world and has a high cost attached to it.

In a sense, we have long been giving ourselves the worst of all combinations: we have been expanding the public economy, and at the same time we have been cynical about the chance of getting much efficiency into that public economy. We have had more than our share of self-fulfilling prophecies. Thus, for example, we have had able men say that waste is inevitably built into all government spending and then we have seen these men help make their statement come true by refusing to lend their talents and time to ways of improving government services. And we have had more than our share of false economies in the public sphere. We extol the virtues of the private corporation which has planners paid well to think about the shape of the business five and ten years from now, but we show reluctance about paying enough to get municipal planners with the vision to make a bold beginning on building better cities for tomorrow. The point can be made in one other way, by contrasting American professional education in business and in public administration. Business education at the graduate school level has undergone profound changes in the past decade; most noteworthy is the way in which some of our ablest behavioral scientists and economists have directed their efforts to building and using fundamental new knowledge in the solution of business administration problems. To date, relatively little of this knowledge has spilled over into the curricula of our graduate schools of public administration. Nor are the ablest students who come out of undergraduate programs rushing to get into these public administration programs. The reasons for this are surely multiple, but one must be the scorn which we have shown too often toward the public servant himself.

CHANGING TIMES ON THE PUBLIC FRONT

But my closing theme is that the times are changing. To pick up that education point first, there are signs of ferment in public administration schools. It seems a safe bet that public administration, including educational administration, will be among the fastest changing professional fields in the years immediately ahead. Then what we have learned elsewhere about the most effective use of resources to accomplish given ends will be introduced into the training of a new generation of administrators of the public's many enterprises.

Moreover, there are noticeable changes of attitude among top men in government and business circles toward one another today. Much of the stereotyped language of the past is dying fast. In its place is growing the new language of men who see their dependence upon one another.

There is a parallel development of greater immediate impact than the forthcoming educational shake-up or the emerging changes in attitudes. This is the dramatic increase in government's own concern about the effectiveness of its endeavors and the willingness of economists to respond to the need for better measures of the impact of alternative programs. "Cost-benefit analysis" is the new fad term of the mid-1960's. President Johnson has seized it with his customary zeal, and is pushing his departments to undertake more searching inquiries into the costs to be incurred versus the benefits to be realized through each of the programs in their jurisdiction. We are growing rapidly in our sophistication in these analyses, and the future process of evaluating public efforts is unlikely to look like the past process. Let me not be misunderstood here: cost-benefit analysis, however refined, is not going to give us any final conclusion on whether or not a particular program is to be pursued in the public sector. In a democracy, that is still a decision to be made by political leaders and representatives, and they will continue to bring a host of considerations—rational and perhaps irrational—to bear on their decisions. What cost-benefit analysis can do is to point up the economic issues more sharply. It can show us what we are likely to get for money spent in one direction against what we might get for that same sum spent some other way. It permits us to ask more intelligent economic questions of our public servants than we could ask before. If they or we decide, all things considered, to ignore what the analysis tells us, so be it. We shall at least have had the chance to appraise the alternatives more rationally.

I have no doubt but that the public-versus-private debate will —and should—continue in the American economy. The bright hope now is that the debate may be lifted in many quarters above its present level. Then free men will use their resources more wisely and their minds more fully.

7 AGRICULTURE: PUZZLES IN PLENTY AND POVERTY

Vernon W. Ruttan

It is an interesting aspect of changing and unchanging America that so much of the values system and, until recently at least, even the political power reflected an agricultural society. Farming lost its dominant position in the economic life of the nation years ago, but farm influence and now farm problems remain. Urbanized America is troubled by the paradox of an agricultural industry with well-above-average productivity increases each year, a closer approach than other industries to the competitive ideal of many small firms producing identical products, and yet income disparities so wide that they have required special aid for the poorest among the farmers. This chapter describes how the "farm problem" came about, what has been done about it, and what the alternative solutions may be from here on.

From the time of the Plymouth and Jamestown settlements until the closing years of the nineteenth century the encounter with the frontier represented a dominant theme in American agricultural development. This encounter created an opportunity for the evolution of an agriculture based on an abundance of land and a relative scarcity of labor. This in turn stimulated the development of an agricultural technology that was primarily directed toward achieving gains in labor productivity rather than gains in land productivity.

Since the closing of the frontier, in the last quarter of the nineteenth century, the encounter with an increasingly dominant urban-industrial sector has emerged as a major theme in American agricultural development. By 1880 nonagricultural employment exceeded agricultural employment. By 1929 manufacturing employment alone exceeded agricultural employment, and by 1970 it seems likely that agricultural employment will be little greater than total unemployment in the United States even during periods of high-level economic activity (see Table 1).

TABLE 1. *Employment by Sector in the United States 1880–1964 and Projections to 1975 (in thousands of workes)*

	AGRICULTURE	TOTAL NON-AGRICULTURE	MANUFACTURING	UNEMPLOYMENT
1880	8,585	8,807	N.A.[1]	N.A.[1]
1929	10,450	37,180	10,534	1,550
1964	4,761	59,097	17,593	3,876
1975 (est.)	3,808	73,871	21,111	3,745

Sources: 1880 and 1929: U.S. Bureau of the Census, *Historical Statistics of the United States, Colonial Times to 1957,* Washington, D. C., 1960.

1964: *Monthly Labor Review,* Vol. 88, No. 6, U.S. Department of Labor, Bureau of Labor Statistics, June 1965.

1975 Projections: Howard Stumbler, "Man Power Needs by Industry to 1975," *Monthly Labor Review,* Vol. 88, No. 3. U.S. Department of Labor, Bureau of Labor Statistics, March 1965. Projections assume a 25 per cent increase in total nonagricultural employment, a 70 per cent increase in employment in manufacturing and a 20 per cent decline in agricultural employment from 1964. Unemployment is estimated at 7 per cent of the labor force.

[1] N.A.: Not available.

We can best visualize the interactions between the farm and the nonfarm sectors that led to this fundamental restructuring of the American economy by looking in turn at each of three sets of market relationships: the *product market,* through which the output of the agricultural sector is transmitted to the nonfarm sector and through which incomes are generated in the farm sector; the *input market,* through which move the manufactured inputs, equipment, and capital used in agricultural production; and the *labor market,* through which labor is allocated between the agricultural and nonagricultural sectors and among firms in each sector.

THE PRODUCT MARKET

Through most of American economic history the product market—the market for things farmers sell—represented the primary link between the farm and the nonfarm sectors of the economy. It was the dominant channel through which international shifts in the terms of trade, national fluctuations in nonfarm income, and local variations in nonfarm demand have flowed into the agricultural sector.

In most low-income countries, where a substantial share of increases in per capita income are devoted to dietary improvement, the product market is still the main link between the peasant and the urban-industrial sector of the economy. As income per person rises, consumption of agricultural products expands less rapidly. At very high income levels there may be no additional food consumed as income continues to rise. In the United States the declining response in consumption of food and fiber to increases in nonfarm income has almost eliminated the commodity market effects of both fluctuations and growth in economic activity in the nonfarm sector.

In addition, monetary and fiscal policy measures have tended to produce rather stable rates of growth in per capita income. Agricultural trade and commodity policies have been designed which insulate agricultural commodity prices, particularly crop prices, from normal trade and market fluctuations.

As a result of these changes the rate of growth of domestic demand for food and fiber products in the American economy now barely exceeds the rate of population growth—approximately 1.5 per cent per year. Growth of foreign demand, except for a few products such as soybeans, is heavily dependent on export subsidies or food aid.

Technological change in agricultural production has been accompanied by institutional changes in the product markets which link the agricultural to the urban-industrial sector. The production of some products has become essentially industrialized. Broiler "factories" have almost entirely replaced farm production of poultry meat. Commercial production of fruits and vegetables is becoming highly concentrated. Regional specialization in production of fruit, vegetables, and animal products, resulting from technological and organizational changes in processing, transportation, and distribution, has reduced the impact of local urban-industrial development on the demand for locally produced farm products. Milk, protected by a series of local market trade barriers, remains a major exception to this generalization.

These developments in the farm sector have been accompanied by the replacement of small-scale retail stores served by local wholesalers by large chain-store distribution systems served by integrated wholesale and retail operations. There is an increasing tendency for these large distributing organizations to establish direct linkage with the large specialized fruit and vegetable producers, poultry producers, and livestock feeders and to bypass traditional market channels.

This type of development has not yet had any substantial impact on the major agricultural commodities, such as wheat, cotton, corn, soybeans, and most hog and beef production. However, the emergence of highway truck transportation, as a major competitor with the railways in the hauling of bulk agricultural commodities, has reduced the importance of many of the older terminal markets.

THE MARKET FOR PURCHASED INPUTS

The markets for manufactured capital equipment and current inputs have become increasingly important in transmitting the effects of changes in the nonfarm economy to agriculture. Much of the new agricultural technology is embodied in the form of new capital equipment or more efficient fertilizer, insecticides, and other manufactured inputs. In 1870 the typical American farm was still a subsistence unit—with inputs purchased from the nonfarm sector amounting to less than 3 per cent of the value of farm production. By 1900 nonfarm inputs still amounted to only 7 per cent. But by the mid 1960's nonfarm inputs amounted to approximately 30 per cent of the value of farm output.

The use of purchased inputs has been closely related to developments in the labor market. The demand for labor, resulting from rapid urban-industrial development, reinforced the economic pressure for the substitution of capital equipment for labor in American agriculture at precisely that period when the frontier was disappearing as a major factor in agricultural development. It was during this period that the tractor, first functioning as the source of motive power for formerly horse-drawn equipment, and later as the power unit around which new equipment was designed, became the symbol of technological change, both in American agriculture and around the world.

The rapid growth of labor productivity in American agriculture was not, at first, accompanied by parallel changes in land productivity. Grain yield per acre in American agriculture remained essentially unchanged between the end of the Civil War in the 1860's until well into the twentieth century. By the mid-1920's, however, the production of fertilizer and other agricultural chemicals was beginning to be reflected in higher yields. Higher yield potentials were also emerging as a result of the application of advances in genetics to plant breeding by scientists in the Land Grant College system and the U.S. Department of Agriculture.

This emergence of a new chemical and biological technology in American agriculture in the 1920's was itself the product of a long sequence of institutional development. Legislation granting public lands to the states which could be used for "support and maintenance of at least one college where the leading object shall be . . . to teach such branches of learning as are related to agriculture and the mechanic arts" was passed by Congress as early as 1862. It was not until 1887, however, that an act establishing agricultural experiment stations in each state, usually at the land grant colleges, was passed.

By the mid-1920's a substantial body of agricultural research embodied in new crop varieties, new production practices, and other forms of new knowledge was beginning to flow from the agricultural education and research system and to be carrried to farmers by the newly organized federal-state extension service. Hybrid corn represented a particularly dramatic prototype of this research.

TABLE 2. *Annual Average Rates of Change in Total Outputs, Inputs, and Productivity in U.S. Agriculture, 1870–1961*

	PER CENT/YEAR			
Item	1870–1900	1900–25	1925–50	1950–64
Farm output	2.9	0.9	1.5	2.0
Total inputs	1.9	1.1	0.3	0.3
Total productivity	1.0	−0.2	1.2	1.9
Labor inputs[1]	1.6	0.5	−1.8	−4.5
Labor productivity	1.3	0.4	3.3	6.6
Land inputs[2]	3.1	0.8	0.1	−0.9
Land productivity	−0.2	0.0	1.4	2.5

Sources: Computed from U.S. Department of Agriculture, *Changes in Farm Production and Efficiency*, Statistical Bulletin 223 (revised), Washington, July 1965; and D. D. Durost and G. T. Barton, *Changing Sources of Farm Output*, U.S. Department of Agriculture, Production Research Report No. 36, Washington, February, 1960.

1 Number of workers, 1870–1910; man-hour basis, 1910–1961.

2 Cropland used for crops, including crop failure and cultivated summer fallow.

The combination of rapid advance in biological research plus a high volume of relatively inexpensive agricultural chemicals created a new dimension in agricultural productivity in the United States. Land productivity, which had experienced no real growth between 1900 and 1925, rose by 1.4 per cent per year for the period 1925–1950 and by 2.5 per cent per year between 1950 and 1964. This higher output per acre combined with continued mechanization to produce a rate of growth of labor productivity of 6.6 per cent per year between 1950 and 1964.

THE LABOR MARKET

The labor market has become an increasingly important channel of interaction between the farm and nonfarm sectors. Technical and economic developments have made it increasingly profitable to substitute inputs purchased from the industrial sector for farm labor. The slow growth in domestic demand for farm products, the insulation of domestic markets from changes in demand in other countries, and the rapid growth in labor productivity all combined to place the burden of balancing the rate growth of agricultural output with the rate of growth in demand for agricultural products on the labor market.

With the demand for agricultural output expanding at less than 2 per cent per year and labor productivity rising by more than 6 per cent per year, the burden of adjustment in the labor market has been extremely heavy. It has been particularly difficult in the low-income agricultural regions where local nonfarm employment has not expanded at a sufficiently rapid rate to absorb both the excess agricultural labor force and the new entrants to the labor force from rural areas.

The labor surplus has been so large, and the obstacles to migration for the older and less well-educated members of rural communities have been so great, that migration has generally not been sufficient to narrow income differentials between farm and nonfarm workers, except where there has been substantial growth in the local nonfarm labor market. It has not been possible to realize the full potentials of rapid growth in agricultural productivity and income per farm worker or per farm family throughout much of the southeastern United States, and in scattered areas throughout the rest of the nation, where local urban-industrial development has lagged.

PROGRESS AND POVERTY IN AMERICAN AGRICULTURE

The technological and institutional changes which have characterized American agriculture in recent decades have been highly successful in achieving three major objectives. One, they have enabled American agriculture to meet national food and fiber requirements at declining real costs to the urban-industrial sector; two, they have permitted a massive transfer of the labor force out of agriculture to meet the needs of an expanding urban-industrial sector; three, they have permitted the emergence of a high-income commercial agricultural sector which participates fully, both culturally and economically, in the advantages of a dynamic urban-industrial society. The families who operate the nation's commercial farms do their shopping at the same supermarkets and suburban shopping centers as the families of urban workers and professionals.

An unanticipated by-product of these changes has been the emergence of a dual structure in the well-being of rural families. There is no sector of American agriculture that can be properly classed as a peasant sector. There is, however, substantial poverty in rural areas. The poverty problem has several dimensions. There is a regional dimension, an occupational dimension, an age dimension, and a racial dimension (see Table 3).

TABLE 3. *Median Money Income of Farm and Nonfarm Families by Region and Color—1964*

				SOUTH		
	UNITED STATES	NORTH-EAST	NORTH CENTRAL	WHITE	NON-WHITE	WEST
1. Median income						
Nonfarm	$6,755	$7,277	$7,101	$6,136	$3,112	$7,378
Farm	3,558	4,804	4,160	3,168	1,721	5,248
Farm median income as a per cent of nonfarm	53%	66%	59%	52%	55%	71%
2. Families with incomes of $5,000 or more						
Nonfarm	68%	74%	72%	62%	24%	72%
Farm	36%	48%	42%	31%	4%	53%
3. Families with incomes of less than $2,500						
Nonfarm	12%	8%	10%	14%	40%	10%
Farm	35%	23%	30%	39%	77%	21%

Source: U.S. Bureau of the Census, "Income in 1964 of Families and Persons in the United States," *Current Population Reports,* Series P-60, No. 47 and unpublished data.

Regionally, approximately half of the nation's low-productivity and low-income farm families are located in the South. There are other substantial pockets of poverty in certain peripheral areas such as the Ozark Mountain area in Missouri and Oklahoma; parts of southern Ohio, Indiana, and Illinois; certain cut-over areas in the northern lake states of Michigan, Wisconsin, and Minnesota; and the areas of Spanish and Indian concentration in the Southwest.

There is also an occupational dimension. Incomes of hired farm workers are substantially lower than incomes of farm operators. The hired farm labor force is the most heterogeneous employee group in the American economy. Incomes of full-time hired workers on commercial farms have increased rapidly. Incomes of part-time and migrant farm workers have, however, failed to keep pace with the income of either full-time farm workers or farm operators. Mechanization of operations formerly performed by hand has actually reduced the number of days worked per year by some categories of hired farm workers.

The rapid growth in the size of commercial farms has also helped create an age dimension to the poverty problem. Many older farm operators have been caught in a situation where they have neither the financial resources to expand their farm operations nor the labor skills necessary to find remunerative off-farm employment. Extension of social security to farmers in the mid-1950's has, however, substantially reduced the disparity between the incomes of older farm and nonfarm families.

Finally there is a racial dimension to the poverty problem. Roughly half of the farm families that fall into the poverty class are located in the South, where the percentage of nonwhite farm families in the poverty class is roughly twice that of white farm families. Although the median income of white farm families in the South is almost twice as high as the median income of the nonwhite, it is only about half that of white urban families.

Rapid growth in the nonfarm labor market is a necessary condition for any successful effort to overcome the regional, occupational, age, and racial dimensions of poverty in American agriculture. Rapid expansion of nonfarm employment encourages migration from low-income regions and to higher-income occupations. During the early 1960's the net migration from farms is estimated at over 800,000 people annually. Included in this migration are large numbers of low-income Negro farm families from the South: nonwhites have accounted for one-third of the total decline in the farm population in recent years. In areas where local nonfarm urban-industrial development has been particularly rapid, older farm operators on low-income farms have shifted into nonfarm employment.

While rapid growth in the nonfarm economy has contributed importantly to the reduction of the low-income problem, neither off-farm migration nor local urban-industrial development is capable, by itself, of fully overcoming the poverty problem in American agriculture. Substantial numbers of the least mobile portion of the farm labor force remain stranded in rural underemployment—on small farms, in part-time employment, and in barely remunerative nonfarm employment.

NEW DIMENSIONS IN AGRICULTURAL POLICY

American agricultural development policies have been uniquely successful in meeting national farm output and productivity objectives, but they have been less successful in meeting the income objectives of all of the families who are engaged in the production of agricultural commodities. One observer has pointed out that the "behavior of rural people, their representatives and their institutions implies a materialistic bias in favor of plants, land, and animals and against people." While this is perhaps overdrawn, it is true that the policies of the past were designed primarily to solve technological and commodity problems rather than to solve the income problems of rural people.

This was a valid choice at the time these policies were established. It was important for United States economic development that the agricultural sector should achieve a sufficiently high rate of output and productivity growth to meet national food and fiber requirements and to release substantial numbers of farm workers and new entrants to the labor force from rural areas for nonfarm employment.

There is no economic reason, however, for the continuation of a dual structure in American agriculture during the last third of the twentieth century. And, in fact, a new set of agricultural policies that are less commodity-oriented are now emerging. There is a shift away from the relatively unsuccessful attempts to improve the income distribution within agriculture through policies designed to maintain or improve commodity prices. And there is growing recognition that rapid technological change, while desirable from the standpoint of efficiency, imposes severe financial and personal adjustment burdens on many farm families and regions.

The extension of social security to farmers in 1955 was an important step in the separation of income support payments from commodity prices. Land retirement programs, which make rental payments to farmers for removing marginal land from intensive crop production, also operated as a mechanism to transfer income to farmers without directly affecting market prices. The Food and Agriculture Act of 1965 goes further than earlier legislation in separating income support payment from production incentive and price stabilization payments.

The use of effective income protection programs employing some criteria of a socially acceptable minimum standard of living and protection against the risks imposed on individuals through product, input, and labor market developments is particularly important in the short run. Such payments permit the program participants to achieve a level of consumption more nearly in line with American standards. But they typically do not meet the additional objective of enabling the participant to contribute effectively to the further growth of the American economy.

To meet this latter objective, a stronger emphasis must be placed on investment in the human agent of production—man. The current pattern of underinvestment in rural health, rural education, and other rural social services must be corrected.

New steps in this direction are now being taken. Government programs emphasizing education and regional economic growth are being developed to assist members of low-income families to increase both their incomes and their contribution to national economic growth. A Manpower Development and Training program is providing some members of rural communities with the skills necessary to compete effectively for nonfarm jobs. The Economic Opportunity Act of 1964 provides health facilities, day camps, and special education programs for the children of migrant workers. Education in rural areas will be improved through the Elementary and Secondary Education Act of 1965, which allocates federal funds to school districts with heavy concentrations of children from low-income families. The Public Works and Economic Development Act of 1965 authorizes funds for new regional economic development programs in low-income areas.

AMERICAN AGRICULTURE IN THE DECADE AHEAD

What kind of agriculture will emerge out of the technological and economic forces that currently impinge on the rural sector of the American economy?

The decline in the number of farms and farm workers will continue. Over the next decade farm employment will probably decline to less than four million workers. Fewer than one million commercial farms will produce 85 to 90 per cent of total farm output. The farm operators and regular farm workers employed on these farms will achieve incomes that will permit them to enjoy the American standard of living. This may require that farm families earn higher incomes than comparable nonfarm families in order to compensate them for the growing locational disadvantages of rural life.

The geographic concentration of agricultural production on fewer acres will continue. Yield increases resulting from biological and chemical innovation will continue to exceed the rate of growth in demand for farm products. Expanded commercial exports and food aid to less developed countries may result in slower declines in area planted than in the last decade, but the trend is not likely to be reversed over any sustained period.

The production and marketing of agricultural commodities will continue to be closely regulated through a combination of restrictions on land use, marketing allotments and quotas, and multiple-price systems. These programs will be less oriented to achieving income goals in the agricultural sector than in the past. They will be directed to a greater extent toward the protection of urban consumers from undue price fluctuations and the achievement of international trade objectives.

Rural poverty will surely be reduced as a result of area development, education, health, and direct income transfer programs. But in spite of continued progress, substantial numbers of the individuals and families who are considered to have substandard income and consumption levels will continue to be found in rural areas. An economy that is increasingly concerned to eliminate such disparities may yet come to see that the poverty problems of both rural and urban sectors are essentially similar in their psychological, sociological, and economic dimensions.

8 THE RICH, THE POOR, AND THE OTHERS

Gerald G. Somers

Throughout these essays, one of the most frequently cited changes in the United States economy is the renewed concern with reducing poverty in the world's wealthiest society. This chapter summarizes the essential background for the other discussions of this topic; it tells what we know now about the characteristics of those in the poverty class and what major lines of public attack are being used in the War on Poverty.

It may seem anomalous that in this period of affluence and unparalleled economic expansion in the United States there should be a growing national concern with the problems of poverty. Even though the per capita income of American families has steadily risen since the brief recession of 1961–1962 and is now at record levels, President Johnson has announced that the reduction of the number of families at poverty levels is a major item of the nation's unfinished business.

There are a number of reasons for the concentration on the problems of poverty at this time. First, in spite of the prosperity of the nation as a whole, it has been established that approximately one-fifth of the country's families receive an income (under $3,000 per year for families and under $1,500 per year for unrelated individuals) which compels a standard of living well below the national average. As President Johnson noted in his Economic Report to the Congress in announcing the "War on Poverty":

> Americans today enjoy the highest standard of living in the history of mankind. But for nearly a fifth of our fellow citizens

> this is a hollow achievement. They often live without hope, below minimum standards of decency. The per capita money income of these thirty-five million, men, women, and children, was only $590 in 1962—against $1,900 per capita for the nation as a whole.

Thus poverty is seen to be a relative concept. Even though the present status of those at the bottom one-fifth of the nation's income ladder is substantially higher than it was in previous decades and parallels the *average* income of a number of countries at the present time, the persons in this lowest income category in the United States are deemed to be in poverty; and programs are called forth to bring them above an established minimum.

The attack on poverty has also stemmed from concern over excessively high rates of unemployment in the United States since the recession of 1957–1958. Serious pockets of unemployment and low incomes persist in a number of depressed areas of the country and in a number of industries undergoing technological change. Finally, the concern with poverty has been closely related to the social and economic problems of the growing number of the aged in our population, and the concern also stems from the "revolution of expectations" of the American Negro.

THE DISTRIBUTION OF INCOME AND WEALTH

In the United States as in all countries there is inequality in the distribution of income and wealth among families and individuals. The lowest one-tenth of the spending units (essentially households) received only 1 per cent of the money income and the lowest 30 per cent of the spending units received only 9 per cent of the total money income before taxes in 1960. At the other extreme of the income scale, the top one-tenth of the income recipients received 27 per cent and the top one-fifth of the recipients received 43 per cent of the total money income before taxes.

The holdings of wealth are also unequally distributed. In 1962, 61 per cent of the nation's wealth was held by the top 10 per cent of families, and the bottom one-fifth held only 7 per cent.

Although there is not complete agreement among the experts on the trends of the distribution of income and wealth, there appears to be some consensus that income equality was greatly furthered during World War II, but that there has been no appreciable change in relative income shares for the last twenty years. Similarly, whereas the share of wealth held by the top 2 per cent of the families in the United States fell steadily from 1929 to 1949, there is evidence that this share has now risen again slightly in the last ten years.

Although long-run changes in the incidence of poverty reflect the concepts used in defining poverty, there appears to be general agreement that there has been steady reduction in the percentage of the population in poverty. This percentage has been falling by about one point per year and is now at 18 per cent of the population, whereas in 1947 it had been estimated that 32 per cent of the families had money incomes which placed them in the poverty classification. However, the rate of reduction in this decade has not been so great as in some earlier years, and there is a general feeling that further reduction in the percentage of the population in poverty will be more difficult to achieve in the future unless extensive government policies are directed toward this objective.

WHO ARE THE POOR?

Even though unemployment contributes significantly to low family income, it should be noted that one-fourth of all the poor families (about two million) were headed by a person who worked full time throughout the year and another one and a half million family heads worked at full-time jobs but did not work throughout the year. Thus, half of today's poor families are headed by a worker whose annual wages are simply too low to support a family.

One-fourth of the nation's families in poverty are headed by a woman, and about one-fourth of the poor are in nonwhite families. Families with aged heads constitute one-fifth of the poverty total.

Special problems of poverty arise when a confluence of these "poverty characteristics" are found in the same family. Thus, about 40 per cent of the nonwhite families in poverty are headed by women, few of whom have year-round, full-time employment.

There are also significant relationships between the education of the family head and the incidence of poverty. Whereas 37 per cent of those families headed by a person with eight or fewer years of education are found in the poverty class, only 8 per cent of the families in which the head had more than twelve years of education are in the poverty category.

Poverty is also relatively concentrated in particular geographic areas of the nation. The incidence of poverty is found to a disproportionate extent in the Southeast, in rural areas in the northern portions of the Great Lakes states, portions of the Southwest, and a few scattered areas throughout the country. More than 15 million of the 35 million people with incomes in the poverty class live in rural areas, and approximately 5¼ million of these people live on farms. These numbers greatly exceed the proportion of rural and farm population in the country as a whole. It is found that the concentrations of poverty in these areas are related to the high incidence of those family characteristics which we have already noted to be responsible for low family income. Thus we see that a relatively large proportion of the poor families in these depressed areas are headed by older persons, Negroes, or women, and that the levels of education in these areas are relatively low.

It has also been found that poverty tends to perpetuate itself in certain families and in certain depressed areas. Low levels of income and education among parents often result in low levels of education and future income among children. Local cultural norms may be established in which dependency on public welfare becomes an accepted fact of life. Many of the policies included in the attack on poverty are designed to break through this "vicious circle" of perpetuation of poverty.

WAR AGAINST POVERTY

Even though the progressive income tax and other measures help to prevent a widening of inequalities in income distribution, the primary approach to these problems in the United States has been in the upgrading of those in the lowest income categories rather than in the downgrading of those in the highest income categories. The current attack on poverty is in this tradition, and the policies established as part of this attack are directed at the causes and characteristics of poor families indicated earlier.

A well-publicized attack on the problems of poverty has been established in the recently enacted Economic Opportunity Act of 1964. Well before this coordinated approach to the problem, however, many federal, state, and local programs have been directed toward the income maintenance of the poor and the enhancement of their employment opportunities.

Since the mid-1930's, a combined federal-state system of unemployment insurance has aided in the income support of workers during periods of unemployment. There have been regular improvements in the coverage and benefits of many of the state plans, and in recent recessions federal programs have been devised to provide additional funds for those workers who exhausted their unemployment benefits under state legislation. The unemployment-insurance system has been increasingly recognized as an important measure of counter-cyclical economic policy as well as a means of income support. Similarly, an extensive program of old-age and survivors' insurance has been in existence since 1935; and the coverage of benefits of this program, too, have been progressively extended in subsequent years. The social security system now covers almost all of the working population and provides a significant form of aid to older persons and widows. Also dating from the 1930's, systems of public welfare assistance have contributed to the income support of poor families through combined federal, state, and local programs.

Whereas these forms of social insurance and welfare payments are designed primarily for those who are unable to work or who are unable to find work, federal minimum-wage legislation, also enacted in the 1930's, attempts to raise the income of those already employed. Since it has been shown that a substantial proportion of the poverty income class is employed—but at levels too low to support their families—some have stressed the need for higher minimum wages and further extension in the coverage of the legislation. In fact, the minimum wages have been steadily increased since the 1930's and will reach at $1.60 per hour shortly. Future action can be expected by Congress and by state legislatures designed to raise the minimum further and to extend the coverage of the minimum wage to millions of additional workers.

Other programs directed at the maintenance of the income of the poor are currently being discussed. These include the possibilities of a system of family allowances, which is enforced in a number of other countries; and, alternatively, a system of negative income taxes whereby those families too poor to benefit fully from exemptions under the present federal income taxes would receive payments from the federal government as part of the tax scheme.

Also antecedent to the Economic Opportunity Act are a series of measures designed to improve mobility and employment opportunities for workers of low skill and low educational levels, many of whom are found in the poverty income class. Foremost in this regard is the effort to bring about full employment through aggregate tax, spending, and monetary policies. The tax cut of 1964—a major measure in these aggregative policies—has contributed to a reduction of over-all unemployment rates, and it is expected that further tax cuts will be enacted if required.

Other measures have been aimed at the reduction of structural unemployment rather than at the indiscriminate expansion of the total demand for labor. Indeed, there has been a virtual revolution in such manpower policies in the last few years. The Area Redevelopment Act of 1961 authorized grants to business and local communities for the provision of employment-creating facilities in depressed areas throughout the country. This legislation has now been renewed, with an emphasis on public works as well as private facilities in such areas.

The high concentration of low-income families in the Appalachian Mountain area, stretching from the southeastern part of the country into northern Pennsylvania and New York State, has focused special interest on a recent federal program to rehabilitate this region. Because of the erosion of many agricultural sections and because of the decline in employment in the coal-mining industry which previously dominated the Appalachian states, the approach to poverty in this area must encompass not only the provision of facilities which will attract new employment opportunities but a total development of natural and human resources. Population data indicate that there has already been considerable out-migration from Appalachia and similar low-income areas, but birth rates are also unusually high and a surplus of unwanted labor persists. Unfortunately, the younger and more ambitious members of the labor force are the ones who tend to migrate, frequently leaving behind the older and less skilled workers who may not be so attractive to potential employers. Although the Area Redevelopment Act has resulted in the creation of substantial new facilities and new jobs in the so-called development areas, widespread poverty is still found in geographic pockets of an otherwise prosperous country.

Because of the demonstrated relationship between poverty and the level of a worker's education and skill, special attention has been centered upon raising educational levels and skill levels, not only in depressed economic regions but in all areas of the country. Many studies have indicated that a person's average lifetime earnings increase progressively and significantly with each additional year of his formal education. As has been already noted, a disproportionately large number of families in the poverty class are headed by a person whose education ended at the elementary school level. In 1964 over 17 million workers, one out of every four in the country, had had no more than eight years of schooling. Approximately 2½ million had not even finished the fifth grade. It has been found that the unemployment rate among workers with no more than an eighth-grade education is about 40 per cent higher than the average rate for the entire labor force.

Nonwhite workers have an exceptionally serious educational handicap. Two-fifths have no more than an eighth-grade education, almost twice the corresponding proportion of white workers.

It is in the light of these educational deficiencies that one must appraise the very substantial programs which have recently been enacted in the field of education and training. Elementary education has been significantly strengthened. The Higher Education Facilities Act of 1963 provides much needed facilities for universities, colleges, and community colleges; more fellowships and other financial aid have been provided for college and university students. And legislation passed in 1965 extended additional federal assistance to the educational system throughout the country.

The burden of poverty should also be reduced as a result of very recent advances in the field of training and vocational education. It has been determined that many of the unemployed are not sufficiently skilled or productive to warrant their employment at existing wage levels. Since the tradition of minimum wages has been established, the reabsorption of these workers into the labor force is contingent upon their acquiring skills which will make them attractive to employers. In 1961 President Kennedy appointed a Panel of Consultants on Vocational Education in order to review and re-evaluate the country's existing vocational education programs. A major finding, reported by the panel in 1963, was that opportunities for vocational education were not sufficient either to serve youths and adults currently in need of training or to meet the projected training needs of a growing labor force. The panel also concluded that vocational education in this country had not been sufficiently realistic in relating courses to current and prospective labor requirements.

The Vocational Education Act of 1963 resulted from the panel's recommendations and provides the means for carrying out those recommendations. The revitalization of the vocational education system is based on the philosophy that all citizens—from the least able and the most disadvantaged to those with the highest levels of technical ability—should have access to high-quality education and training, geared realistically to current and future employment opportunities.

The Manpower Development and Training Act, passed in 1962, provided the first large-scale federal program of subsidies and allowances for the training and retraining of unemployed and underemployed workers throughout the country. By June 1, 1965, almost 350,000 workers had been approved for training in MDTA courses and total costs of over $400 million had been incurred in the training programs. This legislation, too, has been extended and improved to cover a larger proportion of the hard-core unemployed, including programs of basic literacy training as well as occupational courses. The MDTA, as recently amended, has also provided for experimental programs of relocation allowances to encourage the movement of unemployed workers from relatively depressed areas to areas of labor demand.

Because there is a high incidence of poverty among Negroes and other minority groups, special significance can be attached to the fair employment practices provisions recently enacted in federal civil rights legislation. Designed to prevent discrimination in the selection of workers for employment, this 1965 legislation should be of special importance in raising the future income of minority groups now in the poverty category.

The Economic Opportunity Act of 1964 established an Office of Economic Opportunity in the Executive Office of the President. The Director of the OEO is responsible for the coordination of poverty-related programs in all government agencies; and within the OEO separate staffs operate such new programs as a Job Corps, a program for Volunteers in Service to America (the domestic Peace Corps), and a series of community action programs in cooperation with local community authorities. In addition, the OEO distributes funds to existing government agencies for the operation of work-training programs (administered through the Labor Department), work-study programs and adult basic education (administered through the Department of Health, Education and Welfare), special rural anti-poverty programs (through the Department of Agriculture), and small business loans (through the Small Business Administration).

Although the programs directed and encouraged by the new Office of Economic Opportunity will have a widespread impact on low-income families, the principal focus appears to be on the education and training of young people. Over $400 million, out of the total initial authorization of almost $1 billion, is assigned to youth programs; and many additional community action programs are also directed primarily toward youths.

Two of the more interesting OEO programs are the Job Corps and Operation Head Start. Under the Job Corps, conservation camps and residential training centers are being established to provide education, work experience, and vocational training to young men and women, removed from a poverty-stricken home environment. About 100,000 young people were enrolled in such camps and centers in 1965.

Operation Head Start is based on the assumption that the handicaps suffered by children of poverty-stricken families should be reduced as early as possible in their upbringing and education. Under this program thousands of children of pre-school age, drawn primarily from poor families, have been enrolled in special nursery schools designed to put them on a more equal footing with their schoolmates by the time they begin their formal education.

CONCLUSION

It is seen that even though the United States is predominantly a middle-class society, extremes of wealth and poverty exist. Record increases in productive capacity and economic expansion have steadily raised average per capita incomes and are expected to continue in the coming years. In spite of this unparalleled prosperity, however, a significant minority of the population is still suffering from inadequate incomes and living standards. Although there has been little change in the relative shares of income among classes of income recipients in recent years, there has been a steady reduction in the number of those who could reasonably be placed in the poverty class.

Extensive and concentrated efforts are now under way to accelerate the reduction of poverty in the United States. Building on a framework of legislation which has long existed to aid the unemployed and low-income families, recent federal programs are aimed at the eventual elimination of poverty in this country. It has been resolved that the "Affluent Society" will become the society of all Americans.

9 MANPOWER IN THE AMERICAN SCENE

Richard A. Lester

Again in this chapter we encounter an American ambivalence toward government in the economy. It took a long time for Americans to believe that we needed or wanted an active role for government in seeking better balances between labor demand (the available jobs) and labor supply (the available workers). But new rates of economic growth and new concern over the disadvantaged in the 1960's have produced a national concern over our human resources—and as a result national manpower policy is in the making.

This chapter deals with the manpower situation and governmental manpower policy in the United States since 1960. It concentrates on three topics: (1) the upswing toward full employment, with increasing problems of labor shortage and diminishing problems of unemployment; (2) the development of "an active manpower policy," consisting of a national program of manpower planning, vocational training, and improvement in labor mobility; (3) some contrasts between the United States and Western Europe in the manpower field that help to explain significant transatlantic differences in policy and practices—differences that are often overlooked and that can lead to mistaken conclusions. The chapter concludes with a brief discussion of the contribution of university research to the understanding and solution of manpower problems in the United States.

THE SHIFT FROM GENERAL SURPLUS TO SIGNIFICANT SHORTAGES

Since 1960 the United States has experienced a remarkable expansion in employment. In the five years from 1960 to 1965 the number of Americans at work increased by nearly 7 million; in 1965 alone the increase was 2.4 million. The rate of unemployment has dropped from an average of 5.6 per cent in 1960 to under 4 per cent in 1966. Now the unemployment rate is less than 2 per cent for married men.

Repeated declines in the over-all unemployment rate have occurred despite large net increases annually in the nation's labor force. The increase amounted to 1.4 million last year. In 1965 the rate of increase in the working population in the United States was about four times that in the six countries in the European Economic Community taken as a group. One result of rapid population growth is that nearly half of the people in the United States are under twenty-five years of age.

In recent years federal fiscal-monetary policy has been a major factor in bringing better balance between the nation's employment demand and its labor supply. The $14 billion tax cut in 1964 was particularly effective in stimulating expansion in employment. Since 1960, the upswing in employment has occurred in all branches of the economy. Although manufacturing employment was slow to expand in the early 1960's, during 1965 it rose almost a million. Half of the total expansion of 2.4 million in employment last year was in blue-collar jobs.

However, for the past two decades white-collar employment has been growing relative to blue-collar jobs, and employment in the nonprofit sectors of the economy has been expanding much faster than in profit-operated business. Thus, production for profit has been a declining proportion of the American economy. The nonprofit sectors include government employment and employment in such institutions as voluntary hospitals, private colleges and universities, mutual insurance companies, religious and charitable organizations, foundations, and cooperatives. Now one out of every four employed persons works directly in parts of the economy operated for purposes other than profit-making.

As the American economy approaches full employment, labor is becoming tight in certain occupations and localities. Noticeable shortages of qualified workers are reported, for example, in such categories as teachers, nurses, engineers, technicians, skilled metal workers, repairmen, and stenographers. In manufacturing, labor of various types is scarce in many industrial cities in the Great Lakes region.

The existence of troublesome pools of unemployed in the midst of growing labor shortages stresses the need for improvement in programs of vocational education, youth counseling, job training for the unemployed, and geographical mobility for jobless workers. Some sections, like the coal-mining areas in the Appalachian Mountain region, have pockets of unemployed miners and others lacking work in declining communities. By contrast, in the Ruhr Valley coal mining is adjacent to other types of industry.

In the United States the unemployment rate continues high for teenagers, and for adult Negroes; moreover, about one out of every four Negroes in the 14–to–19 age group is jobless at any given time.

The federal government has been attacking the residual unemployment problem with various specific measures. One, it has a program for training as many as 150,000 jobless, mostly adults, each year under the Manpower Development and Training Act and the Area Redevelopment Act. Two, the Poverty Program is now providing full-time or part-time employment and training for perhaps 400,000 persons a year under the Neighborhood Youth Corps, the Work Experience Program, and the Job Corps. Three, a serious effort is being made, with the aid of the Civil Rights Act of 1964, to eliminate discrimination against nonwhites both in employment and in admission to skilled unions. Four, the government is experimenting, under a small program of financial support, with relocation of jobless workers in expanding communities.

A START ON "AN ACTIVE MANPOWER POLICY"

Traditionally, Americans have resisted government intervention in the labor market as contrary to the philosophy of a market economy. Each intervention—laws regarding child labor, work hours and minimum wages, and nondiscrimination in employment—had to win legislative acceptance on its own merits.

The Federal-State Employment Service became established in the Great Depression of the 1930's. Before 1961 it was generally considered a public employment exchange for unskilled and semiskilled manual workers who had lost their jobs and were drawing unemployment insurance.

In 1961 the Kennedy administration sought to change that image. In large cities the Employment Service was divorced from unemployment benefit payment, and separate city employment offices were established for industrial, commercial, and professional workers.

In 1962 the Manpower Development and Training Act was adopted. It provides for an annual report regarding prospective requirements and supplies of different types of manpower, with recommendations for improving the training and utilization of the nation's labor resources.

In his first Manpower Report in 1964, President Johnson began to develop what he termed "an active manpower policy." It includes manpower planning to anticipate and prepare for future manpower needs, and the coordination of separate manpower activities so that they fit into a considered, comprehensive program.

One important element in "an active manpower policy" is improvement of the Federal-State Employment Service so that it can serve as the main instrument for carrying out such a policy. In January of 1966 a Task Force Report on the Employment Service, prepared by a non-government panel, recommended reform of the Employment Service.

Historically, the publicly-operated Employment Service has been joined to the administration of unemployment insurance and has been composed of fifty separate state units. Often referred to as "unemployment offices," the 1,900 local units have not been extensively used by the most prestigious employers or by the best-qualified workers.

The changes already introduced have improved the image and status of the Employment Service. The Task Force report recommends further improvements in the development and dissemination of job information, in interarea recruitment and clearance procedures, in structure and financing, and so forth. Legislation has been introduced to carry out these recommendations and to make the Employment Service a system of "comprehensive manpower agencies."

SPECIAL FEATURES OF EMPLOYMENT IN THE U.S.

Writers tend to stress differences in work life between the United States and Europe. America is assumed to be much more affected by mechanization and by modern industrial practices. It is often supposed that American workers readily shift employers and occupations and that automation is creating mass unemployment in this country. Actually, the differences between the United States and modern Europe with respect to many aspects of employment are often overdrawn.

Important differences in employment practices and manpower policy do, however, exist. Even experts are prone to overlook or discount some of these differences. They include, in particular, a kind of lifetime-welfare concept of employment that limits the applicability of labor-market logic and the special employment problems of youth and minority groups. Let us examine these two unusual aspects of manpower in America.

Since the 1930's a new concept of employment has spread throughout most of modern industry in the United States. Established corporations have assumed large obligations for the welfare of their workers and the workers' dependents. Companies have done so under a program of worklife employment, stimulated by widespread adoption of seniority rights and employee benefits and fostered by protections from discharge, under union-management agreements with a bipartisan grievance procedure ending in arbitration.

The result is that most of modern business in America has assumed responsibilities for the cost of medical and hospital care, life insurance, pensions, sickness and unemployment benefits, and education for the employees, the employees' dependents, and even retirees and their dependents. In many large firms as much as 12 per cent of the cost of employment takes the nonwage form of expenses for employee insurances and welfare payments.

Both company managements and labor unions wish to keep a large part of worker benefits under private control. Neither seems too concerned that mounting company benefits tend to tie employees to the firm and, thus, reduce labor mobility. Practices such as job rights according to seniority (length of service) and wages and benefits fixed for two, three, or more years under long-term labor agreements also help to separate the allocation and compensation of employment from close control by labor-market influences.

Economists have reasoned that the more economic or monopoly power a firm has, the more it will exploit its labor. But in the American environment, with stress on investment in a continuing work force and the welfare of employees, the larger and more powerful the employing unit, the higher the wage scales and employee benefits tend to be. Classical economic theory and Marxian analysis both fail to explain the welfare aspects of industrial relations in large American firms.

And the employees of such firms do not feel particularly exploited or fettered by seniority and benefit ties to a particular company. They regard seniority rights as protection and benefit rights as gains that are more valuable than an equivalent sum in their pay envelopes.

In spelling out employee rights and benefits, labor agreements in this country often run from 100 to 200 pages. Referred to as a "web of rules" by some writers, the rights and benefit provisions of collective agreements are more in the nature of a "cocoon of protections." In the United States "the welfare corporation" competes with "the welfare state" for the workers' favor by ministering to their welfare needs.

Turning now to the second special feature of manpower in America, this country, as already indicated, has had more serious youth and minority employment problems than has been true of

Western Europe. In some respects the West Indian problem in Great Britain resembles the nonwhite employment and unemployment problem in the United States, but there are important differences.

The youth unemployment problem is especially serious in the United States for a number of reasons. One reason is the hiring policies of large firms. Because of the widespread practice of corporate hiring on the assumption of a work career with the company, applicants who are qualified for low-level entrance jobs but who lack good promotion potential are often excluded. Another reason is that, compared with Europe, the United States has not developed extensive bridges for the transition from school to work. Apprenticeship plays an extremely limited role in the United States. It is confined largely to the building and printing trades, and traditionally apprenticeship has been a means of restricting supply and discriminating against minority groups. A third reason for a heavy incidence of unemployment among American youth has been the rapid growth in their numbers in recent years. Youth under twenty-five years of age have been accounting for more than half of the increase in the labor force, rising from 15 to 20 per cent of all workers in the last ten years.

The minority unemployment problem stems largely from unequal educational preparation and discrimination against nonwhites in employment above the most menial jobs. Even in comparable jobs there have been persistent wage differences that work to the disadvantage of nonwhites. True, anti-discrimination laws and new employer attitudes are changing this picture. But the progress still seems painfully slow to those nonwhites who are faced with unemployment at twice the rate for whites and whose median income is less than 60 per cent of the figure for whites.

Education is the most important step in reducing further Negro-white differentials in pay and employment. That is why equality of educational opportunity, through the elimination of segregated public schools in the South and improvement of schools in Negro areas in the North, is so vital for long-run improvement of the Negro element in the nation's work force.

Negroes have been heavily overrepresented in casual and other kinds of short-term employment. A much higher proportion of Negro workers needs to acquire seniority in large corporations and to enjoy the benefits and opportunities of career employment under welfare capitalism. The advantages include company investment in employees' futures, including the benefits of good supervision, on-the-job training, and other preparation for advancement.

In the past few years many large companies have been making special efforts to hire and promote qualified Negroes. For some higher level jobs, managements of large firms, especially those with government contracts, may give Negroes preference in hiring and promotion within management.

THE CONTRIBUTION OF MANPOWER RESEARCH

A significant amount of the country's scholarly resources is devoted to research on manpower, often referred to as labor-market research. Manpower research provides a large part of the contents of three scholarly journals in the labor field and of the annual meetings of the Industrial Relations Research Association, which has more than 2,500 members. The research programs of some forty university labor research agencies usually include some aspect of manpower.

The federal government is spending around $6 million a year on research under the Manpower Development and Training Act. In addition, government funds are spent on research to evaluate the effectiveness of various types of training projects, and especially on research in the field of vocational education.

We in the United States are, to a considerable extent, research-minded. A number of research projects of American scholars have involved study of the manpower programs and experience of European countries during the past decade. The policy-makers in Washington during the last five years have been extremely receptive to new ideas and proposals with respect to manpower policy. University scholars have testified at Congressional hearings, served on task forces and as consultants to the Secretary of Labor, and participated in public meetings and special conferences on manpower problems. Private companies and labor unions also use the results of manpower research. Indeed, through their own staffs, they engage in manpower research.

The findings of manpower research are rapidly distributed to the public and applied, with varying lags of course, by governments and business. As a result, public and private manpower policies in the United States are increasingly subject to careful analysis and evaluation.

Incidentally, a survey of changing fashions in the research of labor economists and other social scientists over the past four decades provides an interesting commentary on progress and problems in American labor. Until just before World War II the most popular subject for research was social insurance and social legislation. The big question then was: How can law be used to cure some of the major hazards to which workers are exposed in both their active and their retirement years? Then, with the growth of strong industrial unions, the focus shifted to union-management relations. The question became: How can a free society find ways to live with the exercise of private power in the hands of large corporations and labor unions? In the 1960's the focus shifted to manpower policy. Now the question is: How can this economy utilize all elements of its manpower resources so as to achieve maximum economic growth and equity of opportunity?

SUMMARY

In this chapter I have attempted to indicate the changes that have occurred in the United States since 1960 in manpower requirements, in manpower thinking, and in manpower policy. Now let me try to summarize.

1. The upswing toward full employment has shifted much of the focus of public policy from the problem of widespread unemployment to means of overcoming labor shortages, especially in the skilled trades and in the technical and professional occupations.

2. During the last five years, under the rubric of "an active manpower policy," the United States has begun the long, slow

move toward a national program for the rational development and utilization of its manpower resources by means of planning, training programs, and improvements in the operation of the Federal-State Employment Service.

3. The program has been adapted to certain special features and problems in the American environment, where company manpower and welfare activities play a most important role and where special problems are created by a large nonwhite element and a growing youth ratio in the labor force.

4. Manpower research, under expanding federal stimulus and support, is playing an increasingly important role in the development of public and private manpower policy.

5. In the manpower field, the United States is in a period of ferment and fresh ideas, seeking to learn from the European experience as well as from experiments in this country.

These are exciting times for those of us interested in manpower policy and research. The concept of investment in labor resources opens up exciting possibilities for the improvement of people and for the development of a work force capable of coping with the rate of progress in our society.

10 PROGRESS AND POWER IN LABOR UNIONS

Myron L. Joseph

It is now almost two decades since a distinguished economist called the American economy "a laboristic society." Some employers believed that to be true at least since 1935; a few union leaders took so much credit for economic progress made since 1935 that they, too, fanned the idea of labor in the driver's seat. In this essay there is a more sober view of the scene, a tallying of the places where organized labor does and does not make a big difference in the contemporary United States. The picture is harder to absorb than one that sees labor leaders as either completely dominant or wholly ineffective, but it is probably more accurate for all that.

There is no question that labor unions are an important economic and political force in the American society. Wages and working conditions are established through the process of collective bargaining in most major industries, and strikes can shut down critical industries and cripple the economy in a relatively short period of time. Labor leaders help select candidates for the highest political offices, they are members of key government committees, and they are consulted by public officials on appointments and major policy matters. But in spite of the visible role of labor unions in the political economy of the nation, in recent Congresses organized labor has been unable to obtain its highest-priority legislative objectives, labor union membership is smaller today in absolute numbers and as a fraction of the labor force than it was in 1956, and there is little evidence that unions have raised the share of total income going to labor.

To understand these apparent contradictions, we must examine the structure of American unions and their role in the American society. Perhaps the best way to do this is to view the labor movement through the eyes of a member. In most cases, if his company is organized, he will be represented by a local of the national union (called an international union if it has locals outside of the United States) that has asserted jurisdiction over his industry or craft. In general, representatives of the national union will work with officers of the local in negotiating a labor agreement that will detail the wages and working conditions for employees of his company. The local union and its members will look to the international for help in policing the labor agreement, and for advice and help in educational, political, social, and community activities. In case of a strike, the national union may provide financial aid as well as organizational leadership. Since it draws its support from a broad base, the national union has the resources to maintain a research and administrative organization which makes it possible for the union to negotiate effectively with management. As a result, major decisions in the larger unions tend to be made at the national union level, although to be effective they must be supported by the locals and the membership.

Our union member will vote for local union officers and either directly, or indirectly through convention delegates, for officers of the national union. His local will send delegates to committees and conventions that help the national union formulate its economic and political policies as well as its bargaining objectives. He will learn of the union's decisions from the union newspaper and through reports that come down to the local from the national union. The union policy-makers may appear remote and the issues may not always be understood, but if a union is to maintain its bargaining strength, the local members must be willing to support their representatives at the top and the officers must be careful to respond to the needs of the members. If the leaders lose touch with the rank and file, even the cumbersome election machinery of the largest unions can be used to unseat the national union officers.

Between contract negotiations our member's contacts with the national union will be infrequent. For most purposes, the loca and its officers are the union. If our member believes he has beer treated unfairly by management or that the labor agreement ha been violated, the local union provides a mechanism for protesting the employer's actions. In fact, in the great majority of cases if the union is not satisfied with management's responses to alleged violations of the agreement, the union can appeal the matter to an impartial arbitrator who is empowered under the term of the labor agreement to make a final and binding decision or the issues in dispute. Although the local union may receive help from national union representatives, the local has the primary responsibility for protecting the members' rights under the terms o the labor agreement. In addition to providing protection agains contract violations and arbitrary management actions, the loca union's activities frequently cover a broad range, including offering advice on community services, political education, socia affairs, and adult education. In spite of the variety of service educational and social activities, most union members have littl contact with their unions, and attendance at most local unior meetings is notoriously low. As long as the union is there when it is needed union members tend to be apathetic about participation in its activities.

THE INFLUENCE OF THE AFL–CIO

Our member will know in a somewhat general way that, in addition to his membership in the local and national union, he belongs to the AFL–CIO—the American Federation of Labor and Congress of Industrial Organizations. With a few key exceptions the national and international unions are affiliated with the labor federation, but the ties are very loose. The AFL–CIO provides a top-level spokesman for organized labor on the national scene. It maintains a mechanism for resolving disputes among its member organizations and performs a number of public relations, research, legal, and political services for the affiliated unions.

But what does it mean to say that the AFL–CIO speaks for the

American labor movement? The 128 affiliated unions represent a wide diversity of often-conflicting interests. The Federation leadership has the difficult task of generating a program that will be backed by the affiliated unions and that will be at least partially responsive to some of the more important narrowly defined interests of the member unions. As a result, the Federation tends to concentrate its focus on general objectives that are considered to be pro-labor such as high employment, low interest rates, and a higher minimum wage, on goals that are related to union organizational strength and status, such as legislation to restore the legality of compulsory union membership; and on objectives that have been traditionally identified with a liberal labor movement, such as civil rights legislation and immigration reform.

To provide a focus for their specialized interests the member unions of the AFL–CIO are organized into departments. The Building and Construction Trades Department, the Maritime Trades Department, and the Metal Trades Department are examples of these specialized organizations. The departments provide an independent base for political action as well as a means for developing policies that represent the special interests of the affiliated unions to be presented for adoption and support by the parent organization. Of particular interest is the Industrial Union Department, which gives the unions that came into the merged Federation from the CIO a relatively independent base for organizing, negotiating, research, and political activities.

With a constituency of highly organized, special-interest groups, the Federation leadership must play a delicate internal political game to get unified support for the highest-priority legislative goals. How powerful a political force is the labor movement and what is the basis of its influence? The record of the 89th Congress (1965–1966) provides some insight into the question. The AFL–CIO Executive Council called the first session of the 89th Congress "the most productive Congressional session ever held." The Director of the AFL–CIO Department of Legislation asserts that "labor's expectations for the 89th Congress were largely fulfilled." And the record shows that many new programs supported by the labor movement were passed into law. These include legislation in the areas of aid to education, housing and urban affairs. Medicare and social security, voting rights protection, encouragement of the arts and conservation, regional public works and immigration reform. None of the new programs is specifically oriented toward labor unions or their members. On the other hand, the Congress in 1965 failed to pass legislation which would legalize compulsory union membership in states where it is illegal, the coverage of the minimum wage law was not extended, unemployment compensation was not increased, overtime penalty rates were not increased, and picketing by construction unions at multi-employer sites was not legalized.* In short, the high-priority labor union items that were more specifically oriented toward labor union goals or the interests of labor union members were not achieved.

There are many factors involved in this very complex political problem but at least part of the explanation can be found in the apparent absence of any strong grass-roots demand on the part of the union members for the Federation's legislative objectives. A recent survey conducted among trade union members in California by a university research team found that in the non-bread-and-butter areas such as automation, support of candidates friendly to labor, and the like, "much of the membership either does not understand or does not sympathize with the position of the union and its leadership." These findings are not surprising. The chain of communication between the union lobbyists in Washington and the local union member is long and tangled. The issues involved are complex and difficult to understand, and in many cases the long-run interests of the organization were involved rather than the more easily understood short-run interest of the members. The ability of labor organizations to communicate with their members is severely limited. Local union attendance is small and educational programs are likely to reach only a very small percentage of the members. It is a tribute to the efforts of organized labor that the California study found that members who are most active as measured by their attendance at meetings are "generally in accord with the union and its leadership on the

* Some part of organized labor's aims on minimum wages and unemployment compensation reform was achieved in the 1966 session of Congress, but the gains were less than the unions hoped for—J.R.C.

broader issues." The general membership is more likely to reflect community attitudes than official union policies.

If, as appears to be the case, union membership does not provide a strong base in support of organized labor's more general objectives, what is the source of labor's political strength? Why are the unions consulted in the formulation of legislative programs and in major political decisions? The answer is probably money and organization. Through labor's political arm, the Committee on Political Education, labor unions provide substantial contribution to political organizations and candidates. The withdrawal of this financial support could be very costly to those who now depend on it in part for their campaign funds. In addition, labor unions in many areas are organized for effective political action at the local level. By this I mean the old-fashioned but essential process of making sure that voters are registered and get to the polls to vote. When this is done effectively among groups which in general are likely to support your candidates, it can be the deciding factor in an election. A majority of the wage earners in a community may support a particular candidate, but he may not win unless they are registered and vote. The normal apathy of voters makes this type of political action an important source of influence. Proper consideration of organized labor's interests by political leaders at the national level helps to ensure their active support where it counts, in the local election district. As was demonstrated in 1965, this influence is most effective when it is in support of programs that have broader appeal to the American people.

THE INTERNATIONAL UNIONS

Although the AFL–CIO is the official spokesman for organized labor and maintains the main lines of communication with the government, the autonomous international unions are the primary centers of union power. The AFL–CIO is simply a loose federation of independent organizations. It does not have a collective bargaining function and has only a modest and informal influence on the policies of its affiliated unions. The national unions are worker organizations whose primary purpose is to use bargaining power in the interests of their members.

Our union member looks to his national union to improve his wages and working conditions and to protect his rights as an employee. Union leaders who stray too far from these goals are inviting opposition. In recent union elections the incumbent officers were voted out after a campaign which included accusations that they worked too closely with management on joint problems. Our labor unions represent their members, not labor as a class. This has been an important source of strength for unions in the United States but it also represents a long-run threat to labor's continuing influence. The principle of concentrating on the mutual interests of the members *as workers* has been part of the American union philosophy since the early days of the American Federation of Labor. The early leaders of the labor federation found that workers recognized their shared interests on the job and would join together to work for those interests. Outside the work place their interests and aspirations were too diversified to provide a sound base for organizational solidarity. This limited focus made it possible for the first time for unions to survive depressions and to avoid the internal conflicts and disruptive activities that had destroyed earlier labor organizations.

The focus on the narrow job interests of their members gave American unions internal strength and stability. But it helps to explain the reluctance of the old-line craft unions in the 1930's to organize the industrial workers in the expanding new industries. It was only when the established unions were threatened by the rival CIO that they recognized the extent to which their future strength was tied to the successful organization of the mass prouction industries. The independence of the national unions and their historical preoccupation with their own organizational problems and the interests of their own members help to explain the difficulty until 1955 of bringing the two parts of the labor movement together again into a merged organization. The relevant question was not "Would it be good for labor?" but rather "Would it be good for the individual organizations, their members and officers?"

After the merger in 1955 and the creation of the AFL–CIO many union leaders anticipated more vigorous organizing activities and a rapid increase in union membership. Instead, labor union membership reached a high of 17.5 million in 1956 and decreased to 16.8 million in 1964. Organized labor slipped from almost 25 per cent of the labor force in 1956 to under 22 per cent in 1964.

In part, at least, this decline can be attributed to organized labor's inability to adjust to a changing economy. Unionized industries and occupations have declined in relative importance as the service industries expanded relative to manufacturing, and white-collar employment overtook and passed blue-collar employment.

The national unions have been more concerned with protecting their members' jobs than with organizing in the industries and occupations of expanding employment. Attempts to organize white-collar workers have not been very successful. Whatever the cause, existing unions have not been able to demonstrate that they can meet the needs of this expanding sector of the labor force. Nor have unions been very successful in trying to organize in the South or among service industry employees.

Some labor leaders believe that organizing should continue to be the responsibility of the individual unions and they are not concerned about the lack of membership growth. Others believe that organized labor will eventually decline in power and influence if unions do not expand with the economy. The focus and structure of the individual unions make it unlikely that they can provide the resources and stimulus for effective union growth. Walter Reuther plans to have the Industrial Union Department, which he heads, run a $6 million organizing drive of white-collar Southern textile and service industry employees. Whether or not our present labor movement can meet the requirements of the potential members in the largely nonunion industries, areas, and occupations remains to be seen.

ECONOMICS AND COLLECTIVE BARGAINING

In spite of the growth problems of organized labor, union strength should not be underestimated. About 30 per cent of nonagricultural workers are union members, and in manufacturing, construction, mining, transportation, and public utilities the great majority of wage earners are union members. To a considerable degree, therefore, wages and working conditions in our economy are set through the process of collective bargaining.

But this joint-decision process operates within the context of the product and labor market environments. Collective bargaining is the means by which market forces are translated into economic decisions. When demand is high and unemployment low, bargained wage increases are more generous than when the economy is in a slump. When profits are high or when market conditions facilitate price increases, it is easier to negotiate substantial wage improvements. When profits are squeezed and cost increases cannot be passed on to buyers, employers show strong resistance to union demands. When many union members are unemployed, job security is given high priority by union negotiators and wage increases are likely to be modest.

Since the basic economic forces are important determinants of relative bargaining power, it is difficult to demonstrate the extent to which the final result should be attributed to effective collective bargaining rather than the underlying market factors. Studies of the impact of unions on relative earnings suggest that on the average in recent years American unions have raised the wages of their members from 10 to 15 per cent higher than those of nonunion workers. The relative effectiveness of unions was apparently greatest in the early stages of the Great Depression of the 1930's when they were able to resist wage cuts which reduced earnings in the nonunion sectors. In periods of rapid expansion and inflation, unions have much less effect on relative earnings and, indeed, may lose some of the effects they previously had.

We have no evidence that bargaining power has been able to increase labor's share of total income. This is understandable when we consider the many market adjustments to wage increases. Substitution of capital for labor and reduced employment in an industry are among the reactions that would forestall any increase in labor's share of total income. In fact, it is possible that as a result of these adjustments capital's relative share could increase.

It would appear that bargaining power has, on the average produced a relatively modest improvement in the earnings of union members, and that their gains have been primarily at the expense of nonunion workers. As a result, the evidence suggests that "they have narrowed the gap between the best paid manual workers and the very rich, and widened the gap between these workers and the very poor."

Three major factors explain the difference between the apparent or alleged economic effects of unions, as evidenced by well-publicized reports of their bargaining accomplishments, and their actual economic impact. First, as explained above, the market forces affect the entire labor force, not just the union sector; second, the economic adjustment process tends to readjust income shares; and finally, money-wage improvements can be wiped out by price increases. It is this last possibility that creates a special problem for the economy. In periods of relative economic slack, if unions are able to use their bargaining power to push wages up faster than labor productivity, the result may be inflationary price increases. Upward pressure on prices from the wage-cost side when unemployment is high makes it more difficult to gain acceptance for and to implement expansive monetary and fiscal policies. As the economy approaches lower unemployment rates, the risks of inflation increase and one way for the inflationary spiral to start would be through an increase in union pressure on wage costs in key industries.

The noninflationary wage-price "Guideposts," first described by the President's Council of Economic Advisers in 1962 and restated many times since, represent an attempt to affect the private decision process by calling public attention to the requirements for price stability. In the present context, with unemployment close to the 4 per cent level, the Administration has placed increased emphasis on the importance of keeping wage and price decisions within the framework of the guideposts. As the economy expands and profits increase, union bargaining power grows. The question is whether the government can forestall inflationary wage bargains by informal influence of the guidepost type, or whether it can prevent an acceleration in wage increases only by slowing down the economy to remove the economic base for labor's bargaining power. In the absence of such action some unions may be able to push their wages up faster than prices, at least in the short run. The possible inflationary effects of such wage hikes are sufficient cause to be concerned with the way unions use their bargaining power.

THE NONECONOMIC IMPACT OF UNIONS

If the economic impact of labor unions has been frequently overstated, the noneconomic importance of collective bargaining has not been given enough importance. The average labor agreement restricts management's freedom of action by imposing constraints based on employee needs and interests. In most unionized plants the employer may not take arbitrary action against his employees, and the workers are aware of the rules that govern their assignments, promotions, and job security. The effective presence of the union to protect workers on the job is in my view the most dramatic result of collective bargaining. Workers are no longer anonymous and defenseless individuals faced by powerful employers who have no obligation other than self-interest to concern themselves with their employees' needs. The union member has achieved personal dignity as a worker with a legitimate claim to having his interests considered in the management of the enterprise.

We pay a cost in reduced efficiency for this achievement. When an employer may not lay off the least efficient first, or when his flexibility is constrained by seniority considerations or restrictive job classifications, production costs are increased. Our acceptance of collective bargaining as an institution protected by law is recognition of our willingness to accept a compromise mixture of human rights and productive efficiency as the appropriate goal for industry. Collective bargaining may not be the only way to achieve this blend, but it must be given credit for dramatic changes in the treatment of employees in many industries.

THE ISSUE OF STRIKES

A more obvious cost of collective bargaining is the loss of income and production due to strikes. Although employers and employees have many common interests, the hard fact is that higher wages for workers represent higher costs for management. Tighter seniority rules for employees are costly restrictions for employers. There are serious conflicts of interest between the parties to labor negotiations, and they cannot be ignored. To resolve these differences, the parties must be able to demonstrate power, and for the union, this means a willingness and ability to strike. But the social costs of strikes tend to be exaggerated. In 1965 about 2 per cent of all labor agreements were affected by strikes, and less than two-tenths of 1 per cent of total U.S. work time was lost by strikers—substantially less than the loss due to illness and accidents. The production and income loss estimates usually ignore the fact that much of the apparent loss is made up either immediately before or after the strike.

Our greatest public concern tends to be about strikes in key industries involving large numbers of workers. If we assume that critical defense and health needs can be taken care of, there is little reason to fear anything greater than inconvenience from even the most extensive strikes. The future of free collective bargaining may depend on our ability to accept strikes as an inherent part of the bargaining process. There has been an increasing tendency for the government to intervene actively in major bargaining situations to avoid strikes. If labor and management learn that strikes will not be permitted by government, they will lose their incentive to bargain realistically. Our acceptance of collective bargaining as part of the economic decision process rests on the belief that decisions arrived at through the private resolution of conflicting objectives will, in general, be in the public interest. There is little reason to believe that agreements forced on the parties by the government to avoid a strike will be closer to the public interest than the agreements the parties would have reached if they had been left to their own resources.

Attempts to avoid inflation and strikes have involved the government increasingly in the collective bargaining process. If the parties to collective bargaining are not responsive to the strong signs of public concern, the government's role in collective bargaining may grow. However, there is a strong and widespread belief in the importance of protecting the private decision process. Unions and management generally object strenuously to "interference" with free collective bargaining. The political force behind the principle of noninterference was demonstrated a few years ago when the White House and Congress juggled the hot potato of a possible railroad strike with obvious reluctance on all sides to accept the responsibility for the final decision to impose arbitration. Free collective bargaining has powerful support and it undoubtedly will continue as the basic decision process in the unionized sectors of the economy. However, public reactions and government responses to collective bargaining decisions will continue to grow in importance as part of the bargaining environment.

American unions today are still an important political and economic force, but their future influence will depend on their ability to adjust their organizations, strategies, and goals to a rapidly changing society.

11 SECURITY IN AN INCENTIVE SOCIETY

Wilbur J. Cohen

The pursuit of goals that are not always compatible with one another is a common enough—and often delightful—aspect of human behavior. This chapter shows how Americans have tried to have things both ways on a key issue, to have a society where men are rewarded for what they do as individuals and to ensure at the same time that the incentive rule is not applied so fully as to leave some people out of the income picture completely. The compromises described here have achieved in workability what they lack in neatness—but they raise new questions about the future.

On this planet of ours, with its many peoples, many lands, and diverse ways of life and government, one common thread extends throughout. This is the quest by each individual for security—security against want.

This has been true as far back as recorded history will take us, and it is a fair assumption that it was true even earlier. And it is true in any land that exists today. Civilization, either complex or rudimentary, free or totalitarian, urban or rural, rests upon the bedrock of some form and some degree of security for each of the people composing each separate tribe, city, or nation.

This individual security can and does take many forms. In the past—as is still true today in some places—security depended on a good harvest. If the crops were not adequate to last until the next harvest, people died. In the past—and in some societies today—security also depended on good health. Life was harsh and total community effort was required to meet the demands for food and shelter. Those who were too old, too sick, or too weak to take from the land those natural resources—animal, vegetable, and mineral—that are necessary to sustain life were often left to die, or were driven from the society.

There are still places in the world, and even in certain sections of the advanced industrialized nations to a degree, where whatever security an individual and his family enjoy comes from their efforts alone as they contend with and draw from their natural environment to maintain life. For the most part, however, industrialization and all that has come with it not only made greater personal security possible but in doing so also profoundly changed the way in which individual security is obtained.

With industrialization came the absolute necessity of interdependence, as the tasks of production and distribution were divided and then subdivided among the individuals composing the society. This brought separation of the majority of the people from the land, and thus security came to depend on a money income. For most people in an industrialized nation a money income comes in the form of wages. A man does one of the thousands of jobs that must be done to drive the technology. In return, he uses the money he earns from that one task to purchase the fruits of the labor of others—his family's food, clothing, shelter, medical care, and so on.

THE AMERICAN BACKGROUND FOR SOCIAL SECURITY

The United States was slower than most countries to recognize and adapt to the fact that, with economic security depending on a money income, individuals were exposed to threats to their security over which they had no control. Up until the 1930's, if earnings were stopped by unemployment, by old age, by sickness, or by injury, only savings and other family resources stood in the way of economic disaster. And most people lacked sufficient savings to cover every possible threat to security.

Strangely enough, however, there were no loud voices raised in the United States in the early part of this century for economic security guaranteed by the federal or state government, or by business and industrial employers as a "fringe benefit." Rather, it was felt that economic security was the responsibility of the individual. Almost all Americans believed that hard work and thrift were all that were needed to obtain economic security. Ideas contrary to this were considered a sign of weakness.

The individual seeking of economic security, it was felt, was one of the incentives that drove our competitive economy. Those holding this view believed that the more one individual contributes in effort, energy, and time to the nation's productive output, the more he will earn, and thus, the more he will receive from the economy, both for today and to save against future need—thus, economic security. They believed that to guarantee even a minimum of economic security without requiring work and thrift would weaken the very force that made the country a strong and growing one. There was, as the saying went, work for anyone who wanted it. And each individual could choose from the alternatives of saving for the future or doing without when he was unable to work. It was his choice and therefore he was responsible for the consequences.

But the depression of the 1930's shattered the myth that workers, or anyone else for that matter, had much individual control over their economic fortunes independent of the general state of the economy and independent of the security of their neighbors.

Almost overnight the people of the United States woke up to the fact that they were dependent on each other; that their economic system was complex and interrelated; that the workingman could no longer pick up the hoe when he lost his job. Labor discovered that good wages and safe working conditions didn't amount to much when there were no jobs. Business found that it wasn't profitable to produce goods if no one had the money to buy them. Consumers found that the nation's excellent productive facilities were useless if they did not have the money to buy what was produced. The nation discovered that its prosperity was the sum of each individual's prosperity. It was a rude awakening —but a necessary step toward the future.

There was a brief period, in fact, during the breakdown of the economic machinery of the United States—and of many countries

—in the 1930's when some seriously questioned whether marketplace considerations could be relied upon to drive a modern, interrelated, interdependent economic system; whether it was possible to provide for individual economic security within the framework of an incentive society.

This country was faced with a dilemma that we are still debating. How do you go about guaranteeing economic security for all and at the same time retain a maximum freedom of choice for each individual and not weaken the incentive to work?

Within the framework of these conflicting thoughts, it is easy to understand the long and still continuing dialogue in America as to how much of an individual's security—his money income—should be determined by his efforts alone and how much should he use his government to guarantee his security when he is unable to satisfy his needs within the conditions of competition.

What does an expanding, competitive society do about the security of an older person, no longer able to work and earn, no longer competitive?

What does such a society do about the child whose family is unable or unwilling to support it?

What does such a society do about a worker who can find no work because he doesn't have a skill that is needed?

A FEDERAL PROGRAM FOR OLD-AGE SECURITY

Beginning in the early thirties, the government of the United States set about to find a means of strengthening individual economic security through government programs, but to do it in a way that would neither interfere with the incentive to work nor lessen the individual freedom of Americans.

That the job was well done is reflected in two general observations about the American people today. They now enjoy the world's highest degree of economic security; they enjoy, individually, a maximum of political freedom.

In 1935 President Franklin D. Roosevelt signed the Social Security Act, which was a first and historic commitment by the federal government to help maintain the economic security of Americans.

I was fortunate enough, as a young man, to have participated in the creation of the Social Security Act, and have been involved, in one way or another, in the operation of the programs created by the act and in the numerous improvements that have been made in it over the past thirty years.

Basically, the Social Security Act established a federal social insurance system of old-age benefits; a federal-state social insurance system of unemployment payments; and a federal-state public welfare program. This initial start proved so successful and so popular that the programs were quickly expanded.

The federal old-age social insurance system is financed by contributions paid by workers on their earnings, with employers required to pay an equal amount. These contributions are paid into trust funds and from these funds monthly payments are made when the worker retires. Since 1935 this cash benefit system has been expanded to include benefits to workers when they become disabled and to the families of workers who are retired, disabled, or die.

In 1966 more than 20,000,000 people are receiving monthly benefits from this federal social insurance program. The system will pay out about $18.5 billion in benefits this year. And—as a result of 1965 changes in the law which took effect in July of 1966—all people in the United States aged sixty-five and over are provided paid-up hospital insurance through the same social insurance system. Hospital benefits, like cash benefits, will be financed by contributions based on workers' earnings, with employers paying an equal amount.

There are three points that I would like to stress about this social insurance system of ours.

First, it is financed by contributions from workers based on their earnings. This means, in effect, that each citizen individually pays for a large part of the insurance he receives from the system, with the difference being made up by what his employer contributes. Social insurance is not a giveaway system; it requires that each individual contribute toward his family's economic security.

Second, the benefits payable under the system are payable as a matter of earned rights. These rights are enforceable in the courts of the United States and are founded in the legislation that created the system. Therefore government, even though it operates the system, can neither withhold benefits from a person who is eligible nor reward him with higher payments than he has actually earned.

Third, the amount of cash benefits is based on the worker's previous earnings. In general, the higher a person's earnings during working years, the higher the benefits to which he will be entitled if he retires, becomes disabled, or dies.

Thus, the same incentive that is supposed to motivate the individual during working years is reflected in both his eligibility to benefits and the amount of such benefits. The structure of the economy in general is reflected in the major system for economic security, as are individual rights and freedom of choice.

The federal social insurance system, although improved many times since 1935, is not yet perfect and will certainly undergo further changes in the future. But it does provide a sound base upon which economic security can be built, and it guarantees to practically all Americans and their dependents at least a modest income when wages stop because of death, disability, or old age, as well as much needed health insurance when they reach the age of sixty-five.

A FEDERAL-STATE SYSTEM FOR UNEMPLOYMENT BENEFITS

The second major program of the Social Security Act of 1935 was the federal-state social insurance system of unemployment benefits. While administratively more complex than the strictly federal system, unemployment insurance works on the same principle. It insures workers against loss of income due to unemployment by making payments available during periods of joblessness. Funds to make the payments come from taxes paid by employers which are placed in trust funds.

Again, in principle, benefit amounts are tied to wages and eligibility depends on a previous history of work and the willingness and the ability of the worker to accept another job when one becomes available.

Wage replacement when unemployment occurs is, of course, a treatment of symptoms. It is made necessary by the technological unemployment that spins off from an advancing technology, but it is no long-range substitute for employment and wages.

As a result, we in the United States are now putting heavy emphasis on the retraining of the unemployed and the updating of the skills of the labor force. This aspect is covered in other chapters in this book; suffice it to say here that unemployment is a problem to a small percentage of Americans, and unemployment insurance is the immediate guarantee of economic security when an individual finds himself without a job.

PROGRAM FOR PUBLIC ASSISTANCE

When the social insurance systems were set up under the Social Security Act, it was apparent that some people would not be able to qualify for benefits under these programs because they would not have worked in employment covered by the social insurance, or would have such a small amount of earnings that their benefits would not be adequate to meet their needs. Moreover, certain risks cannot effectively be covered by social insurance, such as the risk of loss of income to a family if the head of that family willfully refuses to discharge his responsibility for their economic security.

Accordingly, the Social Security Act also provided for public assistance programs to be administered by the separate states with the federal government providing part of the money to make the payments and administer the programs.

Under the public assistance programs—as opposed to the social insurance systems—eligibility for benefits and the amount of benefits are determined by the need, rather than the past history of employment and the previous wage level, of the individual worker. Moreover, the federal funds involved in the program's operation come from the general revenues of the United States, not from earmarked contributions to trust funds, as in the social insurance programs.

Until recently, payments could be made under this program

only to people over sixty-five, the disabled, and children in families where the head of the household was dead, disabled, or had deserted the family. A few years ago the law was modified so that benefits could be paid to unemployed workers and their children, but public assistance payments because of unemployment are available in only a minority of the states at the present time.

The fact that seven million people are dependent on public assistance in a country as prosperous and busy as the United States is, on first glance, one of the major paradoxes of our times. With our economy functioning at a record level; with employment at an all-time high; with incomes at record levels, why should millions of people need to turn to public assistance for their very survival?

The answer is at once easy to find and difficult to understand. Many of the people receiving public assistance are too old or too disabled to work. Some live in areas that have been bypassed by the general prosperity of the country. And some, frankly, have just been unable to fit themselves into the highly technical and complex industrial society into which they were born. In the almost overnight transition from a rural to an urban economy many people were born, raised, trained, and worked on farms much of their adult lives only to find that, with the decreasing need for farm manpower, they must turn to the city for a living.

But in the industrial cities of the United States there is little need for the skills and techniques that are useful on a farm. Living is less relaxed, more complicated. The work that is to be done demands great technical or managerial skill.

So the transition is not easy and the casualties of the process find themselves and their families dependent on public assistance.

As a result, there is in the United States a growing awareness that cash payments are not the real answer to dependency. Rather, we are shifting the emphasis in the public assistance programs from income maintenance to the prevention of dependency and the restoration of economic independence wherever possible. We are rapidly integrating programs of vocational rehabilitation, vocational education, work training, and mental health with the public welfare programs. Moreover, in recognition that the dependent adults of tomorrow are today's neglected children, we are providing greater help and opportunities to the children of dependent families so that they will be able to participate productively in the economy when they become adults.

A SUMMING UP

Thus, economic security in the United States to a great degree rests upon these three major programs: federal social insurance against loss of income due to death, disability, and old age; federal-state social insurance against loss of income due to unemployment; and federal-state public welfare programs to provide money to the needy simply because they are needy.

The social insurance plans were not the absolute break with the past that many sincerely believed they were when they were created. As I have said, eligibility under the programs was based on a past history of work. Benefits were determined by past wage levels. The original incentive to work—the wage that comes with gainful employment—continues to be reflected in the programs that reinforce individual economic security.

Moreover, Americans are encouraged to supplement their protection under the social insurance plans with private insurance, savings, pensions, and other safeguards against the loss of economic security.

In fact, the complex mixture of social insurance and private insurance that has evolved in America sometimes makes it difficult for people from other lands to understand why we do what we do.

For instance, health insurance for the aged was recently added to the social insurance system to protect older people against the high cost of medical care. This was done because the usual methods of private health insurance didn't work for most older people. Besides being bad risks, their incomes were only about half those of younger people; they simply couldn't afford private health insurance when they needed it most. So the government set up a system whereby workers pay small regular sums into trust funds when they are earning, thus accumulating paid-up hospital insurance for their old age.

The great majority of the American people were in favor of using social insurance to provide health insurance for aged Americans, but they would resist extending social insurance to provide health insurance for everyone in the United States, just as they would resist any attempt to socialize medicine. And for a very simple reason. Most Americans are covered by some kind of private health insurance at modest cost. They are able to provide very well for their own economic security in this particular area, and that's the way they want it.

The deeply held belief that people should do as much as possible for themselves has historically played a large part in determining the government's role in furthering the general welfare. In health, in education, in dealing with the problems of unemployment and economic dependency, there is a feeling on the part of the majority that the federal government does have a responsibility, but that this responsibility ends where it is realistic and appropriate to expect the individual, either alone or working through his community or state government, to see to his own welfare.

The line of demarcation as to when, and when not, federal action is necessary to the well-being of the people is a thin and sometimes invisible one. Much of the continuing debate on internal problems centers around the precise definition of this line.

It has long been accepted that the federal government has a responsibility to assure the opportunity of education to the people. We still debate how much federal action is needed to discharge that responsibility.

It has long been accepted that the federal government has a responsibility to assure the opportunity to enjoy good health to the fullest extent possible. Again, the way and form in which this responsibility is discharged continues to be debated.

It has long been accepted that the federal government has a responsibility to assure the opportunity for general well-being, and this responsibility is discharged through the social security programs, through housing programs, through minimum-wage laws, and in numerous other ways. However, we continue to debate the proper role of government under changing conditions.

As a consequence, although the people of the United States

reject the philosophy of the "welfare state," they do recognize the ability of the state to further their welfare in so far as they are unable to do so themselves.

In short, you can have economic security in an incentive society and, at the same time, maintain the motivation to work that is required and the individual freedom that is necessary to the system. This is done through a unique partnership between the individual, his local and state governments, his federal government, and the business and commercial interests.

President Johnson has expressed the conviction that in this direction lies the building of the Great Society—a society where opportunity to work, to learn, to live in good health and economic security is available to all, but always within the context of individual freedom.

12 CAN THE U.S. AVOID DEPRESSIONS AND INFLATION? FISCAL POLICIES

James Tobin

The next three essays shift the focus away from marketplaces and individual economic institutions to look at the over-all functioning of the economy. They deal with the levels of jobs, incomes, production, and prices. Alternating booms and busts are an old story in the United States, but since the Great Depression of the 1930's there has been a new realization of what free men can do to rid themselves of the worst aspects of such fluctuations. Today, economic stability and the interplay of public and private actions to achieve it are matters of common discussion. This essay looks at several decades of experience in an increasingly sophisticated use of government's taxing and spending policies to achieve a more stable economy.

Experience in recent years has produced new optimism about the economic future of the United States. Steady growth at low rates of unemployment and inflation, interrupted only infrequently by minor recessions, now seems an attainable objective. The new optimism is widely shared by economists, businessmen, trade union leaders, government officials, workers, and consumers. Federal fiscal policy is the major reason for the remarkable degree of confidence and consensus in appraisals of U.S. economic prospects.

Thirty years ago the U.S. was still in the early stages of recovery from the Great Depression. In President Roosevelt's dramatic phrase, one-third of the nation was ill fed, ill clad, ill housed. The cruel paradox was that the country had ample resources to meet their needs. One-fifth of the labor force was involuntarily unemployed. Industrial plants stood idle, and land was being deliberately withdrawn from cultivation. The economic system, a decentralized network of private enterprises and free markets, seemed to have failed. The democratic political institutions of the nation seemed incapable of repairing the economic machine. Things are very different now. No basic changes in the country's economic and political institutions have been made. Yet almost no one expects that the U.S. will ever again suffer a major depression.

In 1961 the U.S. was beginning to recover from a business recession, the fourth since the end of World War II. Business cycles, alternating periods of inflationary boom and periods of recession and unemployment, were generally accepted as an unfortunate but inevitable defect of the American economy. Compared to the Great Depression of the 1930's, all the postwar recessions were mild and short. The decline that began in 1929 lasted forty-three months, reduced industrial output by 38 per cent, and raised the unemployment rate to 25 per cent. The longest postwar downswing was thirteen months; the sharpest drop in industrial production was 7 per cent; and the highest unemployment rate was 7 per cent. But by 1961 recessions seemed to be occurring with increasing frequency. The previous expansion had lasted only twenty-five months before it ended in the spring of 1960 with 5 per cent of the labor force still unemployed. Rising unemployment seemed to many a chronic rather than a cyclical condition, due to deep-seated structural changes rather than to fluctuations in business activity.

Both fatalism about business cycles and pessimism about unemployment have proved to be unjustified, and they have largely been replaced by confidence in the steady growth of the economy. The expansion beginning in the winter of 1961 has already lasted longer than any prior peacetime upswing and has already reduced unemployment to rates last experienced before 1954.

Why has the U.S. economy performed so much better since the war than before? Why is it growing more steadily, and now with less unemployment, in the 1960's than in the 1950's? Federal fiscal policy is a major part of the answer to both these questions.

By federal fiscal policy I refer to the impact of federal expenditures and revenues on the rate of total spending, private as well as public, for goods and services. The most relevant aspects of the federal budget are its size and its balance. Its size is indicated by the rate of federal expenditures, including direct purchases of goods and services or transfers of money to individuals, state and local governments, and foreign governments to enable them to make purchases. Balance refers to the relation of total revenues to expenditures, the size of the budget surplus or deficit. By focusing attention on these over-all features of the federal budget, I do not mean to underrate the economic and social importance of the composition of government expenditures and taxes. But most of the story of the budget's relation to economic stability can be told in terms of the aggregate magnitudes.

THE ECONOMICS BACK OF THE BUDGET

The economic principles involved are very simple. The economy's capacity to produce goods and services depends on its labor force, its stocks of capital goods, land, and natural resources, and its technological knowledge. Potential output increases as the labor force grows, capital is accumulated, and technology is improved. In the U.S. it is estimated that potential output grows at from 3.5 to 4 per cent per year. But output will be produced, and labor will be employed to produce it, only if it can be sold—to consumers, to business firms, or to governments. When the total spending of households, businesses, and governments is too small to buy potential output, men and machines are unemployed. When total demand is so large as to strain the manpower and industrial resources of the economy, prices and wages rise.

The rates of spending of households, businesses, and state and local governments can fluctuate for many reasons. One very important influence on their spending is the income they receive or expect to receive. Furthermore, one man's expenditure is another's income. A reduction in total spending multiplies; as people lose sales, jobs, and income, they cut down their spending and cause similar losses for others.

The central government—in the U.S., the federal government

—can act as a balance wheel. When excessive total demand threatens inflation, the central government can use its budget to restrict spending. One way is to diminish its own purchases. This will reduce total demand even if taxes are reduced equally, but it will have a much stronger deflationary effect if taxes are maintained. Another way is to induce private households and businesses or subordinate governments to spend less by raising taxes or curtailing grants. In the opposite case, when total spending is inadequate to buy the output the economy is capable of producing, the central government can raise its outlays or lower taxes.

The key to stabilizing the economy by fiscal policy is for the government to act differently from other economic units. Unlike households, firms, and subordinate governments, the central government must not tailor its expenditures to its income. Inflation is a great tax collector, but the government will only add fuel to the inflation if it spends the added tax revenues inflation brings in. Likewise, when recessions in business activity reduce the yields of existing taxes, the government will deepen the recession if it cuts its spending or tries to recoup its income by raising tax rates.

The central government is uniquely free to break the link between revenue and expenditure. Other economic units must balance their budgets, at least in the long run. They can run deficits only to the extent that their wealth and their income prospects give them good credit standing. The central government can finance deficits in its transactions with its own citizens either by issuing new money or by incurring interest-bearing debt. And the central government alone has the power to coin or print money with which it may discharge its own internal debts. This power can be and sometimes has been abused, but it can also be used to promote economic stability and prosperity.

In the United States federal deficits are financed in the first instance by selling interest-bearing Treasury securities, and federal surpluses by retiring them. The size of the federal debt at any time reflects the cumulative past history of deficits and surpluses. But a part of the debt is "monetized," i.e., repurchased by the central banking agency of the federal government, the Federal Reserve System, in return for currency or deposits in Federal Reserve Banks, which serve as the reserves of the commercial banking system. The Federal Reserve must decide how much debt to monetize; its monetary policies, which will be discussed in the next chapter, are also important for the stability of the economy.

THE MATTER OF THE PUBLIC DEBT

The federal debt has aroused considerable popular and political concern in the U.S. The debt is for the most part a legacy of World War II. The outstanding debt was $230 billion at the end of 1946 and was $270 billion at the end of 1965. Meanwhile Gross National Product has grown from $209 billion to $681 billion. Much of the resistance to deficit financing as a tool of economic stabilization has been based on the alleged dangers of increasing, or failing to reduce, the federal debt. Many people argue by analogy to private families, for whom a large debt means an interest burden and eventually an unhappy day of reckoning. This analogy might apply to a governmental debt to foreign creditors, but it does not apply to the federal debt, which is almost wholly the internal debt of a sovereign government to its own people. Other critics assert that deficit finance immorally shifts the burden of current public expenditure to future generations. This is true only in the sense that alternative policies might build up a greater stock of productive capital for future generations to inherit. However, when deficit finance is used to maintain or restore high rates of economic activity, the result is generally more capital accumulation rather than less.

Finally, the debt is often regarded as a stock of latent inflationary tinder which may at any time burst into flames. Indeed something like this occurred in 1947–1948, when the owners of highly liquid government securities acquired during the war tried to spend them on the scarce civilian goods of which the war had deprived them. However, in normal circumstances the liquidity of the debt can be flexibly managed by Treasury and Federal Reserve authorities so as to prevent any such inflationary outburst. Indeed the occasions when deficit financing is appropriate for fiscal policy are generally times when the salient economic problem is insufficiency of demand rather than inflation.

THE AUTOMATIC STABILIZERS

Let me return to the questions I posed earlier. How has fiscal policy contributed to the improved performance and greater stability of the American economy? There are two main points. The first concerns the automatic contribution of the federal budget to economic stability, while the second relates to deliberate discretionary use of the budget for economic objectives. I shall discuss these points in turn.

Postwar federal budgets have economic stabilizers built into them. This is partly because of their sheer size. Federal outlays on income account were only 2.5 per cent of Gross National Product in 1929, averaged 9.5 per cent of depressed GNP levels from 1933 through 1940, and have averaged nearly 18 per cent of GNP since 1946. Big changes in expenditure programs on short notice are not operationally or politically feasible. The assured continuation of so large a block of national expenditure has made the economy much less vulnerable to self-reinforcing spirals of declining demand.

With the increased size of the budget have come higher tax rates. Federal revenues are sensitive to fluctuations in business activity, the more so because of reliance on corporate profits taxes and progressive personal income taxes. When private incomes move up or down, the after-tax incomes available for spending move much less than before the war. Likewise the social and economic legislation of President Roosevelt's New Deal, extended since the war, established federal programs under which expenditures automatically move counter to the business cycle. Business recessions increase the number of people eligible for social security benefits, unemployment compensation, and public assistance. Federal commitments to support farm prices and incomes require increased expenditure when private demand falls off.

Altogether, the federal fiscal position today absorbs 25 to 30 cents of every dollar change in Gross National Product. Correspondingly, the incomes of spending units other than the federal government—households, businesses, and state and local governments—rise or fall in aggregate only 70 or 75 cents when GNP rises or falls one dollar. In the 1920's and 1930's, by contrast, the federal government absorbed only 5 to 15 per cent of short-run changes in GNP.

The built-in stabilizers are one reason why postwar recessions and inflations have been contained. But valuable as they are, they cannot *prevent* swings in business. They can only moderate them. They offset only fractionally the changes in private spending that generate cyclical fluctuations in business activity. In recent years both President Kennedy and President Johnson have asked Congress to increase the counter-cyclical response of the federal fiscal system. One proposal is to increase the size and duration of unemployment compensation whenever national unemployment exceeds a specified rate. Another proposal is to let a designated rise in unemployment trigger the release of federal funds for certain federal, state, and local public works. The third and most controversial proposal is to make quick, simple, standardized, temporary reductions in income tax rates to avert or arrest recessions. President Kennedy, following the recommendations of a group of influential citizens privately organized as the Commission on Money and Credit, suggested in 1962 that Congress delegate to the President the power to initiate such tax cuts. To avoid the difficult issues of Constitutional prerogative raised by an outright delegation of power, President Johnson has simply asked the Congress to prepare itself to take rapid action on a Presidential request for an anti-recession tax cut. To date no action has been taken on these proposals.

THE DISCRETIONARY STABILIZERS

The automatic response of federal taxes and expenditures to economic fluctuations has helped stabilize the economy, and the contribution of built-in stabilizers can be further increased. But no automatic fiscal mechanism is a substitute for deliberate discretionary adjustment of the federal budget to changing economic circumstances.

Here too there has been a great change. During the Great Depression the instincts of both political parties and both Presidents were to reduce expenditure and raise taxes. The budget must be balanced. When times are hard, the federal government, its income reduced, must economize like anyone else. Thus during the 1929–1933 recession the government did not offset but indeed accentuated the decline in private spending and business activity. As a consequence, its own revenues fell further and its budget was still in deficit.

Fortunately the Roosevelt administration found it difficult to carry out in practice as strict a budgetary policy as it originally espoused. After 1936 the Administration flirted with the new ideas of J. M. Keynes but did not consistently follow them. Ultimately federal spending did end the Depression in 1940–1941, but the spending was not undertaken for that purpose but to prepare for war.

As World War II drew to a close, most people in the United States, as in other countries, were resolved that the Great Depression must never be allowed to happen again. Many Americans feared that demobilization and cutbacks in defense spending would cause serious unemployment. In this atmosphere the Congress enacted, with the support of both parties, the Employment Act of 1946. The Act declared it to be the policy of the federal government to use its powers to promote "maximum employment, production, and purchasing power." It established machinery both in the Executive Office of the President and in the Congress to review annually the state of the economy and the actions of the government, and to appraise them in the light of the Act's declared objectives. But obviously the mandate of the Employment Act is not self-executing. Specific policies to carry it out depend on the federal budget from year to year and on other actions by the President, the Congress, and the Federal Reserve System.

In the early years of the Employment Act the major problem proved, contrary to expectation, to be the control of inflation rather than the prevention of unemployment. This was true in 1947–1948, when pent-up demands for civilian goods poured into markets suddenly freed of rationing and price controls. It was true again in 1950–1951 because of the effects of the Korean War, first in igniting private speculation and then in requiring a large and rapid increase in defense spending. During the first inflation the federal budget achieved a large surplus. Nevertheless President Truman proposed in January 1949 a $4 billion tax increase to check private demand. The Congress did not act—fortunately, as it turned out—because the economy had slid into recession at the end of 1948. During the Korean War taxes were increased in three steps and federal revenues were raised 75 per cent in two years.

During the Eisenhower administration, 1953–1961, a mildly counter-cyclical fiscal policy supplemented the automatic effects of the built-in stabilizers. Some special Korean War taxes were scheduled to expire in 1954; these and other tax reductions enacted by the new administration were fortunately timed, because 1954 was a recession year. Both at this time and in the 1958 recession the Administration accelerated public works and other spending. But President Eisenhower and his administration were strongly committed to the principle of balancing the federal budget. If they did not apply the principle year by year, as had been so disastrously attempted during the depression after 1929, they considered it at least essential to balance federal receipts and expenditures over the course of a business cycle. The recession of 1958 produced a large unexpected deficit—$12.4 billion in the administrative budget—as a natural consequence of the stabilizing sensitivity of the budget to economic activity. Thereafter the Administration earnestly economized so as to produce a surplus during the ensuing recovery. This restrictive turn in fiscal policy appears to be one reason why the recovery ended prematurely in the spring of 1960, with 5 per cent of the labor force still unemployed.

THE RECORD OF THE 1960'S

By 1961, fifteen years after passage of the Employment Act, federal fiscal policy was still not wholeheartedly dedicated to economic stabilization. Understandably, budget balancing had wide moral and political appeal, and the economic role of the budget was not widely understood. The Kennedy administration increased spending cautiously in its efforts to speed recovery from the 1960 recession. Like Roosevelt thirty years before, President Kennedy at first pledged his administration to balance the budget. Nevertheless, international developments led him to expand defense and space spending; as in 1940–1941, noneconomic circumstances fortuitously produced an expansionary fiscal policy in 1961–1963.

In 1962 the recovery slowed down. President Kennedy and his administration became convinced both that balance in the federal budget was unattainable without more rapid and complete recovery and that the large bite of increases in income taken by federal taxes was a severe drag on the needed expansion of private spending. In other words, the built-in stabilizers seemed to be stabilizing the economy at unacceptably low levels of employment and national income. The frustrating and partially self-defeating quest for budget balance was abandoned, and in 1963 the President recommended a cut of $12 billion in personal and corporate income taxes, designed explicitly to stimulate private spending, employment, and production. The income tax cut was finally enacted in 1964 under President Johnson, and took effect in two steps during that year and the next. It was followed by a $3.5 billion reduction in federal excise taxes in 1965.

These measures were a radical new departure in U.S. fiscal policy. They were adopted when the budget was already in deficit, and when the economy was in an upswing. They were not anti-recession or counter-cyclical measures. They were designed rather to sustain and to speed economic expansion. They were very much in the spirit of the Employment Act of 1946. The fiscal powers of the government were used to restore full employment, which the Administration interpreted to correspond, at least for the time being, to 4 per cent unemployment. Thanks in no small part to the sequence of fiscal stimuli since 1960—the buildup in federal spending mainly for defense and space exploration, followed by the series of tax cuts—the economy has enjoyed six years of steady expansion. The unemployment rate, nearly 7 per cent in early 1961, has been reduced to below 4 per cent for the first time since 1953. The apparent success of fiscal management has quieted political and ideological controversy about the federal budget. A considerable consensus now supports the view that flexible fiscal policy, relatively free from inflexible requirements that the budget balance every year or even on average over a period of a few years, can help immensely to stabilize a growing economy at low rates of unemployment.

In a growing full employment economy, the appropriate federal fiscal policy depends on the strength of non-federal demands relative to the resources available for meeting them. Since this balance changes from time to time, fiscal policy must be flexible. When private investment demand is insufficient to employ all the saving generated by full employment personal and corporate incomes, the federal government should run a deficit, borrowing and spending the excessive private saving. Otherwise the economy's willingness to save will be frustrated by unemployment, reduced incomes, and underproduction. When private investment demand exceeds the economy's full employment saving, the government should run a surplus, which will in effect make up the shortage of private saving by public saving. Otherwise there will be excess demand and inflation. For these reasons, it is not possible to say categorically that a full employment fiscal policy always requires a surplus, or a deficit, or an exact balance.

With given tax legislation and constant expenditure programs, the normal growth of the economy tends to make the federal fiscal position more restrictive from one year to the next. At present, in the absence of deliberate action, the annual growth of full employment GNP would yield the government $6 to $8 billion in additional revenues. Each year a decision must be made. Unless private demands are independently expanding faster than private incomes, deliberate action to neutralize the revenue growth is called for. The action can take the form of expenditure increase or tax reduction, or some mixture of the two.

The size of federal expenditures is politically determined on criteria largely unrelated to economic stabilization. The changing requirements of national defense and of domestic programs to build President Johnson's Great Society are currently the main factors. Although total federal expenditures have grown very little since 1963, they are now rising because of the war in Vietnam.

Given the course of federal expenditures, taxes can be adjusted to maintain the appropriate fiscal policy for economic stabilization. This has been the practice in recent years, and there is strong support for the principle that budgetary adjustments for purposes of stabilization should be made on the revenue rather than the expenditure side of the ledger. A number of observers foresee the need, if and when defense expenditures are again stabilized or reduced, for a series of further tax cuts or equivalent measures to dispose of growing federal revenues. Among the competing claimants are plans to share federal revenues with state governments and proposals to pay federal allowances or "negative income taxes" to families with incomes below the poverty line. President Johnson has promised that relief for low-income groups will have high priority in future tax reductions, in view of the benefits given to corporations and high-income individuals by recent tax legislation.

ROUNDING OUT THE ANALYSIS

Before I conclude I must remedy two oversimplifications in my discussion of the relation of fiscal policy to the objective of full employment. First, the choice of the target rate of utilization of manpower and other resources is itself a difficult and controversial issue. It is not true that falling short of a chosen target spells unemployment and no inflation, while overshooting means inflation unaccompanied by higher employment and production. Instead there is a zone within which higher unemployment rates will be accompanied by greater price stability, and lower unemployment by higher rates of price increase. The choice of a target rate of unemployment therefore involves political value judgment of the weights to be attached to the two objectives, high employment and price stability.

Some critics of the economic policies of the Kennedy and Johnson administrations have felt that their "interim" goal of 4 per cent unemployment was too ambitious. The critics feared, on the basis of experience in the mid-1950's, that this goal implied too much inflation, especially unacceptable in view of the deficits in the U.S. external balance of payments.

In 1966 once again the inflationary consequences of low unemployment have become a key problem and issue. The interim unemployment target has been reached, and prices have been rising at 3 to 4 per cent this year. The experience does not seem to be as unfavorable as the 1955–1957 boom, and it is still unclear how much inflation is an inescapable by-product of high rates of employment and production. The Kennedy and Johnson administrations have sought to dampen the inflationary consequences of high utilization rates by two other policies. One is the enunciation and repetition of guideposts for non-inflationary price and wage behavior, addressed to trade unions and managements in concentrated industries. The other is a series of specific measures to improve the adaptation of the labor force—its education, skills, training, and mobility—to the job opportunities available. It remains to be seen how far these measures and other circumstances will permit expansion of aggregate demand to reduce unemployment without giving rise to inflationary pressures which the Administration, the Congress, and the Federal Reserve find unacceptable.

Second, I have oversimplified by speaking of fiscal policy in isolation from monetary policy. In fact, the two should be and generally are coordinated. There are in principle a number of mixtures of the two policies which can achieve a chosen full employment target. If monetary policy is easy and interest rates are low, investment demand will be relatively strong. The appropriate fiscal policy will then be a comparatively restrictive budget; indeed the federal government may need to run a surplus in order to provide enough saving to finance the investment stimulated by low interest rates and abundant credit. This is presumably the kind of policy mixture which would be favored by those concerned with the burden of debt finance on future generations and by others who wish to promote economic growth. However, the opposite combination—high interest rates and deficit budgets—may be forced on a country struggling, like the U.S. in recent years, to reduce a balance-of-payments deficit.

13 CAN THE U.S. AVOID DEPRESSIONS AND INFLATION? MONETARY POLICIES

G. L. Bach

This essay continues the discussion begun in Chapter 12, with the focus for attempting to stabilize the economy shifting now from changes in taxes and public spending to changes in the supply of money. Both chapters contend that our willingness to use the knowledge and tools now at our disposal will be key factors in our attack on instability.

Can capitalism avoid depressions and mass unemployment? Ever since Karl Marx, critics have argued that the downfall of capitalist economies would come through such crises. And this criticism has persisted until today. In spite of the spectacular success of the capitalistic, individual-initiative economies of the West, through much of the world the nagging question remains: Have they really conquered the business cycle and mass depression? And this question is focused more on the United States than on any other nation.

Three decades ago—in the Great Depression of the 1930's—the answer to the question seemed far from clear. One worker out of four, or even more, was out of a job. Faith in the ability of the American economy to restore itself automatically to high level employment waned. Insistence on government action to get the economy going again grew as the depression years wore on. After the depths of 1933, times improved; unemployment dropped; the financial crisis was ended; incomes began to rise again. But it was not until the end of the decade, with war in Europe and greatly increased government spending on defense preparations at home, that the economy moved strongly toward prosperity. And the critics saw little good in this performance. They claimed that this showed that only war could eliminate the cancer of unemployment from the basically private-enterprise American economy.

What is the record since World War II? For more than twenty-five years—a quarter-century—the American economy has moved upward with only intermittent slowdowns. Not since 1939 has there been a major depression. After World War II reconversion to peacetime production and high employment came rapidly and vigorously. Throughout the 1950's the economy grew persistently, although with three small slumps—in 1954, 1958, and 1960. In the present decade the record has been excellent. For six years there has not been even a minor recession. Unemployment has been pared to less than 4 per cent of the labor force—a low figure in a free society which permits people to move from job to job freely and at will. Real output has grown steadily at over 4 per cent a year. The American standard of living has moved even further ahead of that in the rest of the world, even though some other nations have grown faster in percentage terms.

Has the American economy conquered the business cycle? If so, how? The record of the postwar years is encouraging, especially that of the present decade. Shall we attribute the success to modern fiscal policy, effective management of government spending and taxing, as Professor Tobin suggested in the preceding chapter? Shall we give the credit to improved monetary policy—to better and more understanding control over the supply of money and interest rates—the traditional guardian of the stability of the currency and the economy? Have the millions of private businessmen and consumers in the capitalist system learned how to manage their affairs so well as substantially to eliminate booms and depressions? Or has it been just a matter of luck?

Most American economists would answer that it was a combination of all these factors and might give greatest credit to modern fiscal policy, especially for the success of the 1960's. But there is evidence that American monetary policy has also played an important role in helping to reduce employment without inflation Some economists give it the major credit.

HOW DOES MONETARY POLICY WORK?

What is monetary policy? Basically, it is control by the central bank (the Federal Reserve System in the United States) over the amount of money that is created and over the availability and interest cost of that money. Money in the United States consists not only of paper money and coins, but predominantly of bank deposits against which households and businesses write checks to make most of their payments. Thus, primarily, monetary policy consists of controlling the volume of bank deposits (the primary form of money) and influencing the interest cost and availability of bank credit.

FEDERAL RESERVE CONTROL OVER BANK LENDING

The Federal Reserve in the United States corresponds roughly to the Bank of England, the Bank of France, and other central banks. It has the power to control the amount of loans and investments that banks can make because it controls the basic reserves which the banks must hold against their deposits. Thus, if the "Fed" wants to encourage bank lending and an increase in the supply of bank deposits (which are the form in which banks make loans available to their borrowers), it can provide new reserves to the banks through "open market operations"—that is, through buying up government securities in the open market from banks or other sellers. Conversely, the Fed can restrict the amount of bank lending and the creation of new money by limiting or reducing the volume of reserves which the banks have. Without reserves, the banks are not permitted to extend new loans and thus to generate new deposits. The mechanics of the banking system are complex, but they need not be of concern here. You can accept the proposition that the Fed has power to control the amount of bank lending and the volume of deposits in the American economy, within moderate limits. While there is dispute over the details, there is no dispute over the central power.

BANK LENDING, BOOMS, AND DEPRESSIONS

If we agree that the Federal Reserve can control the supply of money within moderate limits, does this mean it can thereby control the level of total spending (by businesses and individuals) in the economy? If the answer is yes, monetary policy gives us a powerful stabilizing tool in a private-enterprise economy. For in our economy, keeping total demand growing roughly in balance with the growing full employment potential capacity of the economy is one vital key to stable economic growth. More total spending means excess demand and inflation. Less total spending means deficient demand, unemployment, and wasted productive potential. A brief answer to this central question is that Federal Reserve monetary policy can help powerfully to keep demand growing stably, especially if it is used in cooperation with fiscal policy and other governmental measures. But it certainly cannot do the job alone. And the Fed faces some serious problems in trying to use monetary policy effectively, even with the full cooperation of other governmental agencies.

The monetary key to avoiding both inflation and depression is gradual growth in bank lending and bank deposits (money), roughly keeping pace with growth in the productive potential of the economy. Experience suggests that this growth in productive potential, which reflects our growing population, increasing capital investment, and technological advance, may be around 4 per cent per year.

As Professor Tobin argued in the preceding chapter, government spending comprises one large element of aggregate demand and we have, hopefully, learned to use this government demand as one major device in helping to keep aggregate demand growing at about the desired stable rate. Increasing or decreasing government spending, without corresponding changes in tax collections, provides a powerful, direct channel of influence over total demand in the economy.

Monetary policy is a more indirect way to influence aggregate demand in a largely private-enterprise economy. By increasing bank reserves, the Fed can encourage banks to make more loans and investments, and thereby to increase the supply of deposits (spendable money). It can by the same actions reduce interest rates and lower the cost of funds to businesses and consumers who want to borrow in order to spend. But obviously, if the main goal is to increase aggregate spending on goods and services, there is a loose and somewhat uncertain causal chain between more bank reserves and more spending by households and businesses. Banks may not use the new reserves to make new loans and investments immediately. Businesses and individuals may not want to borrow. The exact amount of new loans and investments, and of new spendable money, is hard to predict on the basis of any given amount of new reserves. Similarly, lower interest rates will surely have some effect in encouraging new business spending on investment; but just how much is hard to say, and it clearly varies from time to time and industry to industry. On the restrictive side, the power of the Fed is somewhat sharper and more predictable. If it restricts the volume of reserves at the commercial banks, they have no alternative under the law but to limit correspondingly the loans and investments they make. But even here the banks and their borrowers have a moderate degree of flexibility through technical devices that need not concern us at the moment. Monetary policy is a powerful weapon, especially in restricting aggregate spending if the Fed wants to restrict it, but it is one whose timing and exact effects are unfortunately far from precise and certain.

American monetary economists have produced interesting research results over the last decade which suggest that the relationship between bank reserves and aggregate spending is considerably more stable and predictable than we had thought on the basis of evidence available up to a decade or so ago. It seems clear beyond a reasonable doubt that changes in the supply of money have an important effect on at least the spending of business firms, and possibly directly on the spending of households. The record suggests that over the long run a steadily growing stock of money can help substantially to assure steadily growing total demand. It indicates that unless the total stock of money grows, aggregate demand will sooner or later fall behind the productive capacity of the economy. Conversely, if the stock of money grows much more rapidly than the growth in productive potential, barring a major change in the public's money using and spending habits the result will be excess aggregate demand and inflation. This much is clear. But just how to use monetary policy to keep aggregate demand from fluctuating over shorter periods—to keep total spending growing *precisely* on target—is a harder question and one that is at the heart of the American problem of minimizing short-term inflation and deflationary slack. The American economy depends basically on millions of free individual decisions by individual spenders, both households and businesses, and their spending is subject to many different short-run influences. More of this in a moment.

HOW WELL HAS MONETARY POLICY WORKED?

How much credit does improved monetary policy deserve for our steadily improving record of economic performance? Can we count on monetary policy, working with fiscal policy, to assure reasonably stable economic growth in the basically private-enterprise, capitalist society that is the United States? What have we learned from the lessons of monetary experience?

The financial collapse of 1929–1933 was the great failure of monetary policy. With deepening depression and widespread failures of businesses and banks, the people lost confidence in banks and other financial institutions. By the millions, they withdrew their funds from the bank to hoard them against the uncertain future. Banks, though their loans and investments were basically sound, were forced to close their doors in bankruptcy. In retrospect, the behavior of the Federal Reserve was incredibly short-sighted. Instead of providing massive new reserves to the banks by buying up the bonds and loans of the commercial banks, the Fed permitted the great drain on bank reserves through currency withdrawals to continue, and permitted the massive forced liquidation that resulted as banks were forced to call in loans and sell investments in order to get funds to meet their depositors' withdrawals. The result was a contraction of nearly one-third in the nation's outstanding money supply, mainly bank deposits. This massive monetary contraction played a major role in the general financial and economic collapse of 1929–1933. Without it, economists are agreed that the Depression could not have reached anything like the devastating proportions it actually attained.

After 1933, government policy reopened the banks and monetary policy turned to providing adequate reserves and monetary ease. As the banks obtained new reserves, by the inflow of gold from Europe and by open market operations of the Federal Reserve, bank lending did rise, and with it the supply of money. This increase in bank lending and the money stock was paralleled by a rapid rise in total demand and by the improvement in economic conditions after 1933. But it was not until the shadows of war, and then World War II, led to vastly accelerated government spending and huge increases in the nation's money stock as the banks bought the bonds to finance the U.S. war effort, that full recovery came.

From the Great Depression America learned an important lesson. It is that we cannot rely on our basically private enterprise economy *automatically* to restore full employment when the downswing of depression is under way. Thus American economists and the American public increasingly have come to recognize the need for strong, positive governmental action to keep aggregate demand in the economy moving upward, roughly in step with the growth in the nation's basic capacity to produce. To help assure this needed aggregate demand, fiscal and monetary policy are our main governmental weapons.

The lesson of World War II and its aftermath was that, just as monetary policy could provide too few reserves and too little money in the depression days, so it could provide too many reserves and too much money in war days. In retrospect, it is clear that the United States would have been better off to have financed more of its massive war effort through taxes and less through new-money borrowing from the banks. But war pressures are great, taxes are unpopular, and the recourse to inflation in the United States was less than in any other major country involved in the war.

With the return to normality after World War II and the Korean War, the American economy settled into a path of modest, and moderately fluctuating, growth. While total output in Western Europe was growing perhaps at a rate of 5 to 6 per cent a year, the rate in the U.S. was more like 3 per cent a year on the average. In prosperity, business flourished and jobs were plentiful. But intermittently slack developed in the economy as aggregate demand fell short of total productive capacity. The supply of money, which has grown too rapidly during World War II, leaving a heavy excess of money in the hands of buyers at the end of the war, scarcely expanded at all during the middle and late 1950's, as the monetary authorities seemed more concerned with possible inflation than with the unemployment that developed in the recessions of 1954 and 1958. Neither monetary nor fiscal policy played a strong role in assuring a buoyant American economy during the late 1950's.

But the record of the 1960's has been a happy one. After a slight recession in 1960, the American economy has moved steadily and buoyantly upward for six years, the longest and strongest persistent prosperity in American peacetime history. The major tax cut of 1964 and fiscal policy generally deserve important credit for this good performance. But, for the first time in its history, the Federal Reserve also has provided steadily increasing bank reserves to permit a steady increase in bank lending as output has grown, without permitting interest rates to rise substantially or credit to tighten so long as the prosperity did not bring large price increases in its wake.

Thus, since 1961 the money stock has grown at nearly 4 per cent per annum, roughly the same rate of growth as that in real output. Total spending has risen about 5 to 6 per cent per annum. The result has been a steady reduction in the amount of unemployment, a persistent growth in real output, and a small rise in consumer prices of about 1.5 per cent annually in the first half of the 1960's, as aggregate demand has slightly exceeded the increase in total output. In spite of the growing prosperity, credit has been permitted to tighten only moderately.

Economists have no foolproof way of allocating credit as between monetary and fiscal policy for the fine, indeed unprecedented, performance of the American economy for the first half of this decade. But the "new" monetary policy is at least as different as the "new" fiscal policy. The fact that bank reserves and money have grown steadily and that monetary conditions have not been permitted to choke off the boom surely merits a gold star for the monetary authorities. As the prosperity has continued into its sixth year, it seems increasingly clear to many American economists that with proper fiscal and monetary policy to keep aggregate demand growing moderately but stably, there is no necessary reason why we need to have a boom and bust economy.

THE PROBLEMS

The successes of the 1960's have not been without problems. Three dilemmas have plagued the monetary authorities.

High Employment versus Inflation

There is widespread agreement that governmental policy should encourage the stable economic growth that will provide jobs for those seeking work, and do so without inflation. Until recently, this set of goals gave a clear directive. Since unemployment exceeded 5 per cent of those looking for work, inflation was a limited danger and the need was clearly for a moderate stimulus to private spending so as to provide more jobs. Each year, the American economy must provide from three to four million new jobs, partly to absorb the young men and women coming into the labor market with our big upsurge in population, and partly because rapid technological advance makes it possible to produce the same output each year with perhaps 3 per cent fewer workers than in the preceding years. Therefore aggregate demand needed to grow fast enough to provide jobs for the three to four million additional workers each year—and a little faster gradually to absorb the unemployed. And in fact this was just what happened, reflecting both governmental policy and strength in the private economy. Unemployment dropped gradually from nearly 7 per cent in the recession of 1960–61 to just about 4 per cent by the end of 1965. This was a level that seemed to many observers a very respectable one for a basically free-choice, individual-initiative economy in which changing consumer demand and individual preferences will always result in more freedom of movement and flexibility than would be true of a planned society.

But as unemployment dropped, the danger of inflation grew. When there is substantial unemployment and unused capacity, there is little danger that prices will rise much. And in fact, U.S. prices had been amazingly stable since the mid-1950's. Wholesale prices had been basically flat. Consumer prices had crept up gradually, reflecting mainly the steadily rising prices of services (such as those of doctors, lawyers, transportation, and so on). This record was far better than that of most of the Western European nations with which the American economy is commonly compared. But as unemployment approached 4 per cent in 1965, prices began to move up substantially.

Then the monetary authorities were faced with a dilemma—whether to continue permitting bank reserves to grow at about their recent rates or to impose restraint in order to forestall inflation, even though some unemployment remained. Even if monetary policy, coupled with fiscal policy, is completely successful in assuring a steadily growing level of aggregate demand, a nation may face the dilemma posed by prices beginning to rise appreciably before unemployment is reduced to satisfactory levels. The other free societies of Western Europe and Japan, of course, know this dilemma as well as we do. Happily, in the U.S. the dilemma has not been a serious one thus far. And many American economists believe that if we don't push the economy too hard in reducing unemployment still further, it may not become serious. But the evidence is not yet in, and in late 1965 and early 1966 monetary authorities indicated clearly their intention of moderating the rate of growth in bank reserves and money, permitting interest rates to rise gradually as they have done in the upper stages of most past periods of prosperity.

Domestic versus International Objectives

A second dilemma faced by the monetary authorities has been between domestic and international objectives. Since late 1950, America has ended up each year owing more dollars abroad than other nations owed to us, reflecting primarily our large governmental aid programs to other nations and a massive outflow of American private capital for private investment in nations all over the world. Although we have consistently exported far more than we have imported in goods and services, having thus a "favorable" balance of trade, in total we have had a "deficit" in our balance of payments. Thus other nations have gradually built up claims on the United States which, under the international gold reserve standard, they are free to take in the form of gold if they wish to do so.

This persistent American balance-of-payments deficit, with its possible resultant large gold outflow from the United States, has been a persistent worry to our monetary authorities. The traditional remedy for such a deficit is higher interest rates and a restrictive monetary-fiscal policy in the deficit nation. This is expected to hold down inflation at home and to reduce domestic buying power (hopefully without causing a serious depression), so that our exports would increase while our imports fell because of reduced American buying power. But, like other nations, America has been reluctant to adopt such a restrictive policy when we have substantial unemployment at home, as we had through most of the past decade. Thus our monetary authorities have faced a continuing, and serious, domestic-international dilemma. Domestic conditions have called for modestly easy money to stimulate the economy moderately. But the traditional international prescription called for a restrictive monetary policy to reverse our balance-of-payments deficit.

In this dilemma, the monetary authorities have walked a tightrope, letting the money supply move upward steadily but not too fast; and permitting short-term interest rates to rise a bit in the hope of inducing foreigners to keep their balances here rather than withdrawing them in the form of gold shipments. Given this dilemma, America has turned to direct controls over capital exports and other special measures to ease our balance-of-payments position, rather than using the traditional device of tight money, a device that is unacceptable within a slack economy. Most observers agree that the balance-of-payments constraint has been an important one in keeping money somewhat tighter in the United States over the past decade than would otherwise have been called for by domestic conditions. Without this constraint we would probably have moved more rapidly toward the high-employment economy that has been achieved by the mid-1960's.

The Problems of Forecasting and Lags

In addition to these dilemmas posed by conflicting objectives, American monetary authorities have faced another nagging worry. Economic forecasting in a free society is difficult. We never know for sure what economic conditions the future holds, because millions of free households and individual businessmen each make spending decisions. Unless we can forecast reasonably well what private spending will be during the next six to twelve months, it is difficult to know whether monetary policy should be easier or tighter, whether fiscal policy should seek to expand or contract aggregate demand. For monetary policy this is especially serious, since the evidence suggests that there is a substantial lag between monetary action on bank reserves and its final effect on aggregate spending, real output, and employment in the economy. This lag, unfortunately, is only roughly measurable; most research suggests that it may run anywhere from three to nine months, with the effects of monetary action spread out from its immediate impact over perhaps a year or more. Thus, monetary policy must always recognize this uncertain lag, here as in other free societies. The improved performance of the money stock, interest rates, and the economy generally during the present decade is a tribute to the wisdom of our monetary authorities in dealing effectively with the uncertain future.

WHAT OF THE FUTURE?

Even if it recognizes these problems faced by monetary policy, can American capitalism now count on this policy to play a major role in assuring stable economic growth without depressions or inflations? Is the success story of the 1960's evidence for confidence in the future?

The answer is that the outlook is more encouraging than ever before, especially if we view monetary policy and fiscal policy as handmaidens. Neither alone can be counted on to do the job, and without proper coordination they might indeed offset each other.

In conclusion, let me make a few observations on why America and the world can reasonably look to American monetary policy to help stabilize a growing economy.

1. We have learned the big lesson of the Great Depression. American monetary authorities are firm and outspoken in recognizing that their first job is to ensure that the economy does not undergo another massive contraction of money and credit like that of 1929–1933. The monetary authorities have adequate power to live up to this commitment, and there is every reason to believe that they will do so. Thus, a major—indeed probably necessary—factor for a massive depression has been eliminated.

2. From the Great Depression we also learned that we cannot sit back and rely on our free-enterprise system automatically to restore high employment once recession strikes. Thus, both fiscal and monetary policy are widely accepted as valid and essential steps to help avoid undesirably wide fluctuations in aggregate demand. This was not true in the 1930's, and indeed was still debated in the 1940's and 1950's.

3. We now have a much clearer understanding of the role of money and monetary conditions than ever before. Some of the conclusions from experience and research were cited above. Thus, we now have the understanding necessary to use monetary policy more flexibly and effectively than in preceding decades.

4. In conclusion, while there is little reason to suppose that

sound monetary policy can eliminate every fluctuation in the economy, almost everyone agrees that big swings in monetary conditions (especially in the rate of growth of the money stock and interest rates) are generally unhealthy. Put positively, there is wide agreement that the money stock ought to grow in a rather stable fashion, roughly paralleling the growth in real productive capacity in the economy so as to avoid both excessive and insufficient demand. Even with this agreement, it would be foolish indeed to assume that monetary policy is the cure-all for the inflationary booms and depressions which have beset American capitalism in the past. But it would be equally shortsighted not to recognize the major strides that have been taken in the use of this powerful stabilizing tool.

14 PERSPECTIVE ON ECONOMIC GROWTH

Edmund S. Phelps

A combination of forces—some internal and some external—led economists to pay new attention to the issue of the economy's over-all growth in the last decade. Government's role in stabilizing the economy had been much on men's minds since the 1930's, but the now-parallel concern with growth in the total product had to wait another twenty years. This article examines the American growth record, some explanations for that record, and some growth issues which now confront us in public and private arenas.

The rapid growth of the American economy over more than a hundred years presents many puzzles for the economist and the economic historian. The prospects for American economic growth in the future and the manner in which the federal government ought to influence future growth are equally open to question.

By the "growth rate" is usually meant the proportionate rate of increase per year of *national product* or *national income.* This concept of national product is an aggregate measure of the market value of the consumption goods (including services) produced and sold to households, of plant and equipment produced and sold to business firms and of goods produced and supplied to the community by federal, state, and local governments. (Another way to arrive at national product is to add the wages and salaries earned by households to the profits received by businesses.) To be more precise, the economist means by the growth rate the rate of increase of *real* national product—i.e., the money value of national income adjusted for inflation. Unfortunately it is hard to make this adjustment accurately because of quality improvements in goods which justify price increases; this is increasingly a problem as the American economy becomes more and more a service-producing rather than a commodity-producing economy. Finally, the purist in these matters, the academic economist, means by the growth rate the rate of increase of *potential* or *capacity* real national product. This concept can only be estimated, not measured. It is a measure of the real national product that would have been produced in a given year had the economy been employing its resources fully in that year. The "growth economist" is not directly concerned with those cyclical fluctuations in real national product which are caused by variations in the degree to which the labor supply and existing capital goods are utilized.

In addition, the economist is interested in the rate of increase of "productivity," as measured by national product per person employed or per manhour worked.

THE GROWTH STORY

Now a brief look at the record. In 1840 the United States was already at a high economic level, ranking fourth among nations in income per head, below England, France, and Germany. But at about this time there began rapid and fairly continuous growth. By 1870 the United States had surpassed Germany and France.

Between 1871 and 1913 American real national product grew at the very high rate of 4.5 per cent per year. This was by far the highest growth rate of that period. Much of this growth was due to immigration, of course, but even real national product per person employed grew very fast—at the rate of 2.2 per cent per year. This was higher than the rate for all the major industrial countries of the world except Sweden and Japan, which were growing from a much lower initial level. By 1913, and even before, the United States had the highest income per head in the world.

In the years between 1913 and 1959 real national product grew at only 3 per cent per year and the growth rate of national product per employed person was only 1.8 per cent per year. But, with the exception of Japan, this was still a bit above the rate for the other major industrial countries. Thus the United States slightly strengthened its industrial lead over most countries in the twentieth century even though its growth was slower than it had been earlier.

A reason for this slowdown in American growth between 1913 and 1959 is not hard to find: the Great Depression of the 1930's led to a drastic reduction of investment-goods expenditures; as a consequence, the capital stock grew very slowly. In addition, industrial research and development activities of U.S. firms were reduced. During World War II, when the American economy operated at full capacity, investment-goods production that could be used for postwar civilian purposes was still below the normal peacetime level. Therefore the relatively slow pace of American growth rate can also be explained by the war and the preceding

The American economy made up for some of this lost growth in the postwar period. Between 1947 and 1957 potential real national product grew at the rate of 3.9 per cent, well above the twentieth-century average. The rate of increase of output per employed person was very high as well: about 2.5 per cent. This transition from an extraordinarily low to an extraordinarily high growth rate can also be explained by the war and the preceding depression: those events had reduced the capital-output ratio, which made it easy to have rapid proportionate growth of the capital stock in the postwar period. In addition, the capital stock had grown old and obsolete by the end of World War II, so that the postwar investments had a great effect in modernizing the economy's capital stock.

Before turning attention to future growth prospects, let us ask what can be said to explain America's rapid growth over this long period from 1840. There is considerable agreement by economists that an important part of the explanation was America's quickness to develop new techniques of production and new products from theoretical scientific advances then occurring and to put these new techniques and products into industrial practice. This quickness must have been due, in part, to scientific expertise, especially in industrial management, to a well-educated population, to an adequate amount of competition and incentive, as well as to a host of other noneconomic influences. Though the details of this mechanism are not yet known, and may never be, it is especially agreed that America's tendency over most of these years to invest about 15 per cent of national product in tangible capital goods—plant and equipment—has not been the prime mover in its economic growth. For without continued technological progress, the persistent investment of a constant fraction of national product would lead eventually to a constant level of national product per head. It is true that some small portion of the difference between national income per head in America and national income per head in the other major industrial countries is due to a higher capital stock per head in the U.S. But this difference in capital per head is largely due to America's higher income per head and hence to its past technological progressiveness, not to its greater propensity to invest in capital hardware.

WHAT OF THE FUTURE?

I come now to America's prospects for growth in the future. Undoubtedly, American economic growth over the far future will depend in large measure upon the underlying advances in science that are going to take place. It is probably safer to predict America's growth rate over, say, the next fifteen years, to 1981. But even that prediction is fraught with difficulties.

In making such predictions, economists usually assume that there will be no war nor any prolonged "depression" during this period. Frequently, they further assume that America will continue to invest about 15 per cent of its national product each year in new tangible capital goods. Making these assumptions, it might be argued (and has been argued) that the rate of increase of productivity—of real national product per employee—will be about 2.2 per cent per year. This was the rate experienced in the pre-World War I period and approximately the rate experienced in the period 1900–1929 before the Depression, World War II, and the postwar recovery. In addition, the labor force is expected to grow at about 1.8 per cent per year until 1975, perhaps until 1980. Adding together these two rates, we obtain a growth rate of real national product of approximately 4 per cent per year.

There is a more optimistic school which argues that our growth rate will be nearer to 4.5 per cent per year, thanks to a faster rise in productivity. This school puts much more weight on the unusually rapid increase in productivity during the postwar period. Pointing to the ever enlarging expenditures on technological research and development by both private business and the federal government, it stresses the steady advance of technology.

Whichever school is right—the pessimists or the optimists—we can expect the gap between per capita income in America and that in several of the other industrial countries to be somewhat narrowed over the next fifteen years. Certainly Japan and probably the Soviet Union, West Germany, France, and Italy, to mention a few, will catch up with America to some degree. These countries have enjoyed more rapid growth of potential national product than has America since the war, including the past few years, but as they approach American technological practice they may find it increasingly difficult to close the remaining gap.

GOVERNMENT AND THE RATE OF GROWTH

The possibility that America may lose its relative economic position has led some American economists to urge governmental action to increase America's rate of growth. This has raised many questions. What is the most efficient way to increase growth: By increased investment in tangible capital goods? By increased research? Or by increased education? And how expensive would it be in terms of consumption goods—in terms of present enjoyment—to increase America's rate of growth by one percentage point over the next fifteen years? Is faster economic growth worth the necessary sacrifices?

Actually the question of how much growth concerns even the majority of economists who are not worried about America's relative position. Since economics is largely the study of the allocation of scarce resources to satisfy competing ends, it is natural that economists would be concerned about the division of resources between those uses that satisfy current wants and those uses that contribute to growth and hence to satisfying future wants. Yet this concern about the "right" rate of growth is only some ten years old in the United States.

The late eighteenth- and nineteenth-century English political economists, who are intellectual ancestors of American economists, realized that the central government could reduce economic growth by running a "budgetary deficit"—by taxing less than enough to cover expenditures; this would stimulate consumption and choke off investment. But these classical economists considered budgetary deficits (and surpluses) to be immoral and hence put an end to any discussion of the best rate of investment or the best rate of growth.

John Maynard Keynes, the great English economist of this century, produced a revolution against classical thinking. His argument was that a budgetary deficit or surplus will usually be needed to maintain full employment. Keynes appeared to believe that, usually, there would be just one budgetary deficit consistent with full employment, not a whole range of deficits each one having different consequences for growth.

American economists have interpreted Keynes's view of the economic system somewhat differently. Many of them believe that full employment can be achieved by a budgetary deficit (low taxes) and "tight money" (high interest rates) *or* by a budgetary surplus (high taxes) and "easy money" (low interest rates). If the government chooses high taxes and low interest rates, consumption expenditures by the heavily taxed households will be small while the low interest rates will stimulate large investment expenditures and hence produce a high rate of growth. Tangible investment expenditures as well as expenditures for research and for education may be stimulated.

In addition to these general controls, the federal government is recognized to have specific controls over research, tangible capital expenditures, and education. It carries out and subsidizes a great deal of "basic" scientific research and allows private business firms to treat research-and-development outlays as a current expense to be deducted from taxable profits; recently it instituted a "tax credit" on business expenditures for capital equipment. The federal government has also been giving increasing stimulus to education, which was once almost exclusively the province of the state governments and of private colleges and universities.

Thus it is now widely felt by American economists that the government can bring about the desired level of employment and at the same time control the division of resources between comsumption and growth-producing investments and even to control the broad division of resources among tangible investment, technological research, and education. In view of these government controls, American economists are now very much interested in two questions: "How fast should America seek to grow?"—i.e., how much present consumption goods should we sacrifice in return for growth and future consumption? And, second, "What is the least expensive, most efficient way to grow at a specified rate?" That is, what is the best "mixture" of research, education, and tangible capital formation?

HOW MUCH GROWTH IS BEST?

There is no agreement on the part of American economists on the first question, "How much growth?" One minority school of thought argues that the question itself is a bad one. These people, who include some economists, argue that it is not a proper function of the government to decide—or for the American electorate to decide through the polls—how fast the economy ought to grow. They contend that the government should pursue a "neutral" policy toward growth, leaving it to the private marketplace to determine the amount of investment and consumption, hence to determine the rate of growth. Unfortunately, there are so many imperfections in the private marketplace that a neutral policy would not be ideal; indeed, even if markets were perfect, there probably would exist government policies that would make the presently living population better off than would a neutral policy.

The discussion of "How much growth?" raises the fundamental question of what should we *mean* by "optimal" growth or the "right" rate of growth? How should the "growth optimum" be defined? Many mathematical economists in America and abroad have explored the concept of a growth optimum which involves assigning certain weights to the consumption or to the enjoyment of the consumers living at the present time and assumed to be living at each year in the future. But it is not indicated how these weights are to be chosen—whether dictatorially or through some improbable ethical consensus. Further, it may be unrealistic to expect future generations to behave as is assumed in this approach: future generations may pursue their own self-interests. Nevertheless these mathematical exercises may sometime prove to have been useful in the development of a concept of a growth optimum.

While the academic economists reflect, the government continues to make decisions about the use of its controls, conscious or unconscious of the consequences of these decisions for America's future growth. What consequences have these decisions had for growth? The Kennedy administration and the Johnson administration saw their principal economic problem as the task of reducing the large volume of unemployment that plagued the American economy in the first half of this decade. To reduce unemployment, the government could have stimulated mainly investment expenditures by means of low interest rates and tax measures, or the government could have stimulated mainly consumption expenditures by the reduction of personal income tax rates. In fact, the government chose a combination of measures which may have stimulated consumption a little more, percentagewise, than investment. But, of course, the resulting increase in capacity utilization and business profits induced a substantial rise in investment expenditures.

What measures did the government take to reduce unemployment? There was a substantial reduction of personal income tax rates, which increased consumption expenditures. To stimulate investment, the government took a number of steps: it introduced the new fiscal device of a tax credit (or tax reduction) given to certain businesses making investment expenditures; it liberalized the depreciation schedules which businesses could use in figuring their profits for tax purposes; and it reduced tax rates on corporate profits. The total reduction of business income taxation, taking these measures together, was about equal proportionately to the reduction of taxation on the personal income of households. But probably consumption responded more strongly to these tax reductions than investment did.

The American government did not reduce interest rate and ease credit to stimulate investment. America's balance-of-payments troubles played a role here. Although the Johnson administration might have liked to have lower interest rates, the Federal Reserve System—the nation's central bank, which can operate independently of the Executive Branch of the government—chose high interest rates to prevent an outflow of short-term capital abroad. There is some question, however, whether this policy of high interest rates has been very effective. When the Federal Reserve System raised interest rates during America's emergence from the situation of low employment and depressed business conditions, foreign central banks were free to raise their interest rates in response, so as to nullify the effect of America's action. The end result may largely have been an all-round rise of interest rates in America, Europe, and other financial centers, with the main consequence being a reduction of growth in many countries and little alteration of the international payments imbalances.

The second question of interest is how to grow efficiently, at minimum cost. Given the total amount that is being spent on investments of all kinds, should we have more research and less plant and equipment expenditure? More education and less research? What is the right combination? To this question, at least, economists have some theoretical and conceptual answers. In a laissez-faire economy there is a presumption that there will be too little research relative to investment in tangible capital goods because research is risky and because it rewards society more than it rewards the individual business firm that undertakes it. But the American economy is not laissez-faire; the government already gives much support to research and to education—more support than to plant and equipment expenditures. Whether the federal government should tip the scales even more in favor of research or education is an open question. Economists are trying to answer this question by statistical analysis of "rates of return," but it is a formidable task.

It is clear, then, that America is a long way from finding answers to these perplexing questions of economic growth. But there is new and increasing interest in these questions and it may be that we will have tolerably good answers to them before this century has passed.

15 COULD THE U.S. AFFORD DISARMAMENT?

Murray L. Weidenbaum

While some Americans ask if we can afford our current level of defense expenditures, some critics of this nation ask if we could have prosperity without that spending. A number of economists in recent years have made intensive efforts to see what disarmament would in fact do to the domestic economy. Here is a summary of a widely held view and a menu of choices that we face when and if men move to more peaceful paths to reconcile their differences.

Many studies in the past few years have been devoted to the possible repercussions on the American economy of arms control, arms reduction, and disarmament. Intermittent developments have periodically renewed public and professional interest in the subject. These have included the nuclear test ban treaty, the establishment of a direct communications link (the so-called "hot line") between Washington and Moscow, the adoption of the United Nations resolution against weapons in space, and the Antarctica Treaty, setting that continent aside as a military-free science preserve. The trend of international relations has not, of course, moved steadily toward the lessening of tensions. The required expansion of the U.S. commitment in Vietnam is a current and strong reminder of the underlying external pressures for raising rather than lowering the level of American military preparedness.

Most of the studies of the economic implications of disarmament attempt to answer facets of one basic question: How can the American economy successfully adjust to a major reduction in defense spending? This presentation attempts to deal both with the aggregate problem and with its important components.

THE NATIONAL ASPECT

Studies of the impact of moderate or time-phased reductions in defense spending—such as have been contained in the disarmament proposals of the United States government to the U.N.—have almost universally concluded that the United States is fully capable of making the necessary economic adjustments to fundamental reductions in the level of national security expenditures. That is, after an initial period of adjustment, a rapid rate of growth of employment, income, and output can be maintained through sufficient aggregate demand for the potential production of goods and services by the American economy.

The limitations are considered to be mainly in the political sphere—the willingness of the nation to take measures of sufficient magnitude and promptness to utilize the resources that would be released in such eventuality.

The possible resulting annual reductions in defense spending—which generally have been estimated in the neighborhood of $5 to $6 billion a year—would be roughly equivalent to a mild inventory recession or a poor automobile year, economic situations which this nation has repeatedly and successfully faced in the period since World War II.

The major problem of economic planning would be to choose an initial policy which is sufficiently prompt to prevent serious unemployment and excess industrial capacity from developing; such negative influences, if unchecked, could accelerate into a major recession or possibly depression. There is a wide range of fiscal and monetary policies which have the necessary stimulating impact on aggregate demand but different effects on the composition of output and on the allocation of income among the different groups in American society.

The balance struck between tax reduction and increased government spending would be influenced by the relative importance accorded to the private versus the public sector—to private demand for such goods and services as food, clothing, housing, recreation, health, and education—as against public demand for roads, space exploration, urban renewal, area development, public health, and social services.

Perhaps insufficient attention has been given to the fundamental economic climate which would encourage private business to take the initiative in making the necessary and difficult changes in product lines and markets served so as to convert from military to commercial production.

Most of the discussion thus far has centered on the possibilities for expanding government programs to take up the economic slack resulting from disarmament. Little has been done in the planning work to date concerning alternative types of tax reform and other possible improvements in the general operating environment in the private sector of the economy.

Numerous estimates have been made of the funds that could usefully be channeled into social welfare, foreign aid, natural resource development, and many other public sector programs. To achieve a balance between government spending and tax reduction, research may need to be devoted to such other questions as the proper role of downward adjustments in both corporate and individual income tax rates in a general program of tax reform; the types of liberalized depreciation systems that would provide the most effective incentive to increase business investment, and, hence, economic growth; and the necessary encouragement to new business investments, including changes in capital gains and dividend taxation.

The various economic regulatory agencies of the federal government represent another neglected facet of the problem. There are enough examples in their past performance—particularly with reference to the renegotiation of defense contracts—to cause considerable concern that, if ignored, the operations of these specialized agencies might offset many of the positive actions being taken to effectuate a successful economic adjustment to disarmament.

Historical experience testifies to the ability of the American economy to adjust rapidly to major reductions in defense expenditures. However, a look back to the period during World War II shows that many observers then doubted the ability of the American economy to demobilize without experiencing very serious problems of transition. At the time, defense outlays accounted for 40 per cent of total production (measured in terms of Gross National Product).

Yet, this nation demobilized extremely rapidly and suffered no sizable unemployment. Between 1945 and 1946 military spending was reduced by 80 per cent, a far more rapid rate than envisioned in current step-by-step disarmament proposals being offered by the United States government in the United Nations. This reduction was equivalent to about 30 per cent of the Gross National Product of the United States in 1945, and three times the present ratio of defense to GNP. Between June 1945 and June 1946, over nine million men were released from the armed forces, more than three times the present total of U.S. military personnel.

Despite the size and pace of the post-World War II demobilization, unemployment in the immediate postwar year remained below 4 per cent of the labor force. While defense spending fell, business investment more than doubled and consumer outlays and nondefense government programs rose to fill much of the gap. The vast reservoirs of unfilled needs and purchasing power which had been accumulated by both business and consumers during World War II exercised a very positive influence on the ensuing economic developments.

The process of postwar economic adjustment was helped significantly by effective governmental policy. Taxes were reduced substantially. There was a great increase in veterans' cash benefits and in payments for the veterans' training and education programs. Also, a large loan program was established to encourage veterans to purchase businesses, homes, and farms; quick settlements were made so that they could devote their efforts to civilian work with a minimum of delay. The net result was that, despite the massive decline in defense spending, the over-all income of individuals in the United States hardly fell at all.

The experience of the American economy following the end of he Korean conflict involved a much smaller reduction in defense pending, which itself started from a much lower peak than after World War II. Reductions in tax schedules prevented the decline in defense spending from dragging down consumer income and personal consumption spending. The net result was that after the Korean War the decline in GNP was smaller than the decline in defense spending. By 1955, the over-all level of economic activity had completely recovered in the face of further cutbacks in defense spending and had advanced to record heights. Unemployment, after rising to 5.6 per cent of the labor force in 1954, declined to 4.4 per cent in 1955.

More recently, the leveling off in the total of defense spending in 1964–1965 was accompanied by an actual decline in the national unemployment rate, indicating the continuing capability of the American economy to adjust rapidly at least to moderate declines in national security expenditures.

THE INDUSTRIAL BASE FOR DEFENSE WORK

Under the American system of free enterprise, the task of converting industrial production from defense to civilian uses would in the main rest on the individual business firms which presently manufacture the great bulk of the equipment required by the armed forces. The essential problem from the viewpoint of disarmament impact is the strong tendency for defense work to be concentrated in a few industries and in precisely those that have shown the most rapid pattern of growth and technological innovation in the period since World War II.

Only a relatively few hard-goods-producing industries account for the bulk of defense contracts: aircraft, electronics, motor vehicles, petroleum refining, chemicals, rubber, and construction. Conversely, the extent of industrial dependence on defense work varies widely. It is estimated that 98 per cent of ordnance production is consumed by defense, 90 per cent of aerospace, 60 per cent of shipbuilding, and 50 per cent of electronics. In contrast, the proportion is less than 5 per cent for many important industries including food, apparel, leather, lumber and wood, wholesale and retail trade, services, finance, and construction.

It is likely that the economic adjustment problems arising from disarmament would center in the handful of defense-dependen industries. The other industries would stand to benefit from increases in business and consumer after-tax income and the resultant expenditures and investments. The problem would be accentuated by the restricted operating experience of the defense firms and their limited familiarity with commercial markets. In contrast with the situation during World War II, and even with that during the Korean conflict, a far greater share—the majority—of defense work currently is performed in highly specialized facilities which have been specifically built for the purpose, often at the initiative of the military establishment. The Department of Defense still actually owns many of these factories and the highly technical equipment in them.

Moreover, many of the companies involved, especially in the aerospace and electronics industries, were set up for, and much of their experience is limited to, the design and production of military weapon systems and related aerospace vehicles. Their attempts to use their technology and other defense-derived skills to penetrate commercial markets have frequently been unsuccessful. The abandoned attempts at defense industry diversification literally range from canoes to computers to coffins.

A variety of reasons has been offered for the inability of these large, specialized defense companies to utilize their resources in profitable commercial endeavors. These include their lack of marketing capability and their inability to produce large numbers of items at low unit prices. Of course, these weaknesses are not necessarily handicaps in defense work. Their lack of commercial marketing capability results from their preoccupation with meeting the rigorous technical requirements of the military customer. Their inability to produce large volumes at low cost also reflects their unique capability to design small numbers of large-scale systems of great technical complexity.

Major reductions in defense orders resulting from disarmament might necessitate public decisions as to the proper actions to be taken to put to use the research and development, systems management, and related skills of defense contractors and their employees that would become available.

One possible type of government program would be various attempts to aid defense contractors in diversifying into commercial markets. Another method of taking up the slack could consist of efforts to transfer the resources of defense firms to companies and organizations in other parts of the economy. It is likely that this kind of decision would not involve an either-or choice but some combination of the two approaches.

There are numerous ways which could be chosen to help defense contractors diversify. One possibility would be for the federal government to award them large amounts of nondefense research and development contracts. Another way would be to establish new requirements for nondefense products which these companies could manufacture and sell to the government, such as civilian space systems, transportation equipment, and electronic teaching facilities. The extent to which any of these steps would be taken might be influenced by how much the companies themselves had invested their own efforts and funds in some of these programs to show that there would be the possibility of significant payoffs from large-scale government financing.

Another approach to encouraging defense industry diversification could be taken in conjunction with existing military contracts; the Department of Defense could consider as an allowable cost of such contracts the creation of a general commercial marketing capability on the part of the specialized defense contractors.

Alternatively, the nation could give attention to the desirability and possibility of encouraging the movement of defense industry personnel and other resources to the so-called "under-researched" industries in the private economy. Some ways of so converting the defense economy might resemble existing programs of government assistance to private industry. One possible method would be a tax rebate for industrial research and development similar to the tax credits currently given to encourage business to invest in new equipment. Another alternative would be loans and loan guarantees to help finance new technology-based business ventures. Such aids would be similar to the financing programs of the federal government's Small Business Administration and the Export-Import Bank. Alternatively, a cost-sharing plan could be established; this would be analogous to the mining exploration program of the Department of the Interior whereby the government pays part of the cost of high-risk new undertakings but is reimbursed out of any proceeds of the results—in this case if the research and development would lead to profitable production. Still another alternative might be programs of technical assistance to show nondefense companies how they could profitably apply defense-originated scientific and technological advances to their industries and markets.

THE GEOGRAPHIC DISTRIBUTION OF DEFENSE WORK

The tendency for the major defense contractors to cluster in a relatively few regions of the country would pose an important geographic adjustment problem in the event of large reductions in military outlays.

Certain states and communities, because of their relatively high degree of dependence on defense work and on the payrolls of military installations, would be especially hard hit. Six states depend on defense work for at least 10 per cent of personal income—Virginia, Utah, Washington, California, Alaska, and Hawaii. (Conversely, for the other forty-four states the relationship is far less important.) Within some metropolitan areas—Washington, Boston, Wichita, Huntsville, Cape Kennedy, Los Angeles, San Diego, and Seattle are examples—the reliance on defense contracts and military bases for employment and income is much greater than in any of the six states. For some of these cities, virtually the total economic growth in the period since World War II can be traced, either directly or indirectly, to defense spending in their areas.

Available studies indicate that the location of expanding employment opportunities in the nondefense sectors of the economy might well be at locations different from those affected by defense cutbacks. Clearly an expanded reclamation program in the Great Plains region would have little need for the defense industry personnel and other resources presently located on the Pacific Coast. Increased consumer requirements for food, clothing and automobiles—to cite another possibility—would be met primarily by existing production complexes in the northeastern part of the nation.

The advent of a general disarmament program likely would generate strong local pressures for governmental assistance to the communities now most heavily dependent on defense work. The 1964–1965 defense cutbacks resulted in such programs on a small scale; these included establishment by the Atomic Energy Commission of an Office of Economic Impact and Conversion and the expansion of the Department of Defense's Office of Economic Adjustment. The latter agency sends out representatives to communities adversely affected by defense reductions to assist the local people in launching or expanding industrial development and in other promotional efforts designed to reorient the area to civilian work.

Any substantial concentration of unemployed former defense workers in these affected areas might accentuate the need to choose promptly among alternative public policies which would create employment and income for those directly affected by disarmament as well as contribute to an efficient, growing economy. So-called "income maintenance programs"—unemployment compensation, public assistance, and other welfare payments of various kinds—might be the most rapid way of meeting the short-term needs for jobs or income. However, sole emphasis on this approach might limit the nation's ability to utilize productively the resources released by disarmament and thus make a successful long-term transition to a lower level of defense spending.

Other suggested measures to aid the people hurt by defense reductions include relocation payments to unemployed defense workers and their families, and government purchase of their homes to enhance their ability to move to locations where jobs may be expanding.

In choosing from among alternative public policies to adjust to the economic impacts of disarmament, it may be helpful to keep in mind some over-all or fundamental criteria by which to judge specific policy suggestions. One criterion could be consistency with standards of fairness and equity among various sectors of the economy and regions of the country—that is, do the suggested policies avoid singling out particular groups for special benefits not available to others in similar circumstances? This of course raises the question whether unemployed defense workers should receive more generous treatment than other unemployed persons.

A second standard might be consistency with efficient allocation of the nation's resources. Do the proposals avoid creating long-run inefficiencies in the economy when dealing with short-term problems? Any policy of maintaining obsolete defense facilities in order to avoid temporary unemployment might be affected by this criterion.

A third principle might be consistency with emphasis on local and private initiative. Is the suggestion likely to encourage and assist, rather than replace, the efforts of those state and local governments and private organizations which attempt to offset the adverse economic consequences of defense reductions? This, of course, opens up the whole question of private sector versus public sector orientation in a disarmament adjustment program.

A final screening criterion could be consistency with the national security. Would the proposed action maintain the capability of the nation to respond effectively to future changes in the requirements of national security programs, whether toward further disarmament or toward rearmament? This latter consideration might be particularly pertinent during the early stages of a disarmament agreement when both sides have only begun dismantling their military establishments and an atmosphere of mutual trust has not fully developed.

A SUMMARY VIEW

Perhaps the fundamental policy decision that would be required in the field of economics in the event of disarmament would be the choice of emphasis between (a) aggregate adjustment of the economy as a whole, in terms of maintaining total employment or the GNP growth rate, versus (b) the desirability of focusing on pockets of geographic or industrial hardship resulting from closing or phasing down specific military bases and defense plants.

Certainly, the bulk of the population, area, and industry of the United States is only marginally influenced by defense spending and would be affected by disarmament in a very limited way.

Only a relatively few companies in a few regions tend to be either greatly benefited or adversely affected by expansions, contractions, or shifts in defense programs. For those companies and regions, of course—and for their employees and their families—the impacts, certainly the initial effects, are likely to be substantial. However, a national perspective may be necessary, although difficult to maintain, in determining appropriate public policies.

A final thought is that from time to time the question is raised as to how much national security spending the American economy can afford. It turns out that there is no simple or generally agreed on method for measuring or determining the "burden" of defense programs on the economy, much less what, if any, economic ceiling exists on such government spending.

Using a comparison of defense spending to the Gross National Product, it appears that the portion of the nation's resources devoted to armaments has tended to diminish rather than increase in recent years; the ratio to GNP fell from 10.5 per cent in 1957 to 8.5 per cent in 1964. During this recent period considerable unutilized or underutilized manpower and industrial capacity existed in the American economy, far more than was generally desired. Price inflation was not particularly troublesome; the wholesale price index fluctuated within the narrow range of 99.0 to 100.7 from 1957 to 1964 (base of 1957–1959 = 100). Hence, it would appear that there was little curtailment of civilian demand in order to meet the requirements of the defense program or that the nation was straining its resources.

Overall, available analyses of the "burden" of defense spending have generally concluded that, if necessary for military or political reasons, the American economy could handle, with a minimum of dislocation or hardship, a far higher level of such spending than has been the case in recent years. The recent experience of the Vietnam buildup appears to bear this out.

Similarly, most of these economic analyses conclude that the long-term growth and prosperity of the United States do not require even the current level of defense spending. It is generally believed that, after a period of adjustment, the level of economic activity would be higher in the absence of military outlays because of the greater productivity of investments in industrial facilities. Hence, economic constraints do not appear to be an important real limitation on the level of defense spending, on either the up or the down side. Recent American history tends to confirm this essentially optimistic conclusion rather strongly.

16 AUTOMATION IN PERSPECTIVE

Lloyd Ulman

The catchword "automation" draws to itself a catchall of extreme conclusions on what technology is doing to jobs and production. The present essay avoids the easy generalizations and the scary headlines; it takes a hard look at the evidence now on hand to test what automation's impact has been. Such a sober approach was rare until recently, but now a similar analysis has appeared from a Presidential commission.

A British manufacturer at the close of the nineteenth century complained that England, "the land of strikes and holidays," was being overtaken in international competition "by Germany, where the laboring man works like a machine, and by America, where machines work like men." The contemporary descriptive validity of this tart judgment is not at issue here, but it is relevant to note that a half-century later, in all three countries, the intensity of industrial strife has abated, holidays have increased, men have, on the whole, been working less like machines, and machines have been working more and more like men. The latter tendency, in fact, has become sufficiently prominent to warrant special designation.

Automation is the name given to the new technology, and it is frequently distinguished from the older type of technological change which dates back to the Industrial Revolution, on the grounds that the new change involves the mechanization of work formerly done by the human brain. This, however, is an oversimplification, since old-fashioned mechanization, in substituting achine guidance of tools for manual guidance, has frequently placed human cunning as well as muscle; it has often dispensed ith skilled craftsmen as well as unskilled labor in favor of ma-inery tended by semiskilled operatives. On the other hand, me-anical sensing and control—the ability of machines to check rformance against pre-set standards and to correct its own mis-kes—is a unique attribute of automation.

A question arises, however, as to whether or not this technolog-al distinction implies economic difference. The question origi-ated in political debate and not as a matter of academic specula-on. At issue was the nature of unemployment in the postwar nited States and the type of policy best designed to reduce un-nployment to levels more consistent with the objectives of naximum employment, production, and purchasing power" set rth in the Employment Act of 1946. By the end of the 1950's, it as not only apparent that unemployment had moved to a much gher plateau in the second half of the postwar period than it cupied in the years immediately following World War II and compassing the Korean War; it seemed, in addition, that it had een trending upward during the last two-thirds of the decade. uring the peak month of the cyclical upswing of 1949–1953, the nemployment rate stood at 2.7 per cent; at the peak of the llowing upswing from 1954 to 1957, it was 4.2 per cent; and at e cyclical peak in 1960, it was 5.1 per cent. In the post-Korean eriod 1953–1960, the average rate of unemployment was 4.9 per nt (as opposed to 4 per cent in 1947–1953); between 1957 and 960, moreover, unemployment averaged 5.6 per cent. Since price vels—which had moved sharply upward in 1946–1948, 1950, nd 1955–1957—stabilized after 1957, fear of "creeping inflation" bated, but only to give way to fear of "creeping unemployment."

President Kennedy's Council of Economic Advisers regarded ese high and rising levels of unemployment as symptomatic of eneral deficiency in effective demand for goods and services. his deficiency resulted in the failure of the economy to live up its potential and to utilize fully or at optimum levels the man-ower and capital resources at its disposal. This view of unem-loyment, which is shared by most academic economists, was con-stent with other aspects of the economy's behavior, including the fact that each of the last two cyclical upswings referred t above was shorter and weaker (in terms of the growth of indu trial production) than its predecessor, and the average annu rate of increase in Gross National Product (measured in 195 prices) declined from 4.6 per cent in 1947–1953 to 2.6 per cent i 1953–1960. The immediate cause of this decline was a slowdow in the rate of increase in spending by business firms on plant an equipment, especially after the investment boom of 1955–195 This in turn was attributed to the economic policies pursued b the fiscal and monetary authorities. As a result of these policie which were either actively restrictive or unresponsive to emergin deflationary pressures, demand failed to grow sufficiently aft mid-1957 to utilize fully the extra capacity created during th boom; during the next upswing (1958–1960) private investmer demand remained stunted by excess capacity and thus did nc constitute a sufficient offset to the increased total of private an public saving which was allowed to develop.

Thus, when the Kennedy administration took office at th onset of a fresh cyclical recovery, a new Council of Economic Ac visers vigorously opposed suggestions, first, that credit be tigh ened, and next, that taxes be raised to offset the increased defens expenditures associated with the Berlin crisis in the summer c 1961. Moreover, the Council was an early advocate of liberalize depreciation allowances and of a tax credit to stimulate privat investment spending and to raise the share of investment in tot spending once full employment was achieved. And later, after th upswing began to falter in early 1962, the Council inspired a su cessful campaign under Presidents Kennedy and Johnson to ir crease private spending and reduce the volume of public wit drawals from the income stream (the so-called "fiscal drag") b cutting taxes—corporate and personal income taxes in 1964 an excise taxes in 1965—in the face of actual and contemplated def cits in the federal budget.

Criticism of this generally Keynesian approach to the probler of unemployment flared up at various points of the political cor pass. One line of criticism, which proceeded from a traditiona aversion to unbalanced budgets, emanated most strongly fror the financial community (and was reflected, for a while, from th

Treasury Department). But it also aroused a conservative response among other groups of citizens in whose bosoms there lurked what, in a moment of unfortunate felicity, the Chairman of the Council of Economic Advisers referred to as "the Puritan ethic." A quite different line of criticism proceeded from the belief that automation and related technological phenomena had transformed significant sectors of the American economy so as to create a new strain of unemployment that was impervious to public policies designed to increase aggregate money demand. This and related viewpoints were not confined to ethical Puritans but found—and still find—exponents in a wide variety of political and economic groups: Republicans and Democrats; radicals and conservatives; trade unionists, business managers, and engineers.

THE FEARS ON AUTOMATION

One argument holds that changes in technology and shifts in product demand have combined with changes in the age, sex, and color composition of the work force to produce a type of unemployment which is largely "structural" in nature. In contrast to a hypothetical case of "pure" cyclical unemployment in which each unemployed worker might regain his old job with the return of prosperity, structural unemployment is said to be characterized by a mismatching of worker capabilities and job requirements, producing an unhappy coexistence of unfillable job vacancies and unemployable idle workers. At the beginning of the recovery in 1961 the Federal Reserve Board, concerned that a policy of continued monetary ease might generate a renewal of price inflation, argued that most of the increase in unemployment after 1957 (when the unemployment rate fell to 4 per cent) had been of such a structural nature; and one leading Republican member of the Joint Economic Committee of the Congress vigorously propounded the opinion that there were as many job vacancies as there were unemployed people, so that no deficiency of demand existed. Similarly, some conservative opponents of the tax cuts argued that increasing aggregate demand would merely increase the number of skill bottlenecks in the economy and thus produce inflation without reducing unemployment. But not all who initially entertained reservations about the ability of tax cuts to achieve full employment were averse to the expansion of aggregate demand by fiscal policy. Trade union representatives and some economists who specialized in the study of labor markets, while agreeing that increased demand was a necessary condition for reducing unemployment, doubted that tax cuts could effect a sufficient recovery for production workers—especially semiskilled factory operatives—whose employment had declined absolutely and relatively in the entire labor force ever since 1953. For many adherents to this version of the structural unemployment thesis the answer lay in the direct creation of jobs, under government spending programs, for workers whose capabilities were not in demand in private industry.

To the extent that automation causes structural unemployment, it tends to restrict the potential output of the economy, at least in the sense that fuller utilization of the labor force could be achieved only by incurring the cost of programs designed to make the structurally unemployed worth hiring. On the other hand, to the extent that automation results in increased productivity, it contributes to increased potential output. Yet this latter effect (which presumably is greater than the former) is also regarded in some quarters as evidence that automation has been creating a new brand of noncyclical unemployment which, like structural unemployment, is strongly resistant to fiscal-monetary policies of the variety advocated and put into effect in the Kennedy and Johnson administrations. This conclusion rests on two assertions.

The first assertion is that the new automated technology will be diffused throughout the economy so rapidly that massive displacements of labor will occur simultaneously in virtually all industries and occupations (including many of the professions). And the second assertion is that, notwithstanding the creation of such widespread unemployment, the new technologies will satisfy existing private consumer wants more rapidly than (employed) people will be able to develop new wants. This view has been expressed most forcefully by a group of citizens known as the "Ad Hoc Committee on the Triple Revolution." They conclude that the traditional link between jobs and incomes is being broken," ɔ that a new system of income distribution is required to elimi-ate the poverty arising out of unemployment and other causes. Iore prosaically, they also argue for more government spending rograms to satisfy the nonmarket communal needs of the citi-enry out of the productive potential which automation has made vailable.

But even under these circumstances—which the Triple Revo-ıtionaries regard as "radically new"—it is presumably not antic-ɔated that total demand would sustain employment at present evels. What some writers in this vein appear to envisage is a ıodern analogue to a slave economy, with mechanical instead of uman slaves producing virtually all of the goods desired and ith the human beneficiaries of the new technology freed for eisure-time pursuits. They argue that, in order to encourage peo-le to withdraw from the labor markets, new and socially desira-le ways of utilizing this great potential leisure time must be ɔund or else people may be driven by boredom—not economic ecessity—to resume or continue a largely fruitless quest for work nd thus be counted as unemployed rather than as "not in the ıbor force." (Hence, a state of full employment in a fully auto-ıated or "cybernated" economy would be characterized by a ıarply lower level of employment and a correspondingly lower labor force participation rate" than is envisaged under more onventional objectives.)

How well supported are these arguments concerning the eco-omic and other social effects of automation and related techni-al change and their alleged implications for economic stabiliza-ion policy? The issues involved are extremely complex, and olitical discussion has not always served to clarify them. Hence ıe following comments can do little more than hint at a few road lines of reasoning and the nature of some of the evidence dduced by the contributors to the rather extensive literature on ıis subject.

It would be well to post four cautionary signposts at the outset. n the first place, some of the numerical data which would con-eivably be most relevant to important questions are either not vailable at all or not sufficiently reliable or adapted to the purpose at hand. Second, experience with the new technology is stil limited, so that in this case comparisons between the present anc the recent past—let alone the more distant past—may afford a particularly unreliable basis for projections into the future Third, and related to this last point, not all of the disputants are agreed on the definition of the problem under dispute. To the Council of Economic Advisers the question has been whether o not most of the *increase* in unemployment occurring afte 1956–1957 has been "structural" in nature, for 1957 was the las year in which unemployment averaged below 5 per cent; it actu ally stood at 4.3 per cent in 1957, and thus was close to the Ad ministration's "interim" target of 4 per cent that was assumed to be attainable without price inflation. (This formulation, i should be noted, does not deny the existence of structural unem ployment, even of a sizable amount of structural unemployment indeed, the noninflationary target of 4 per cent supports the in ference that a major fraction of total unemployment may be structural in nature. It merely calls into question whether or no the structural share of unemployment increased in the latter hal of the 1950's.) But others are more concerned with the rathe different question of whether structural or technological unem ployment had increased over the entire postwar period. Finally the three phenomena under discussion—deficient demand, struc tural unemployment, and accelerated increase in productivity— are not mutually incompatible. Indeed, various conceivable com binations among them may reflect different causal relationships and the latter may carry distinctive policy implications.

IS DEFICIENCY OF DEMAND THE PROBLEM?

To begin with, what evidence has there been of a deficiency in demand, beginning shortly after the mid-1950's? Exponents of thi viewpoint have contented themselves with citing the record of the declines which occurred in actual Gross National Product relative to potential product and in the latter itself. But recital of these facts does not constitute evidence supporting their cause; for a major increase in structural unemployment—assuming this to have occurred—could have slowed down the rate of growth in output by restricting supply (rather than demand). In this case, however, if money demand had indeed been buoyant, we should have expected the slowdown in growth and the high rate of unemployment to have been accompanied by inflation: instead of raising output and employment, increased demand would have leaked out in price rises. But in fact prices were quite stable; and this price stability—in a manner akin to the silence of the celebrated dog in one of Sherlock Holmes's cases—constitutes strong evidence that demand was indeed deficient.

Nevertheless, an increase in unemployment due to insufficient demand might be accompanied by some increase in structural unemployment. On the one hand, deficient demand might itself produce some structural joblessness. It has been suggested that one cause of long-term unemployment is the "rusting" of skills of workers laid off in cyclical downswings during which technology continues to advance; as a result, these workers are unable to fill job vacancies which increase during ensuing recoveries. Such structural unemployment would be induced by inadequate demand; however, it could not be eliminated simply by reflating the economy, as could other forms of unemployment. On the other hand, deficient demand might be the result of structural changes in employment. If the latter consist of the replacement in production processes of less skilled, low-paid workers with a high propensity to spend their incomes by more highly trained and highly paid people with a high propensity to save their money, the resulting redistributions of income would tend to reduce aggregate demand. Hence demonstration of the existence of demand deficiency does not relieve one of the necessity to produce and examine evidence bearing directly on the existence of increased structural unemployment; and in fact most of the battles have been joined on this ground.

Is there evidence that structural unemployment increased significantly after the mid-1950's? Since structural unemployment describes a state of coexistence between unemployed people and unfilled jobs, it can in principle be measured directly from data on unemployment and job vacancies. Unfortunately, no adequate statistics on job vacancies are collected in the United

States. Therefore, attempts to ascertain whether or not structural unemployment has changed over time have necessarily involved recourse to data on employment, unemployment, labor force, and productivity. Some of these studies reflect considerable effort and great ingenuity, and some of the results have consequently been suggestive. In the light of this basic deficiency in data, however, it is understandable that, on the whole, the results must be regarded as less than satisfactory.

Analysis of the composition of the labor force reveals that employment of manual workers in the nonagricultural economy—especially semiskilled factory operatives and laborers—underwent a sharp decline relative to service and white-collar workers during the 1950's. This has been widely regarded as evidence of increasing structural unemployment and also of the effects of automation in displacing nonskilled workers and increasing demand for highly skilled workers, especially professionals and technicians. In the light of many dramatic and highly publicized instances of technological change, this is not an implausible inference from these data on changes in the composition of employment.

Yet changes in the composition of employment hardly constitute conclusive evidence of increases in either structural or technological unemployment. In the first place, increasing structural unemployment (if we assume this to be the case) may result from changing patterns of consumer demand—as in the case of increased preference for services relative to manufactures—as well as from automation or technological change. Conversely, technologically caused displacement, or unemployment, is not necessarily structural in nature: it depends on how readily the displaced workers can fill jobs in other industries or occupations. In this connection, a study of some plants which found that the introduction of automated processes required no appreciable increases in skill levels and no extensive retraining of the labor forces involved is of great interest; these findings, moreover, are consistent with results of some studies in the United Kingdom. A recent news story of the installation in the city of Reading, England, of an automated newspaper plant combining computer control with photographic typesetting and offset color printing is a case in point, for it resulted in the displacement of twenty-four skilled linotype operators by twelve typists punching tape.

But if reference to the changing composition of employment fails to establish the case for increasing structural and technological unemployment, analysis of the composition of unemployment cannot be regarded as establishing the case against. Several extensive studies have concluded that structural unemployment has not increased because they have found no evidence of greater dispersion of unemployment rates among industries, occupations, and geographic regions in the latter part of the 1950's. This conclusion is based on the argument that increasing structural unemployment would be reflected in *particularly* sharp increases in unemployment in the sectors and occupational groups most heavily affected by technological change and that such unevenness would show up in greater dispersion among occupational, industrial, and geographic unemployment rates. It has been pointed out, however, that, if technological change impinged most heavily in sectors where unemployment had been relatively low to begin with, the effect would be to reduce—rather than to increase—the variation among unemployment rates. Moreover, we might note here that, even if automation impinges most heavily on industries with traditionally high unemployment levels, if the latter were (by reducing prices) to take business away from low-unemployment industries, they could, in effect, export unemployment—including structural unemployment—to industries with characteristically lower levels of unemployment; the statistical result would be a narrowing of the structure of unemployment.

Thus, as is frequently the case in disputes of this nature, each side has enjoyed greater success in challenging claims made by the other than in establishing positions of its own. Fortunately, however, the economy—with the help of tax cuts and a generally expansionary economic policy followed by the Administration—has provided us with a laboratory experiment which demonstrated its ability to reach at least 4 per cent unemployment without experiencing serious price inflation. Moreover, some of the greatest reductions in unemployment were obtained in durable goods manufacturing, in the manual occupations, among nonwhites, and among the long-term unemployed—which are among the sectors allegedly most susceptible to structural unemployment.

Now this does not suggest the absence of grave problems of

structural unemployment. Negro unemployment rates, despite their relative improvement from recession levels, remain double that of whites; unemployment among young people is more than three times as high as among experienced wage earners, and the unemployment rate of nonwhite young people is five times the national average. To reduce unemployment among these groups to acceptable levels without raising unemployment elsewhere will require a reduction in over-all unemployment well below the "interim target" of 4 per cent; and this might well result in bottleneck inflation unless the capabilities and skills of these disadvantaged workers are sufficiently enhanced. That is the task of manpower policy—under the Manpower Development and Training Act, the Economic Opportunities Act, and legislation providing governmental aid to educational institutions. But under peacetime conditions, such labor market policies may well require supplementation by expansionary fiscal-monetary policies, or else, as we have found, they will arouse resentment and frustration among people who are trained with no jobs in prospect and opposition among trade unionists and other job holders who are fearful of a potential threat to their own economic security.

IS NEW TECHNOLOGY THE PROBLEM?

What of the argument that the increase in unemployment in the latter half of the 1950's—whether structural in nature or due to deficient demand—was caused by the new technology? Such unemployment would presumably be associated with accelerated rates in the growth of productivity or with output per manhour. Moreover, in the short run at least, unemployment might be expected to increase most rapidly in those sectors experiencing the highest rates of technological change. Now little evidence has been found of significant negative (or, for that matter, positive) relationships between changes in employment and changes in productivity among industries; and this has led some to the conclusion that even modern advances in technology have not given rise to increased unemployment.

But this does not necessarily follow, because changes in productivity are not a reliable indicator of technological change. Increases in productivity can occur without changes in technology, simply because of more complete and efficient utilization of existing plant and equipment during business cycle recoveries; thus a positive correlation between increases in employment and productivity may exist in the absence of a similar relationship between changes in employment and technology. On the other hand, changes in technology may not be reflected in observed increases in output per employee, or per man hour. Automation might occur in a declining industry; but if the latter experiences equal proportionate reductions in output and in employment, no increase in productivity is recorded in the data. Yet, had this industry continued to produce its original output, it could have done so with fewer workers. In this case absence of an observed relationship between changes in employment and in productivity obscures a possibly strong relationship between employment and improved technology. Whether this relationship is negative or positive depends on whether the effect of the technological change in reducing the amount of labor required to produce any given amount of output is stronger or weaker than its effect in limiting the industry's decline in output by enabling it to compete more successfully than would otherwise have been the case.

Cases where increased productivity has been produced by increases in output and reductions in employment have been widely regarded as dramatic evidence of net labor-displacing effects of automation. Examples are not difficult to find. In 1964, 123,000 more motor vehicles were produced with 150,000 fewer employees and 188,000 fewer production workers than in 1955; 46 million more tires were produced in the former year than in the latter, with 19,000 fewer employees and 50,000 fewer production workers; 13.4 million more tons of iron ore were mined in 1964 than in 1958, while total employment in the industry declined by 4,000 and employment of manual labor was down 3,300.

But can we conclude from such examples that current technological improvements are sufficiently different in their economic effects from technological change in the past to lend credence to the apprehensions of the Triple Revolutionaries? During the 1957–1960 upswing, output per manhour in both the private nonfarm economy and in manufacturing rose somewhat more rapidly than in 1948–1957 (although less rapidly than in the postwar upswing of 1948–1953). During the recovery which began in 1961, productivity rose rapidly, but, according to the Council of Economic Advisers, "The recent performance does not provide clear evidence that the long-run trend of productivity growth has changed, but there is some evidence that it may have risen slightly in recent years." Trends based on three- and five-year averages in the postwar period lend support to this cautious conclusion.

However, in the postwar period considered as a whole, productivity definitely has been increasing more rapidly than it did over the first half of this century. From an annual average rate of increase of 2 per cent for the period 1909–1947, output per manhour in the private economy rose to an average rate of 3 per cent a year over 1947–1964. Excluding the agricultural sector, where postwar increases in productivity were dramatic, we still find that, in the private nonagricultural sector of the economy, the annual rate of increase rose from 1.9 per cent to 2.4 per cent—a gain of more than 25 per cent.

These data are clearly not inconsistent with the hypothesis that the new technology has made a difference in the performance of the economy since the end of World War II. But before we can accept this as the sole or even the principal explanation, we must balance these historical contrasts in productivity trends with some relevant historical similarities.

In the first place, a comparison with the 1920's reveals little difference from the postwar era as far as rates of productivity increase in both the total private and private nonfarm sectors are concerned, with higher rates in agriculture and railroads in recent times balanced by somewhat lower rates in manufacturing. It has been argued that historical excursions into the prewar world are irrelevant to questions concerning the possible increase in structural unemployment in the latter part of the 1950's, since it is entirely conceivable that structural jumps might have occurred in both the 1920's and the 1950's. This observation strikes one as valid; nevertheless it also suggests that contemporary technological change, including automation, may not be very dissimilar in the totality of its economic manifestations from technological change in bygone times.

Specifically, one hesitates to accept the claim that automation is capable of much more rapid diffusion throughout the economy than was old-fashioned mechanization. For there is no reason to believe that automation is not subject to those forces which have tended historically to retard the rate of introduction of new technology. Among the most important of these forces is observance of the principle that technologically outmoded plant or equipment is not economically obsolete and will not be scrapped as long as its operating costs alone remain below the total (operating plus capital) costs of new plant. While automated equipment frequently results in striking savings in operating costs, the capital costs associated with automation are often very high. Thus it is doubtful whether its diffusion throughout the economy will be as rapid and its impact on over-all productivity trends as unprecedented as is sometimes claimed. In this connection, it is pertinent to point out that, on the average, gross investment has increased manufacturing capacity by only about 10 per cent a year.

Another area of continuity with the past consists in the fact that some of the most dramatic innovations in the postwar period —such as the diesel locomotive and the oxygen furnace in basic steel, to say nothing of the innovations which made agriculture the most rapidly improving sector of all—are examples of old-style technological change and not of automation, although almost every technical change these days goes by the name of automation. And the contributions to the high over-all rates of increase in productivity in the past two decades made by these and thousands of other nonautomated innovations doubtless considerably exceeds the contributions properly credited to automation thus far.

In view of these historical similarities one is tempted to suggest an alternative explanation for the higher rates of productivity growth in the contemporary era. A clue is found in the equally high rates during the 1920's, to which I have already referred. For the greater part of that period was, like the present and recent past, unblemished by severe depression—by high rates of unemployment and by low rates of investment in new, and therefore most modern, plant and equipment. This suggested explanation, it should be noted, regards high rates of technological change and productivity growth as resulting from full employment rather than as causing unemployment by making output expand more rapidly than the human appetite.

But technological change has been raising the productivity of capital as well as labor; this tendency toward declining capital requirements per unit of output has been held primarily responsible for a decline in the ratio of business fixed investment to (potential) Gross National Product; and this decline in the share of investment was mainly responsible for the disappointing performance of the economy after the end of the Korean War. In this respect, technological change might well have contributed to a deficiency of demand. But this is quite different from an oversupply relative to consumer wants. For notwithstanding the downward trend in unit capital requirements, the increase in demand during the most recent upswing was strong enough to drive the unemployment rate well below 4.5 per cent, reversing the upward creep in unemployment to which I referred earlier. From developments in the economy prior to the recent jump in defense expenditures it would appear that, given sufficiently strong demand, "the traditional link between jobs and income" is still capable of providing full employment. Moreover, the declining trend in capital-output ratios began around World War I; it is not a recent phenomenon of the contemporary period in which automation has become important.

To suggest that the economic differences between the new and the older forms of technology may not be as great as some have claimed is not to disparage the importance of what might in all accuracy be regarded as the Automation Revolution. But it may be urged that, in their preoccupation with the wonders and problems of the new Industrial Revolution, some social scientists, reformers, engineers, and journalists have been doing less than full justice to the wonders and problems of the old. After all, the steam locomotive, the steamship, and the internal combustion engine were pretty wonderful inventions, too. And as for associated problems, it is too frequently forgotten that considerable segments of the public blamed the high rates of unemployment in the 1930's on technical change. Indeed, they received strong support from a group of engineers and allied social scientists known as the Technocrats; the latter were the Triple Revolutionaries of the interwar era.

Nevertheless, the lesson to be learned from the past is not that historic trends will necessarily stretch forth into the future. On the contrary, should we achieve full employment of our resources and maintain it more successfully in the future than in the past, then the continued influence of certain historic determinants of technological change might well ensure higher rates of productivity in the future than have been generally experienced in the past. These determinants include the rate of investment in new capital stock and the current and prospective rates of increase in wages relative to capital costs, and the achievement of substantially lower rates of unemployment in the future will definitely increase the former and probably cause the latter to increase as well. But under these circumstances, I repeat, higher rates of technological change would be regarded as resulting from full employment rather than as causing unemployment.

This, in the final analysis, is probably the main reason why, in the 1950's, countries in Western Europe have experienced higher rates of economic growth than the U.S. and, at the same time, why they have experienced far less social concern over "automation." Nor need the U.S. experience represent what must lie ahead for Europe, as some apparently fear; such will be the case only if the other industrialized countries abandon the progressive economic policies which should serve as a model for us.

WHO BEARS THE BURDEN OF CHANGE?

These generally favorable (although necessarily tentative) judgments on the over-all effects of automation must not be allowed to obscure serious and often tragic dislocations suffered by particular groups who have thereby borne a disproportionate share of the costs of technological advance, the benefits of which accrue to the community as a whole. Among these adverse effects three require explicit mention. The first of these is loss in wages to those workers who either have been demoted within the company as a result of technological change or have been discharged and unable to find employment at their old wage levels. (In view of the relative reduction in employment in the manufacturing sector in the postwar years, the probability that a displaced semiskilled factory or mine worker will be able to find new employment at his old wage is not high if he is obliged to take work in a service trade. In addition, the absence of skill bottlenecks in many of the new automated processes means that the latter can employ lower-paid labor.) A second adverse effect of automation is frequently alleged to consist in increased effort required by those employed on the new processes; this may take the form of greater concentration required by the machine-paced and computerized flow of production and not necessarily of increased physical effort. (In many cases, however, increase in physical effort results from the abandonment of old work rules.) Finally, even where automation does not entail the displacement of incumbent employees, it may dispense with their replacement upon resignation or retirement; and, of course, it obtains increased output with fewer additional employees. Some trade union economists call this effect "silent firings," the victims of which are workers—frequently young people and Negroes—who are denied employment in relatively high-wage industries.

All three types of dislocation have placed many trade unions and collective bargaining arrangements under severe strain, but at the same time they have frequently furnished the occasion for the exercise of great ingenuity and institutional adaptability. Confronted with technological change, American unions have adopted a variety of policies aimed at one or more of the following objectives: opposition, encouragement, and control. Policies of obstruction, which may take the form of setting uneconomically high wages on jobs associated with the new machine, or refusing to work with it efficiently or at all, are occasionally pursued by craft unions, where the rank-and-file membership exercise strong control over policy. However, a policy of opposition is not frequently pursued by American unions because experienced officers know that it is not likely to be successful and because, in the case of industrial unions composed of various occupational groups, technological change may affect only a small proportion of jobs and provide increased compensation for the rest.

Policies designed to enable the old process to compete effectively with the new by abandoning restrictive working practices or, more infrequently, by accepting wage reductions are also followed at times. For the most part, however, such concessions, especially when made in the face of an imminent closing of the plant, are designed with the objective of encouraging and enabling high-cost employers to invest in new equipment. Another method of encouragement consists of raising compensation to such high levels that the employer is effectively induced to invest in new techniques in order to displace labor; this method was pursued most vigorously by the United Mine Workers under the leadership of John L. Lewis.

But the most characteristic approach consists of the method of control whereby unions adjust to the process of technological change by retaining control over the jobs on new processes for purposes of providing employment for their members and by bargaining with the employers for a share in the economic gains from such a change. Since much technological change has occurred in high-wage sectors with rather high unemployment, many unions concentrated their bargaining on issues more immediately related to employment than wages. Attempts to maximize the employment by the imposition or retention of various working rules or by challenging standards of production devised by management were frequent in the past decade among local unions, which often conducted unauthorized strikes or obliged the national unions with whom they were affiliated to lead or support industrywide strikes over these issues. Many of the most intensive industrial conflicts in recent years involved issues relating to productivity and technological change: these included the long steel strike in 1959 which lasted 116 days, an even longer newspaper strike in New York in 1962 as well as other strikes in that industry, the strikes over "local issues" in the automotive industry in 1961 and 1964, and stubborn disputes in the railroads, in maritime and longshoring, and in the petrochemical industry.

On the other hand, bargaining for measures which would hav
the effect of reducing labor supplies—including liberalized pe
sions and vacations—has been conducted more amicably and su
cessfully by the leadership of the national unions, althoug
industrial management has thus far been generally successfu
(with the notable exception of some local construction trades) i
resisting reductions in standard working hours. Policies of contr
have also included the liberalization of privately bargained su
plements to unemployment benefits, the provision for "severanc
pay" (or lump-sum payments on termination of employment
and even, in a few instances, "rate maintenance" (or the guara
tee of earnings for employees who are reduced in grade as th
result of technological change). In some industries preference
extended to displaced employees in the filling of vacancies i
other departments or plants; this may be accompanied by retrai
ing or even relocation at company expense. More frequently, th
principle of "attrition" is followed: this provides that no job re
dered superfluous by technological change be destroyed until c
unless the incumbent either quits voluntarily in the course c
time or is discharged for misconduct or inefficiency. These an
other manifestations of the policy of control constitute a uniqu
contribution by collective bargaining to the solution of problem
created by technological dislocation. In providing compensatio
to those most directly affected in an adverse way, it establishes a
once a civilized alternative to the summary judgment of the com
petitive market and an efficient alternative to restrictive and ob
structionist responses frequently found in nonunion as well a
organized work places.

17 THE ECONOMICS OF EDUCATION

Gary S. Becker

Here, too, is a new frontier in economic analysis. For all of the tremendous investment in education year after year, it is only very recently that economists have begun to analyze the costs and benefits of this investment. Capital resources represent a well-studied field, but human resources are only now coming into their own. This chapter illustrates some of the more important applications of a fundamental economic principle as it applies to the costs of education.

Although the great economists of the past, starting with Adam Smith, usually recognized the economic significance of education and other training, the past decade has witnessed an unprecedented burgeoning of interest. This interest extends to underdeveloped as well as developed countries, socialist and communist as well as capitalist countries, and to public officials, journalists, and laymen as well as scholars. Several examples can be taken from recent experience in the United States. The 1962 report of the President's Council of Economic Advisers was the first to include a section on the economic effects of education. The 1964 conference of the Great Cities Program for School Improvement, an association of the superintendents and Boards of Education of the public school systems in fifteen large cities, was the first to have a session on the economics of education. As a final example, note that three of the twenty founding members of the National Academy of Education, an organization primarily of scholars recently formed to encourage research in education, are economists.

SOME BASIC CONCEPTS

Education, on-the-job training, and learning through experience all use public or private resources to raise earnings and productivity. As such they are important examples of a general process that economists call "investing in human capital." This process can be illustrated by considering college education in the United States. In recent years a typical year of college costs approximately $3,500, which means about $14,000 to send a high school graduate through four years of college. This sum should be compared to the series of economic benefits produced by a college education: for example, a typical college graduate has his annual income raised some $4,500 by the time he reaches age forty and some $6,500 by the time he reaches age fifty. The economics of education, and, indeed, of other human capital as well, consists to a large extent of the study of such benefits and costs.

Various studies of educational benefits have already been undertaken, including comparisons of those from high school and college, liberal and vocational education, or expensive and cheap schools, as well as benefits accruing to persons of different abilities, race, and sex. The evidence overwhelmingly indicates that the economic benefits of education are real and generally sizable and vary in a systematic way by level of schooling, sex, and so forth. Only limitations of data have precluded even more far-reaching studies, including such difficult subjects as the benefits from lengthening the school year, from pre-kindergarten school programs, or from different methods of selecting persons to enter higher education.

Private direct expenditures on elementary and secondary schooling are small in most countries of the world because of the heavy subsidies by governments and churches. Great Britain and countries in the British tradition have been something of an exception—less so recently—while in the United States privately supported schooling has grown at a relatively rapid rate in recent years. Private expenditures, mainly in the form of tuition and other fees, have been more important in higher education, although here too governments and private philanthropy assume major burdens. For example, tuition and fees cover only about a third of the total expenditures by colleges and universities in the United States, one of the bastions of private higher education.

A neglected cost of education until the recent emphasis on economic effects is what has been called "foregone earnings," which are the earnings forfeited by students because they are in school rather than in the labor force. These are clearly greatest at the secondary and higher education levels because the students are old enough to be forfeiting significant amounts. It has been estimated, for example, that foregone earnings account for about half of the total costs of higher education in the United States and Great Britain.

The importance of the concept of foregone earnings is revealed not only by such calculations but also its success in explaining some otherwise puzzling facts. It is easy to understand why free tuition generally reduces but does not eliminate economic impediments to school attendance as soon as one realizes that onerous costs still remain, namely, earnings that must be foregone. In recent years many countries have had relatively few persons in the sixteen to twenty-one age group because of wartime-induced reductions in the birth rate. Since this implies a relatively small addition to the labor force, some of the countries, including the Soviet Union, have been forced to retrench on their educational plans in order to prevent any further reduction in the labor force and earnings. As another example, take the increased high school and college enrollments that have usually occurred in the United States during recessions and in depressed areas. If direct costs alone were considered, unemployment and the accompanying family difficulties should, if anything, discourage school attendance. Increased enrollments are easy to understand, however, when one recognizes that periods of unemployment may greatly reduce the cost of attending school because then the foregone earnings of students would be reduced if not eliminated entirely. As a final example, note that many communities in the United States have tried to encourage elementary and secondary schoolteachers to improve their educational preparation by offering higher salaries to those with greater education. Yet a study of one city, New York, found that very few teachers entered the public school system with more than the minimum education required. An important part of the explanation certainly is that present value earnings forfeited by extending one's education an additional year or two exceed the present value of the higher salaries.

APPLYING THE CONCEPTS

The most well-known and possibly also most important application of the analysis relating to human capital has been to economic growth and development. Not too long ago perhaps most economists believed that investment in physical capital was the main vehicle of economic development. Then a series of studies in the United States, soon confirmed by studies in several other countries, indicated that physical capital as conventionally measured was responsible for only a small part of the growth in per capita incomes. Moreover, in spite of widespread damage to physical capital during World War II, many countries, especially Japan, Germany, and the Soviet Union, managed remarkably rapid recoveries in the postwar period.

These findings led to a search for other explanations, and the quality of the labor force, as evidenced by its education, training and health, has received considerable attention. Surely labor ir the United States is much more productive today than it was ir 1900 partly because its average level of schooling has increase from below nine to about twelve years, and its health has increased perhaps even more rapidly. Indeed, a recent study suggests that the increase in education alone may explain almost one third of the increase in per capita incomes in the United State since 1929. Although education may not have been equally impotant elsewhere—some evidence, for example, indicates that it wa less important in Canadian growth—increased investment in som kinds of human capital has probably been a major factor in th economic growth of most countries.

In the last few years the subject of optimal education policy ha elicited substantial discussion throughout the world. Should sel interest lead people to invest more in high school or college education, to major in engineering and pure science rather than in the humanities and the social sciences, to take liberal arts rather than more specialized programs, and so on? Or if the social interest conflicts with self-interest, should people be encouraged or even required to make changes in their educational plans?

Although answers to these questions are not easy to come by, economists have made several worthwhile contributions to the discussion. In the first place they have introduced the concept of a rate of return to education, which is simply that rate of discount which equates the stream of benefits with costs. For example, if a college education having a total private cost, including forgone earnings, of $10,000 would raise earnings by $2,000 a year for forty years, the private money rate of return would be approximately 2,000/10,000, or 20 per cent. Psychic benefits and costs could easily in principle be added to the monetary benefits and costs in order to calculate a full private rate of return, although one should emphasize that so far they have not yielded to efforts at quantitative measurement. The social rate of return could be calculated in exactly the same way if government and other subsidies were added to private costs to get social costs, and indirect contributions to social welfare were added to private benefits to get social benefits.

Underinvestment in an educational activity exists when its rate of return exceeds that of the next best alternative, while overinvestment exists when the opposite occurs. Calculations for the United States indicate that private rates of return on high school and college education have exceeded those on alternative investments. The rapid increase in the number of students going through high school and college can be interpreted, therefore, as a rational response to profitable opportunities. The social rates of return are much more difficult to calculate, but the available evidence certainly does not indicate that they are lower for high school and college than, say, for physical capital.

Almost three-quarters of the costs of higher education in the United States are borne by students and their families, mainly because they pay most of the foregone earnings; as already indicated, these account for about half of the total costs. Direct outlays by institutions of higher education account for most of the remainder, and students pay only about a third of these. The other two-thirds of direct outlays comes from gifts by alumni, foundations, and corporations and from public tax collections.

The public contribution has been primarily concentrated at the state level: more than half of all students are in state-run colleges and universities, while practically all students in rapidly growing states such as California are in such institutions. In recent years the federal government has also taken a much more active role through scholarship programs and the support of research. Indeed, the latter has transformed many universities into multi-product organizations that spend as much effort on research as they do on instruction. Even such private institutions as my own Columbia University have about half their budgets contributed by federal support for research and related programs, and the fraction exceeds three-quarters in the private Massachusetts Institute of Technology.

Students at primary and secondary schools contribute a smaller fraction of the costs because foregone earnings are less important and their direct outlays are minimal. Gifts are also less important, since almost all students are enrolled either in public institutions or in those connected with religious bodies, especially the Catholic Church. These public institutions, unlike those at higher levels, are run by city, village, and other local governments and are mainly financed by locally imposed property taxes. Even here, however, state governments and even the federal government have been increasingly active in recent years in helping to finance the rapidly increasing expenditures and by setting minimum educational standards.

A very different example relates to international trade. Businessmen, labor unions, and others in high-wage countries often complain that they have difficulty competing with goods from low-wage countries. In view of these complaints, it would be reasonable to expect that relatively high-wage industries within a country would face stiffer competition from imports unless they succeeded in getting high tariffs imposed, while low-wage industries would be more successful at exporting unless tariff barriers were erected abroad. And yet the facts in the United States are almost precisely the opposite! High-wage industries are more successful at exporting, while low-wage industries face stiffer competition from imports and are more protected by high tariffs.

A promising line of explanation demonstrates once again the value of the current emphasis on human capital. It has been shown that export industries in the United States pay high wages primarily because they use skilled labor, as measured by education and training, and not because they pay more for labor of given quality. Similarly, import competing industries pay low wages primarily because they use less skilled labor, and not because they pay less for labor of given quality. Indeed, to the extent that different amounts are paid to labor of the same quality, there probably is a negative relation between the amount paid and exports.

Consequently the United States can be said primarily to export goods produced with much education and other human capital and to import goods produced with little human capital. This generalization from the evidence is not only sensible but is also quite consistent with the accepted theory of international specialization. According to this theory, countries export goods using large amounts of their abundant factors of production and import goods using large amounts of their scarce factors. Now the United States has certainly invested more in human capital than other countries have, and the differences may be even greater than the corresponding differences for physical capital. It follows from the accepted theory, therefore, that the United States would specialize in goods using much human capital and imports other goods, which would explain the observed pattern of exports and imports.

In every society regardless of political institutions there is considerable inequality in the distribution of education. This is partly the result of unequal ability and attitudes; it is also partly the result of very unequal access to educational opportunities. Discussions in the United States have particularly stressed the barriers created by limited financial means, and one of the most persuasive arguments for highly subsidized education in this country has been its effect in equalizing access to education.

Of course, substantial inequality in the distribution of income has also existed practically everywhere, and many observers have not hesitated to relate the inequality in income to education. Indeed, by reducing the inequality in educational opportunities, subsidized education was supposed to reduce the inequality in incomes. Nevertheless, systematic study of the relationship between the two has only begun in the last few years. A combination of the rates of the return from, and the distribution of, education appears to explain a significant part of the distribution of income in certain regions of the United States. For example, they explain about 10 per cent of the income inequality in the northern states and about 20 per cent in the southern ones.

Education is even more important in helping to understand differences in income inequality between geographical areas. Differences in ability, luck, motivation, and so on undoubtedly explain a considerable fraction of the income differences within an area, but usually they do not vary sufficiently to explain much of the differences between areas, such as the considerably greater inequality in the South and then in the North. Rates of return and the distribution of education, on the other hand, do vary substantially between areas because of differences in demand for educated personnel, subsidies to education, and other factors. Some calculations confirm this for the United States: about half of the differences in income inequality between the North and the South or among all fifty states is explained by differences in rates of return and the distribution of education.

IN CONCLUSION

In conclusion let me stress that I have considered briefly only a few examples involving education and other human capital: the importance of foregone earnings, economic growth, optimal investment policy, international specialization, and the personal distribution of income. If space permitted, many other factors could have been discussed: for example, the tendency, at least in developed countries, for unskilled workers to be more unemployed than skilled ones appears to be related to the greater educational and other human capital of the latter.

Throughout the world scholars are busy trying to sharpen the analytical concepts, improve the quantitative measures, and extend the range of applications. Unlike many other developments in economics, with education and other human capital the direction of causation has almost invariably been from possible applications to concepts and measures, as economists struggle to make coherent sense out of a puzzling world.

18 THE U.S. IN WORLD MARKETS

Charles P. Kindleberger

The next two chapters look at the American economy in the context of a rapidly changing world situation. The first of the essays deals with a series of issues on the U.S. as a buyer and seller of goods in world markets, as an investor in other nations, and as an influence in shaping international monetary reforms. In each of the issues, the need for new initiatives crowds out policies that were once good enough to get along with.

The year 1966 saw the United States propose new policies in several international economic fields. President Johnson's messages to Congress have recommended a revision of the regulations governing East-West trade, and a new program of Food for Peace. Still further initiatives are likely to be forthcoming. Yet our economic foreign policy at the end of 1965 was losing momentum. The important question is when and how that momentum is to be regained.

Three short years ago the United States had a program for world initiative in the economic field. The Trade Expansion Act of 1962 was designed to lower tariffs and expand trade. On another front the internationalization of aid to the less developed countries was taking place through the Development Assistance Committee of the Organization of Economic Cooperation and Development in Paris. In a third area—the strengthening of the world's international payments mechanism and the provision of larger reserves—the United States did not believe in substantial initiatives and was content to enlarge the quotas of the International Monetary Fund. On the whole and despite the British concern on the point, it did not believe it necessary to undertake any drastic reform, as many economists and some politicians thought important.

TALK ON TARIFFS

Today the initiative embodied in the Trade Expansion Act has slowed down to a walk. The exclusion of Britain from the Common Market in January, 1963, destroyed one of the major assumptions on which the program for lowering tariffs was based. French theoretical questions as to the best way to reduce tariffs caused a six months' delay. Then the failure of the Common Market to adopt the French program for agriculture and France's temporary withdrawal from Common Market meetings have made it impossible to go forward on the agricultural agreement which the United States insisted was a vital element in the total bargain. The Kennedy round of negotiations still goes forward at Geneva, but so slowly that there is a possibility that the five-year limit in America's authorizing legislation may run out before a bargain is concluded. And the bright hopes for a wide elimination of tariffs on manufactured goods among the highly industrialized countries, and the halving of most of the rest, will surely not be realized. In present circumstances the cross-the-board tariff reductions, from which certain items are excluded altogether, will be on the order of 25 or 30 per cent, far short of the bright hopes of the Kennedy era.

Tariffs are no longer what they used to be. In an earlier year, before the world shrank to its present size, tariffs were a device for protecting innocent businesses from competition which came upon them suddenly and unexpectedly. In particular, the disruption of trade by wars gave birth to some firms which needed protection afterwards when international trade began again. The United States raised tariffs after every major war up to 1945. But in the world as small as it has now become a responsible businessman must broaden the horizon he scans for potential competition from the town, the region, or the country he lives in to the entire world. Tariffs to protect against events which lie over the horizon are no longer needed in a world where the horizon of business men has stretched around the world. There are some industries which are protected in spite of their acknowledged inefficiency because of defense considerations, because the resources devoted to them have few alternative uses, or because of their political strength. But they are losing out. The intellectual opposition to lower tariffs has been defeated. President Kennedy had a relatively easy time getting the Trade Expansion Act of 1962 on the statute books, but it would be difficult to extend the Presidential powers of tariff reduction if no headway is made in using it.

Indeed, the initiative in trade reform seems to have shifted to the less developed countries. These met in a major conference in Geneva in 1964, the so-called UNCTAD, or United Nations Conference on Trade and Development. There, seventy-seven less developed countries (out of more than a hundred such countries in the world) called for more help from the developed countries. In a world where the American position had been against trade discrimination, they wanted discrimination in favor of the less developed countries. For example, they asked that, in the developed countries, tariffs on textiles, shoes, and other simple manufactures either be very low or be eliminated altogether insofar as imports from the developing countries were concerned. In addition they came out strongly for programs of maintaining the prices of primary products which the less developed countries sold in world markets, for automatic access to the assets of the International Monetary Fund for countries whose exports had declined sharply in value because of falling prices, and for a host of other measures which would favor the less developed countries and, in the usual case, cost something to the developed. In some cases, the price would have been political, such as that implied by tariff reductions in textiles and shoes, industries which are marked in the developed countries by low-income labor and high unemployment. In others, the cost would have been financial, either through budget expenditures for stockpiling of imported materials, or, in Europe, where excise taxes are levied on coffee, tea, and cocoa, the loss of regular sources of revenue. The slogan of "Trade Not Aid," which Europe adopted in the middle 1950's, was taken over by the less developed countries, even though some of the proposals put forward had all the earmarks of being merely different types of aid.

THE ROLE OF FOREIGN AID

The question of aid policies is treated separately in Chapter 19. Yet that question cannot be separated completely from trade policies. For the loss of U.S. initiative in trade seems to me to have a parallel in a loss of initiative in aid, too. Apart from the "Food for Peace" program, United States initiative in aid has been replaced not so much by that of some other country or group of countries as by a total loss of forward motion. Proponents of foreign aid can point to a few successes, such as Taiwan, Israel, Mexico, and Peru, but for the most part these are exceptions. The Alliance for Progress in Latin America seems to have run into difficulty: the notion of providing aid to countries which undertake economic reforms is easy to understand in principle, but hard to apply in practice. The Latin American countries want to undertake the highly explosive task of reform only if aid is forthcoming, whereas the United States as the donor wants the aid to be conditional on achievement of reform. The result is often inadequate aid and no reform. Key legislators, once staunch friends of foreign aid, are now expressing doubts or even outright opposition. The countries of Europe have most often given a cold answer to America's warm argument that their shares in aid should be increased because of new strength in their balances of payments. For these and other reasons, over wide parts of the world the bright hopes for rapid economic and political growth and stability which foreign aid was expected to produce have been dimmed. The processes of development are now seen to be more complex and slow than must men had believed. Foreign aid continues, of course, but the uncertainties in the aid policies, when combined with loss of initiative in promoting freer trade, suggest an America looking out at the world in a way that is at once sober, perplexed, and anxious.

EAST-WEST TRADE

There is still another area in which United States policies have encountered decreasing interest and sympathy with its trading partners. This is the field of East-West trade. Under the Battle Act of 1951, which is still the governing legislation on the books, we restrict trade with Eastern Europe in so-called strategic items, and forbid United States trade with China and Cuba. Our allies are less and less interested in going along with these measures. Canada sells large amounts of wheat to China, and can point to the fact that the United States itself has sold wheat to the Soviet Union. Britain has sold buses to Cuba. In trade with the Soviet Union and Eastern Europe, this country has now adopted the view that more trade in nonstrategic items is highly desirable and constitutes a force for peace. United States firms have even received State Department encouragement to set up plants in Czechoslovakia and Rumania, where, it is felt, more normal trade relations would support forces working for independence from the Soviet Union.

But while the forces making for embargo have weakened, the United States and the world are a long way from an effective means of conducting trade with the Soviet bloc. Indeed, the Soviet bloc has difficulty conducting trade among its own members. Each country is planned separately, and when the several plans are added together, there is no assurance, or even a likelihood, that each has provided what the other wanted, and that the value of goods sold equals that of goods bought. Moreover, in a system of thought which abhors capital there is difficulty in providing for the movement of international capital at interest. Some parts of the world, such as West Germany, have more interest in East-West trade than others. For the United States, the interest, except perhaps in wheat, is limited. But strong political attitudes among some Americans plus difficulties in the Soviet bloc prevent working out a reasonable solution to the problem of East-West trade. The United States has abdicated leadership in the problem, but no other country has taken it over. In his January 1966 State of e Union message, President Lyndon Johnson called for further eps to promote East-West trade. But it will take much persua- on to overcome Congressional fears about this particular form f trade.

AMERICAN INVESTMENT ABROAD

Not only has the United States lost the trade initiative; in some reas it is on the defensive. One such is direct investment. Under ıe Eisenhower administration, private corporate foreign invest- ıent was regarded as the major contribution which this country ould make to economic development in the less developed coun- ries. American firms establishing subsidiaries abroad brought not nly capital but technical capacity, and trained the labor force of he host country in modern productive and management tech- iques. Foreign opinion has blown hot and cold on this issue. In ome parts of the world where socialist doctrines prevail Ameri- an enterprise has been accused of subversive activities. In others, he complaint is rather that the American firms make too much ıoney, are too big, too strong, too ready to take over. The earliest oncern about American direct investment was recorded in Aus- ralia and Canada. In the last few years some European countries, ut by no means all, have reacted against the rush of American ompanies to establish branches and subsidiaries in the Common Market, or in Europe more generally, to take advantage of prefer- ntial duties on the one hand and the rapid rates of European conomic growth on the other. The French in particular have xpressed the universal ambivalence toward these large, power- ul, and efficient companies. They want to acquire the economic apacity the firms bring, but they worry about the competitive ffects. In the second half of 1965 European concern over the in- asion by American companies diminished from its previous ıeight, partly as a result of the action taken by the United States o restrain it.

THE BALANCE-OF-PAYMENTS PROBLEM

This leads us to the other significant area where the United States has been on the defensive in the foreign economic area, its balance of payments. The balance of payments of a country is a rather elusive concept and, in particular, the deficit in the balance of payments as it is defined in the United States is hard to comprehend at first hearing. One way in which a country can be in deficit is because it is consuming and investing too much—buying from abroad more than it sells and more than its power to borrow. This is called "living beyond one's means." But this is not the sort of deficit the United States has. On the contrary, the United States buys from abroad a lot less than it sells, even after allowing for its military expenditures and foreign aid. Its balance of payments on current account, that is, is positive. In 1965 it amounted in fact to about $7.1 billion, and in 1964 to $8.6 billion. The difficulty is that the United States has been trying to invest abroad—through corporate investment, purchases of outstanding securities, purchases of newly issued bonds, and short-term loans, including deposits abroad in dollars—more than its current-account surplus. The result is that foreigners, both private and central banks, have been acquiring more dollars than they would like to hold. Some of these dollars, in fact, they have been converted into gold. The gold lost by the United States and the increase in dollars acquired by foreigners constitute the deficit.

There is a variety of ways of looking at this deficit, and some people—both Americans and non-Americans—take it more seriously than others. I, for one, do not think it is a very serious matter. That is, I think of the United States as a bank and accept it as normal for a bank to have its deposits (which are, after all, what it owes to others) go up year after year. The rules that define a deficit for, say, a manufacturing firm do not apply to a bank. As a "bank," the money and capital markets of the United States make a contribution to world liquidity, including the liquidity of European firms, individuals, local governments, national governments, and international institutions, which used to be able to borrow more cheaply in New York than in Europe. But the European central bankers do not think it appropriate for the United States financial intermediary to operate in Europe, and the United States government officials don't either. European central banks have been exerting pressure on the United States by converting dollars into gold, with the result that our gold stock has declined in recent years from $22 billion immediately after World War II to less than $14 billion today. The initial losses were useful in that they redistributed international reserves more evenly around the world. The trouble with the more recent losses is that the world may become alarmed by the weakening of the dollar and reduce its supply of dollars by converting them into gold. The United States has attempted to meet this fear by trying to halt the outflow of capital. A tax was levied on purchases of foreign securities, taking effect in July, 1963. The same law was extended in early 1965 to bank loans of more than a year. Thereafter the Voluntary Credit Restraint Program was imposed in the United States in February, 1965, with the Federal Reserve Board and the Department of Commerce laying down guidelines to limit the outflow of capital by banks and United States corporations. There was a total exemption for Canada and a partial one for Japan, two countries which depend greatly on the United States capital market for finance. But the capital outflow has not slowed down as a result of these measures as much as United States authorities wanted. The deficit was cut from something like $3 billion in 1964 to $1.5 in 1965, but it still remains.

THE NEED FOR LIQUID RESERVES

On July 10, 1965, Secretary of the Treasury Henry H. Fowler made an important speech in which he observed that, while the United States was taking steps to correct its deficit, this deficit had served the function of providing the world with liquidity. When the deficit was gone, he feared that the world would not expand reserves as rapidly as it needed for reasonable comfort in meeting imbalances in international payments. Thus the United States became converted to the view that there was or would be a problem of insufficient liquidity, a position held by various individuals and the British government as far back as January, 195 Secretary Fowler urged, and the governors of the Internationa Monetary Fund agreed in September, 1965, that the experts of th leading financial countries, the so-called Group of Ten, shoul prepare a plan for creating additional international reserves.

There are a wide number of issues tied up in this questio which the world will hear a great deal more about in the month and even years to come. Some experts want to reduce the need fo international reserves, letting exchange rates move when pay ments tend to be out of balance. A country in deficit would hav its rate depreciate to the point where imports were cut o enough, and exports sufficiently stimulated, to restore balanc But this flexible or floating exchange rate is widely opposed, espe cially by central bankers. They believe that the uncertainty o exchanges enhances speculation and exchange instability, whic are disruptive of international trade. A compromise between flexible rate and a fixed rate has attracted a certain amount o support, not least in the powerful Joint Economic Committee o Congress, which would widen the limits within which rates fluc tuated—the so-called band proposal.

The less developed countries have got into the act, too. group of experts called together for the purpose by the Unite Nations Trade and Development Organization, created as a re sult of the Conference on Trade and Development, want to us the need for more reserves as a means of getting more aid to th developing nations. They would enlarge the quotas of all coun tries at the International Monetary Fund and then ask that th quotas of the developed countries be made available to the Inter national Bank for Reconstruction and Development for lendin to the less developed countries, thus expanding aid. The less de veloped countries would presumably spend these newly create reserves in the developed countries, so that the latter would ad to their reserves. But the assets underlying these newly create reserves would be claims on the less developed countries whic they would be unable to repay for years to come.

The French suggestion was to limit international settlements t gold. Since there was not enough gold, the price of gold could b raised, as numbers of British, South African, and more recentl even Soviet experts, have called for, or the same result could b accomplished by issuing certificates equivalent in value to an ounce of gold. Early in 1965 the French started to put their plan into practice by themselves, converting their dollar holdings into gold—except for working balances—at the rate of $300 million a month. But most of the world is out of step with the French, and even they, as realists first and foremost, understand that running a balance-of-payments surplus (at some cost in economic growth) is an excellent device to put pressure on the United States and advance French foreign policy, but does not make much economic sense. In fact, it is very expensive for the French people.

This recital of fields of activity in which the United States used to exert leadership and has lost it, where it is on the defensive (as in direct investment and the balance of payments), or where it is seeking to exercise leadership (as in the expansion of world liquidity), may suggest that the U.S. has lost its capacity to exert economic leadership in the world. This is not at all the case. In fact the contrary is true. United States economic expansion has been under way for fifty-nine months, giving the nation rapid growth, at faster rates than prevail in Europe or in the less developed countries, and doing so with price stability. The extraordinary rates of growth in Europe which used to be combined with surpluses in the balance of payments are now a thing of the past. Having run out of labor, the Continent's "Go-Go" economic growth has given way to the "Stop-Go" variety under which Britain has been suffering for virtually the entire postwar period. United States exports flourish because of price stability at home in the years since 1959, while European prices have been rising. Although there is concern that pressure on resources in the United States may now take hold and lead to substantial price increases and hence to worsening of the competitive position of United States goods in world markets, this will merely reduce this country to the European condition, not set it back relatively.

THE U.S. AND WORLD ECONOMIC LEADERSHIP

No. The United States no longer formulates world economic policies as it did in the days of Lend-Lease, Bretton Woods, the Atlantic Charter, the Marshall Plan, and Point IV. This is largely a result of the success of those early policies. Europe, then pro trate, is now vigorous and inevitably independent in its point c view. The less developed countries, then passive, are now asser ing themselves. The United States used to be what a French ecor omist called "a dominant economy." No longer do we tell then however; we ask them. International economic policy is today two-way street, a give-and-take affair.

But while the United States is no longer dominant, its leade ship is required. If it pulls in its horns and retreats into isolatior ism, it seems unlikely that a consensus for policy and action wi quickly emerge elsewhere. Other interests and voices diverg rather than converge. The French have failed to crystallize a independent third force in economic affairs about their rathe idiosyncratic view. The rest of the world can unite behind o against United States leadership, but it probably cannot functio without it.

This is the basis for the United States initiative in the field c international monetary reform, an initiative which seems to pr vide much more room for effective exchanges of views both wit Europe and with the less developed countries than was true i policy formulation ten years ago. Further initiatives are neede There is only a little time left to see whether the Kennedy roun of tariff negotiations will amount to anything. Before the Pres dent's powers to negotiate lower trade barriers expire in Jun 1967, however, this country will have to decide whether to pres for a tariff bargain which includes the European Common Ma ket or to conclude that French resistance makes it necessary t look elsewhere, perhaps to mutual reductions among the Britis the European free-trade area outside the Common Market, an the Commonwealth—Canada, Australia, and New Zealand.

This, then, is a year of big decisions. What the shape of then will be is still not discernible—but it is a safe bet that the nex challenge to American leadership in economic policies will b every bit as complicated as the past ones have been.

19 THE U.S. AND FOREIGN AID

Max F. Millikan

Two decades after the American entry into the business of extending foreign aid through government on a large scale, many Americans are still asking what it is all about. Oversold on what results this aid would bring, or perhaps never sold at all, they ask some basic questions once again: "What difference does aid make to us and to the developing countries?" "What are the preconditions for making aid more effective?" This chapter speaks to those questions.

Foreign aid is historically a brand-new tool in the foreign policy kit of the United States. Apart from some emergency relief after World War I and occasional succor offered to other countries after natural catastrophes, there was no such thing as foreign aid until World War II. In the twenty-five years since it was invented we have behaved rather like a child with a new toy, discovering every so often new uses to which this instrument, the offering of money by our government to other governments on other than bankers' terms, could be put.

It all started with the Lend-Lease Program during World War II, an arrangement designed to strengthen the military capabilities of our European allies to fight a major war against the Nazis. The next major phase, after an interval of primarily humanitarian postwar relief, was the Marshall Plan, a multiyear program of capital exports designed to put the war-torn economies of the developed European countries back on the path of self-sustaining economic growth from which the war had diverted them. The Marshall Plan, while wholly different in concept and purpose from our present aid program, represented an extraordianary innovation in foreign policy thinking. Some of its elements have carried over into our present policy of aiding the growth efforts of the underdeveloped countries.

First, the Marshall Plan was (in the best sense of the word) like current economic development aid in that it was fundamentally political in its motivation. We were deeply concerned in 1946 and 1947 that the economic disruption of Europe resulting from the war might lead to an abandonment of the open democratic societies which had characterized most of Western Europe and a drift, of which there were powerful signs, toward extremist movements and notably toward communism. Second, we attempted to use American money in the Marshall Plan not to buy a specific kind of foreign policy performance on the part of the recipients but rather to attempt to help them, by strengthening their economies, to achieve an orderly political evolution of their own choosing but of a sort which would be consistent with a peaceful and mutually cooperative world. Our immediate goal was to promote the economic rather than the political performance of the European countries, but we did this in the conviction that economic health and growth were essential prerequisites for political stability. This conviction was and is an important element in the support which the American electorate gives to current economic development aid.

Third, we recognized from the beginning that the economic reconstruction of Europe was a long-term process which would take some years to accomplish. While Marshall Plan appropriations were on a one-year basis, both we and the recipients entered into the program on the clear understanding that to achieve results it would have to extend over a considerable number of years. We and they both made our plans on this assumption. As the subsequent performance of Western Europe, both economic and political, has demonstrated, the Marshall Plan was an overwhelming success. Yet, over the years, as we have discovered many new uses for the aid instrument, we have tended to forget some of the key lessons which this successful experiment should have taught us.

THE USES OF AID

What are some of these other new uses? We have used aid in a number of places, starting with Greece and Turkey and continuing most notably today in Vietnam to counter Communist-supported guerrilla insurgency. We have used it in such countries as Spain and Morocco as the price we paid to acquire rights to establish bases for our own military forces to strengthen our strategic defenses. We have used it in part in such countries as Egypt, Indonesia, Burma, and Cambodia to attempt to maintain the goodwill of neutralist powers and communications with them. We have used it in Eastern Europe and to some extent in a few of the underdeveloped countries to provide an alternative source of support to countries which appeared to be threatened with exclusive economic dependence on the Soviet Union and thus implicitly with political dependence as well. We have used it widely in Africa and elsewhere as a token of friendship and good will to new countries freshly freed from their colonial bonds to try to demonstrate that we were not in league with their former colonial masters.

We have used substantial amounts of military and economic aid to support the capacity of such developing countries as South Korea and Taiwan to resist threatened external aggression. We have on occasion used it—some of us think unwisely—to provide current budgetary support to regimes friendly to us and sympathetic to our purposes but often widely regarded as neither progressive nor democratic, and to permit such regimes to survive in the face of threatened takeover by what were believed to be Communist-dominated elements. Finally, and most important, we have used it increasingly in recent years to provide major support to such countries as India, Nigeria, and Chile which are attempting consistently and systematically to promote their own economic growth and development and which we believed would be unable to do this without substantial outside economic assistance. Many other factors have influenced our aid policy, not the least of which has been a moral conviction that the wealthier and more successful countries of the world have an obligation to assist those less fortunate to better their condition.

In the balance of this essay, I would like to concentrate attention on what I shall call developmental assistance designed primarily to promote the self-sustaining economic growth of the recipient. But in appraising our foreign aid program it is important to bear in mind that this is only one element in a complex of purposes to which we have in fact, wisely or not, devoted the multipurpose instrument which we call foreign aid. The effectiveness of our aid programs has frequently suffered from our failure to recognize that some of these objectives may be in conflict with each other, and that to get results it may be necessary in each case to decide what our priority objective is and then to concentrate singlemindedly upon it.

DOES AID MAKE SENSE FOR THE U.S.?

Economics has very little to do with a good many of the purposes of foreign aid which I have discussed. However, it has a great deal to say about the problem of the economic development of the underdeveloped countries and the role that aid can play in promoting such development. But let me say a little bit more first about the United States' interest in that development, about what is in the best sense of the word a long-term political interest. The view is sometimes put forward by serious U.S. observers of international affairs that we have in recent years been too concerned with the underdeveloped world. These people argue that while the developing countries contain, to be sure, two-thirds of the world's population, they command neither the economic resources nor the military power to pose any very serious threats to vital American interests. The underdeveloped world, so runs this line of thinking, will inevitably be turbulent and chaotic for some years to come and our best course would be to concentrate our attention and energies on the important countries of Europe, Japan, and the Soviet bloc and leave the underdeveloped world to find its own answers to its very special problems.

The trouble with this approach is that it neglects the extent to which the world has shrunk in the last thirty years under the impact of modern transportation and communication. We are now so interdependent that serious instability and outbreaks of violence anywhere are increasingly difficult to confine and isolate. Beyond this, modern weaponry includes such efficient engines of destruction that the almost inevitable escalation of local conflict poses very great dangers to the whole civilized world. One has only to reflect on the fact that most of the international crises since the close of World War II which have seemed ominous and threatening to Washington, London, Paris, and Moscow have had their proximate origins in underdeveloped countries. The list includes Korea, Suez, the Congo, Algeria, Cuba, Kashmir, Cyprus, the Dominican Republic, and many others, including most recently and notably Vietnam. The only important exceptions are West Germany and Hungary. If there is any way in which the developed countries can make the transition to modernity which the underdeveloped world is increasingly determined to undertake less explosive and destabilizing, it is certainly in our interest to do so. Specifically, if by spending less than 1 per cent of our Gross National Product to promote successful economic development, we can even marginally reduce the risk that we may have to spend 10, 15, 20, or even 50 per cent, plus many lives, on military security, it is a chance worth taking.

THE ECONOMICS AND POLITICS OF DEVELOPMENT

This leads us into a set of thorny and in large part unresolved questions concerning the relationship between economic progress and political behavior. There are certainly no simple correlations here. The simple Marxist view, held by many profoundly conservative anti-Marxists, that poverty breeds revolt and that increasing the availability of food, clothing, housing, and consumer goods will in itself be stabilizing is clearly erroneous. Indeed there is a large body of literature—which there is no time to review here—that documents the wide variety of ways in which the pursuit of economic development objectives is responsible for much of the instability in the underdeveloped world.

On the other hand, it is equally clear that, where aspirations for patterns of living radically different from the traditional ones have suddenly been generated and where the society appears to offer few opportunities for its members to work toward the satisfaction of those aspirations, the resulting frustration is a breeding ground for violence and protest. What does this have to do with economic growth? Most of the things which people throughout the underdeveloped world have newly come to want and which the members of traditional societies never perceived as within the range of possibilities for them—all of the things that are summed up in the phrase "the revolution of rising expectations"—can be supplied only in the context of a fairly rapid rate of economic growth. Rising standards of consumption for the average man clearly require a growing Gross National Product, but these are only a part, and in many cases the less important part, of what he wants. Next to enough food, his highest priority is usually education for his children, if not for himself. Once educated, he wants to use his newly acquired training and skills to shape for himself new career patterns which will lift him out of the status in society that his parents had always regarded as inescapable. He wants new respect, new mobility, new opportunity to participate in the making of the important decisions affecting his life. All these things are possible for the mass of the population only in a society that is experiencing fairly rapid economic growth and an expansion both of material resources and of job opportunities. In sum, then, while we have no assurance that prosperous countries will be peaceful countries (and indeed there are many instances to the contrary), we can be quite sure that, once the taste for modernization has taken firm root, economic stagnation will sooner or later bring serious political trouble. In other words, in the world of the 1960's economic development is a necessary though not a sufficient condition for nonviolent and progressive political evolution.

The pattern and shape of economic development when it occurs can have a great deal to do with its political consequences. We need to know a great deal more than we now do about this, but some things are already becoming clear. For democratic politics to be successful, the fruits of development and, more imporcantly, the opportunities for employment and for entrance into the modern world must become broadly available to any group in that society whose perception of alternatives has been newly widened. And this must be done without too great a lag.

FOREIGN AID AND SOME VICIOUS CIRCLES

But we must get back to our central theme. What does foreign aid have to do with all this? Why is the availability of additional resources from outside so necessary to the development process? Cannot these countries lift themselves by their own bootstraps if they are sufficiently determined to do so without help from us? There are important answers to these questions on both the resources and the incentive side. Let us look at the resources side first.

Three vicious circles confront the leadership of an underdeveloped country in its efforts to launch a process of self-sustaining economic growth. The first of these involves human resources. The most serious shortage confronting countries at the beginning of the economic growth process is a shortage of human skills and talents of all sorts. These include technical skills, professional skills, administrative and managerial skills, and entrepreneurial skills across the whole range of functions of an economy from agriculture through trade, commerce, transport and communications, to industry and government.

These skills are developed in each new generation in a mature economy in two ways. They are transmitted partly through formal education and partly through on-the-job experience. But a radical expansion of formal education requires a great many teachers who already possess the skills to be taught. Where there are few people who have these skills, enough of them cannot be spared for teaching. On-the-job training requires a large number of employment opportunities in already well-run and effectively operating enterprises. These simply do not exist in a country at the beginning of its growth experience. Thus there is a vicious circle. In the absence of help in the form of technical assistance from the outside, this vicious circle can be broken only over a very long period of time. If some people can be sent abroad for training and experience, and if skilled managers, technicians, and teachers can be brought in from the outside, the process can be enormously accelerated. This is the role which technical assistance, public and private, in its broadest sense can play in the development process. And the rate at which human skills of all sorts can be expanded in turn sets a limit on the rate at which investment in physical capital can expand.

The second vicious circle has to do with the rate of this physical capital formation. As the skill limit is pushed back, jobs can be provided for the newly trained workers only as fast as the capital equipment with which they can work is expanded. If the country is to grow without outside help, it must devote a substantial fraction of its productive activity each year to the building of plant, equipment, machinery, and tools—that is, to capital formation. But, if a country is producing only enough to meet the bare subsistence needs of its population, it cannot divert resources from consumption to capital formation without risking disaster. Once it has begun to grow, it can decide to apply a large fraction of each year's increase in output to toolmaking, but the process of growth must be started first. When started, the rate of investment, if wholly dependent on domestic savings, will grow very slowly. Capital resources from the outside in the form of foreign aid can greatly speed up the process. If a high rate of growth can be maintained in this fashion over a reasonable period of years, and if as the country becomes richer it increases its rate of domestic saving and investment, it can, after a point, continue to grow without further outside help.

The third vicious circle relates to foreign exchange. Even if the country is rich enough to withhold from consumption an adequate fraction of its resources for investment, it will in the early stages be unable to produce within its own borders the range of capital goods which it requires. Some things it must buy from outside. It could expand imports without outside aid if only it could expand exports in payment. But the traditional exports of many underdeveloped countries, primarily raw materials, have reached ceilings that cannot easily be penetrated. These countries' best hope of expanded exports lies in moving into new fields of production in which they have formerly not been active. But to get into these new fields of exports itself requires greatly expanded imports of capital goods to get the new export industries established. Similarly, economizing on imports, making things at home that were formerly imported, requires an expansion of capital goods imports to establish the import-substituting industries. Thus, except for those few fortunate countries with resources of oil or some other raw material with unlimited foreign demand, most underdeveloped countries must run large balance-of-payments deficits for a period of years in order to get their development started.

One function of aid is to make possible an escape from all of these vicious circles. Again, it is necessary to bear in mind that aid does not ensure the escape but only makes it possible. The escape occurs only when the recipient country takes the necessary and sometimes very difficult steps to make the aid effective.

AID AND THE INCENTIVE TO GROW

Now we come to the incentive effects of aid programs. While virtually all underdeveloped country leaders talk a good development line, a real commitment to follow policies that will, in fact, promote effective development takes great political courage. It means taking unpopular measures to increase taxes and restrict consumption, to prevent luxury imports, to pursue austere monetary and fiscal policies, and to challenge the special interests of many groups that have considerable political power. There are ways for leaders to stay in power in the short run that look a good deal easier than mounting a really effective economic development program. It is easier, for example, to train a police force to keep the lid on dissent, or to focus the attention of the population on external adventure or fancied external threats to the national integrity. Yet there are, in almost all underdeveloped countries, some elements of leadership ready to devote themselves seriously to constructive economic development programs. A skillfully designed foreign aid program can provide powerful incentives for such leaders to do so.

If these incentive effects of aid programs, which are among

their most important potential effects, are to be effective, aid programs must have certain characteristics. In the first place, they must be big enough to have some chance of doing the job. In my view, it is very doubtful whether the present economic development aid program from the United States and all other sources can meet this test. Responsible estimates of the necessary increase in development aid budgets for this purpose range from 30 to 100 per cent. Note incidentally that, even were our own U.S. economic aid program to be doubled, it would still cost us less than 1 per cent of our Gross National Product. Second, aid programs must be singlemindedly based on criteria that reflect the objective of promoting the economic development of the recipient. Our current focus on this objective is much better than it once was, but we still have a considerable distance to go. In particular, we cannot use aid for short-run political purposes and still expect it to do the development job. Third, aid programs must have a time horizon not of one or two or even five years, but of a period long enough to hold out a prospect of seeing the aided country move into self-sustaining economic growth. The United States' aid program lamentably fails this test.

Finally, there must be much clearer public understanding in all the developed countries about the purposes and the requisite characteristics of development aid programs. Otherwise these programs cannot perform the long-term constructive purposes of which I believe them to be capable.

20 THE INDIVIDUAL AND THE CHANGING ECONOMY

Leonard S. Silk

This chapter tackles an elusive but critical issue: in all of the changes that take place in the American economy, how does the individual fare? We pride ourselves on elevating the individual to an exalted place little known through most of man's history—but is this pride still warranted? The balance struck here may be an optimistic one, but it has important cautions attached to it.

Thomas Jefferson, the leading philosopher of the American Revolution, thought that the way to ensure that the United States would remain a nation of free men was to keep the economy essentially agrarian. Freedom, he thought, would flourish amid the beauty of the countryside, on the open plains, in the vast river valleys. He feared the contaminating effects of building an urban and industrial society. "The mobs of great cities," said Jefferson, "are like sores on the human body." If Americans are "piled upon one another in large cities, as in Europe," he said, "they shall become corrupt, as in Europe."

This notion that individual freedom could flourish only in the country and the wilderness was widely held in Jefferson's day—and not only in America. The English poet William Blake asked:

Why should I care for the men of Thames
And the cheating waters of chartered streams
Or shrink at the little blasts of fear
That the hireling blows into mine ear?

Though born on the cheating banks of Thames—
Though his waters bathed my infant limbs—

The Ohio shall wash his stains from me;
I was born a slave, but I go to be free.

Today it might be pretty risky to bathe any infant's limbs in th Ohio. That stream is part of the widespread American problem o water pollution. And the factories along the Ohio add their shar to the American problem of air pollution. Along the Ohio an Mississippi, beside the Great Lakes, down the Atlantic and Pacifi coasts, even in the Lone Star State, one finds sprawling cities– sometimes called megalopolises—that dwarf the European citie of Jefferson's day.

And we have become a nation of employees—"hirelings," a Blake put it. When this nation was founded, more than fou fifths of the working people were independent farmers—and mo of the rest were independent tradesmen or handicraftsmen. To day more than four-fifths of the labor force are paid employees only 7 per cent are employed in agriculture and fewer still ar what might be called "independent farmers."

A number of private companies are as rich as small nation The 500 largest American industrial corporations, with assets o over $250 billion, employ more than 10 million people—three fifths of all those who work in manufacturing and mining. Ther are also great corporations in the fields of retailing, transporta tion, utilities, finance, even publishing. Fifty-five corporation have annual sales of more than $1 billion each.

Government—the feared enemy of freedom to liberals lik Jefferson—has also become a huge employer; today more than 1 million Americans work for federal, state, or local government Total government spending accounts for one-fifth of nationa output, and government's regulatory and other activities signif cantly affect a still larger share of business and individual behav ior.

Labor unions—almost unknown in Jefferson's day—today num ber more than 18 million members in their ranks. It is commonl said that this has become an organizational society.

How does the freedom of the individual fare in this land, now that the weight of big business, big labor, and big governmen has become so evident?

If Jefferson had been right in supposing that there was a vital nk between individual freedom and an individualistic agrarian onomy, then freedom would have long since vanished from this untry. My own view is that it has not—because the crucial link not between freedom and agriculture but between freedom and nation's legal and political institutions.

FREEDOM AND THE LAW OF PROPERTY

The authors of the U.S. Constitution looked upon one institu-ion as absolutely fundamental to individual freedom: the insti-ution of private property. (Curiously enough, the enemies of apitalism have looked upon private property exactly the other ay round; the Communists have declared that they would liber-te the working class from their capitalist oppressors by abolish-ng private property.)

The Founders of this country, at the Constitutional Conven-ion of 1787, saw private property as not so much one right, to be ecured like other rights of citizenship, but, rather, as the early ineteenth-century historian Richard Hildreth put it, as "the reat and chief right, of more importance than all others." This nay have been an overstatement. However, the Constitution did leclare, in one of its most famous clauses, that no person "shall be leprived of life, liberty, or property without due process of law," nd it clearly considered property to be a vital element in safe-uarding the individual against the state—or "the mob."

Private property was seen as the necessary material underpin-ning of the other precious freedoms of the individual—his free-lom of speech, of religion, of assembly, and of voluntary associ-tion with his friends.

To the authors of the Constitution liberty did not mean merely najority rule in political elections. More fundamentally, it meant ninority rights—individual rights—even when the individual vas in a minority of one.

For, if a man knew that he was secure in his property and could not be deprived of his means of livelihood so long as he broke no aw, then he could stand up to any man and to any officer of government. He could not be frightened or coerced into submission. That was the essence of individual freedom.

Property was therefore held to be a *natural* right, not requiring theoretical justification. The Supreme Court ultimately did justify property rights in terms of the doctrine of John Locke and Adam Smith that property derived from a man's own labor and so belonged to him and not to the state. (It is worth noting, once again, that the Communists turned this doctrine around, arguing that, since property belonged to those who labored to create it the working *class,* it was being expropriated by the capitalists. The Communists viewed production as the fruit of manual labor alone, not of capital or of the managerial or inventive or entrepreneurial activities of capitalists—a notion that for a long time played hob with Communist economic planning and resource allocation.)

Although the specific meaning of property rights is complex and has undergone important modifications over time, as Professor A. A. Berle has stressed, it seems to me that the belief of the authors of the Constitution that property rights are essential to individual freedom has far from lost its validity. This is made perfectly clear by the actual experience of Communist societies regardless of the propositions of Communist theory.

The right to own property is basic to the operation of private businesses. And individual freedom can survive only if the individual has alternative private means of gaining a livelihood even if he incurs the disfavor of the state—that is, of the bureaucracy that controls the state. If one sympathizes with Blake in disliking "the little blasts of fear that the hireling blows into mine ear," how much more one should loathe the mighty blasts of fear that the dictatorship of a monolithic state can blow!

Property rights are thus important to safeguard the freedom even of individuals who own little property themselves. For a man's ability to change his job if he incurs the displeasure of his employer (or if the employer incurs his employee's displeasure) is essential to the individual's independence and honesty.

THE RIGHTS OF THE INDIVIDUAL

If individuals are to be free, it is crucial that they be protected from being spied upon or invaded by any agency of the state without due process of law. The Bill of Rights, in Article IV, proclaims the rights of individuals "to be secure in their persons, houses, papers, and effects, against unreasonable searches and seizures." The mark of a society that deprives the individual of his freedom is its secret police and its informers, spying on the "citizens" or breaking down their doors in the middle of the night.

Most important of all to the defense of individual freedom may well be the writ of habeas corpus—which requires a court to test the legality of any form of detention, whether by the military, the police, the warden of a prison, the head of a mental institution, one's own parents, or anyone else who wishes to restrain the freedom of another person. The writ of habeas corpus, as Winston Churchill once observed, is the true distinguishing feature of free societies, and its absence is the true test of the presence of tyranny.

But individual freedom is not simply a negative thing, a denial to the state or to any force within the state of the power to interfere with the person or property of the individual. If freedom is to have positive content—a deep spiritual and creative content—it must imply the existence of a will to search for the truth and to express what one finds or believes.

It is particularly important that a nation's writers and artists and scholars and scientists do their work with dedication and complete integrity. It is similarly important that the intellectual, cultural, and religious institutions of the nation be protected from arbitrary governmental interference—and from the pressures of any group within the society, including political or vigilante groups.

Indeed, this country, like every other, faces grave and continuous problems in preserving free institutions. In my view, the growth in the role of government also poses certain problems and risks for individual freedom, and I think it would be foolish to pretend otherwise.

THE HAND OF GOVERNMENT

Many Americans worry about various aspects of governmen interference. Some see our growing federal support for educatio and research as a threat to the independence of the scholar an the researcher. Farm programs are seen by some as inhibiting th rights of the individual farmer. Welfare programs are condemne by some as destructive of individual initiative.

In fact, we might make a long list of the charges that our citi zens make against the alleged encroachments upon individua freedom of government units, federal, state, and local, such a taxation of various types ("the power to tax is the power to de stroy"), the military draft (some youths now burn their draf cards), invasions of privacy by investigatory agencies, zoning reg ulations, loyalty oaths, licensing laws (that deny individual entry to particular occupations), interference with the mails, wire tapping, and so on. The list is so long that I cannot name all th items here, let alone document each of the charges and attempt t pass judgment on their validity.

Some encroachments on individual freedom are the conse quence of hot wars and cold wars and of the fears they stir u over our national security. Others are a consequence of the diff culties of keeping a crowded industrial society operational—an preventing one man's exercise of freedom from reducing an other's freedom. A century ago John Stuart Mill said, "The onl freedom which deserves the name is that of pursuing our ow good in our own way, so long as we do not attempt to depriv others of theirs." But his "so long" clause has become more an more of an obstruction as economic development has proceede

For our urban and industrial society, the complexity and inte dependence of individual freedoms was stated by Presiden Woodrow Wilson in this way:

> I have long had an image in my mind of what constitutes li erty. Suppose that I were building a great piece of powerfu machinery, and suppose that I should so awkwardly and u skilfully assemble the parts of it that every time one part trie

> to move it would be interfered with by the others, and the whole thing would be buckled up and be checked. Liberty for the several parts would consist in the best possible assembling and adjustment of them all, would it not? If you want the great piston of the engine to run with absolute freedom, give it absolutely perfect alignment and adjustment with the other parts of the machine, so that it is free not because it is let alone or isolated, but because it has been associated most skilfully and carefully with the other parts of the great structure. . . . Human freedom consists in perfect adjustments of human interests and human activities and human energies.

We are continually searching for new institutional arrangeents that will permit our society to grow and function efficiently -and still preserve the freedom of the individual. As the philosoher John Dewey observed, the United States "has steadily loved from an earlier pioneer individualism to a condition of ominant corporateness." But, while Dewey thought that the lder individualism was "bankrupt," he felt that those who were ware of the breakdown were making a serious mistake in supposig that individualism itself was over and done with.

Yet it is far from sure that we know how to deal with the new roblems that our very success as a nation has created. For inance, economic and industrial growth has created serious urban roblems. All those who know American cities will share Jefferon's fear that "the mobs of great cities" might become corrupt. rime is a real problem in our cities. So is misery, loneliness, povty. And—in both our cities and rural districts—economic rowth has in some sense aggravated the unhappiness of the poor, ose left behind in the growth race, and increased their distance om those able to move ahead.

CULTURE IN A CHANGING ECONOMY

We worry a lot in America about our cultural condition. Many servers of the American scene fear that our massive corporaons, branded products, standardized goods, mass communications edia are turning the typical American into an "organization man," a timid nonentity, a processed and programmed Consume or Employee. They see the individual American as the victim nc merely of the organization in which he is involved but, eve worse, as the product of a mass culture and a technology that in hibit his choices, actions, tastes, opinions, values. They conside the symbol of this cultural tyranny to be the enormous supe market, standing bleak and alone near the suburbs, surrounde by parking lots—and within it, the tons of packaged goods, pile row on row, patrolled by the Consumers pushing their wire cart. American artists—pop artists—are the revolutionaries who toda are most sharply attacking this packaged and processed cultur

Other observers see the arch symbol of the new cultural ty anny and depravity as the television set—the "idiot tube"—b fore which much of the nation sprawls for hours every day.

It is easy enough to say that such concerns are those of th intellectuals, who have never had any use for popular cultur anyway. And of course it is true that Americans who go to supe markets or watch stupid television programs do so voluntarily; n one has forced them. They have the freedom to shop in smal stores if they don't like bargains. They have the freedom to wal to work, to buy what they want, to live where they please. I ar afraid that this is too easy a dismissal of the problem. For the fac is that technological and economic change does frequently seer to engulf the individual and affect his entire life. Practicall speaking, one cannot choose to walk to work through a tunne crowded with cars and trucks; one can only choose whether t ride in one's car or in a bus. One can no longer solve all of one' cultural or esthetic or social or economic problems by dependin on oneself; one is necessarily involved in social choices and socia actions, and the task of furthering individual freedom is mor difficult than once it was.

FREEDOM PAST AND PRESENT

This is not to say that the past was necessarily better than th present—certainly not in all respects—or that we make no prog ress. For instance, this country's Constitution made one terribl mission: despite its magnificent defense of individual rights and iberties, it tacitly accepted slavery. It took the holocaust of Civil Var to free the Negro slaves—and change the Constitution. After hat war, during the Reconstruction, Negroes were again denied qual citizenship rights in many states, whether by state laws or y discriminatory practices that the laws—and the law enforcenent officers—did not prevent.

It has since taken new legislation, new interpretations of the Constitution, and new actions by federal officers to extend the ights of citizenship to all our people, regardless of race. We are till far from having achieved that goal. It is significant, however, hat the struggle to secure those rights for all Americans finds our overnment and our Supreme Court a prime mover for change—ommitted to the expansion of individual freedom—rather than reactionary force. We are using government to expand freedom, ot infringe it.

In declaring the intention of our people to "secure the Blessings f Liberty to ourselves and our posterity," the Constitution proided the means for making changes in our political system and n our economy. The efforts to achieve our fundamental objecives—a more perfect union, justice, tranquillity, national deense, welfare, and liberty—have involved the American people n a continuous process of change, experiment, and trial—with nany failures along the way. But we mean to go on.

21 THE ECONOMICS PROFESSION TODAY

Harold F. Williamson

The economists have had their say, both in this book an elsewhere. But who are these people? What do they do? An what difference do they make in the American scene toda This article looks at some of the statistics and some of th activities of a profession increasingly in the news.

As earlier chapters in this book have shown, there is currentl widespread and active interest in economics in the United State This concern by Americans with economic problems is, howeve by no means new. It was evidenced, for example, during th eighteenth century in discussions over the influence of the Britis Navigation Acts on the economic well-being of the British colo nies in North America. It was revealed after the American Revo lution in certain provisions of the Constitution adopted by th newly independent nation and in the controversy generated b Alexander Hamilton's suggestion for the establishment of a stabl monetary system and his recommendations for the adoption o governmental policies designed to encourage the growth of indus try and commerce. Throughout succeeding decades a continuin interest in economics and economic problems was reflected in de bates over such issues as taxation, monetary and tariff policies governmental aid for internal improvements, and public contro of private business.

Until late in the nineteenth century, however, economics wa not recognized as a separate academic discipline in the Unite States and its practitioners were frequently individuals withou formal training in the subject. It is true that the discussion o conomic issues was influenced by the writings of such British conomists as Adam Smith, Thomas Malthus, and David Ri-ardo. Yet the approach of individuals most influential in affect-ıg economic policies was essentially pragmatic, not theoretical. 'heir chief interest was to resolve questions of immediate and ractical concern to business, industry, commerce, and agricul-ıre.

The emergence of economics both as a separate academic disci-line and as a profession in the United States began during the 880's when an increasing number of American scholars, most of ıem trained at German universities, were appointed to the facul-ies of American universities and colleges. By 1885 there was suffi-ient interest among members of this group to organize a profes-ional society, The American Economic Association, which a year ıter had a total membership of 182. From this modest beginning ıe number of individuals specializing in the subject continued to row, with the result that, at the present time, economics ranks mong the leading scientific professions in the United States.

WHO ARE THE ECONOMISTS?

The following comments on the nature and current status of ıe profession will be directed toward answering such questions s who are the members of the profession, what is their number, 'hat do they do, how do they make their influence felt, and how re future members being trained.

Actually it is quite difficult to provide any very accurate an-wers to the first two questions. This is largely because of the roblem of identifying those persons who, on the basis of their raining and experience, should be included as members of the conomics profession. To be sure, it is generally assumed that to chieve professional status as an economist, an individual must emonstrate his understanding of an accepted body of economic ıeory or principles and how they can be applied to explain and nalyze economic phenomena. It is also generally assumed that ıese standards have been met by everyone who has completed a ırmal educational program in the field at the graduate level. No one, for example, is likely to question seriously the professiona competence of individuals who hold a master's or doctoral degre in economics from an accredited university. This likewise tends t be true of those who have passed examinations in economics re quired of candidates for certain positions in government or whos responsibilities in government or business obviously require high degree of professional competence.

These tests or measures of professional competence, howeve are not uniform nor are they universally applied. It is true tha colleges and universities generally require the members of thei economics faculties to hold a Master's or a Ph.D. degree in th subject and that these same standards are frequently applied t candidates for certain positions in government as well as in pr vate industry and research organizations. Yet economists, unlik lawyers and doctors in the United States, do not have to obtain license to practice their profession. Nor do associations of econo mists attempt to certify the professional competence of thei members. The oldest and largest professional organization, Th American Economic Association, with an enrollment of mor than 14,000 individuals, requires simply that its members be in terested in encouraging economic research and the publication o articles and books on economic subjects. As a result, there ar many individuals employed as economists by business, govern ment, and even by educational institutions who, in terms of thei training or experience, should not be identified as professiona economists.

This problem of professional identification is illustrated by th wide divergence between the results of two recent surveys whic attempted to measure the number of economists in the Unite States. The first of these was made in 1960 by the United State Bureau of the Census. In that year, according to the results of th survey, there were 22,424 economists in what was described a "the experienced labor force in the United States." The secon estimate, based on a Survey of Scientific Personnel in the Unite States made four years later, put the number of economists in th U.S. in 1964 at 12,143.

This difference of more than 10,000 between the two estimate was not the result of any decline in the membership of the profe ion between 1960 and 1964. Rather it is explainable by the differences in the purposes of the two surveys and the criteria used by each to identify economists. The Census survey, for example, was designed to classify the entire United States labor force according to a standardized list of some 297 occupational titles. Anyone whose work activity fitted an occupation with an economics title was therefore identified an economist. No minimum standards of economic education, extent of experience, proficiency, or attachment to the profession were used to refine the brief and sometimes inflated job titles initially supplied by individuals to Census enumerators.

By contrast, the major purpose of the Survey of Scientific Personnel was to develop a National Register of Scientific Personnel by locating and identifying experts in a number of scientific fields. To be included in the Register as an economist, individuals had to meet three qualifications: first, they had to be actively associated with a professional association of economists; second, they had to have either a Master's or a Ph.D. degree in the field, or its equivalent in terms of professional experience; finally, they had to designate a special subject in economics as their field of greatest professional competence.

The standards used by the Survey of Scientific Personnel quite obviously provided a more accurate measure of professional competence than those used by the Bureau of the Census. Even allowing for the fact that a number of eligible candidates were excluded from the Register of Scientific Personnel, a reasonable estimate would suggest that there are currently between 12,000 and 13,000 professionally qualified economists in the United States.

An analysis of the data available on economists who were included in the Register of Scientific Personnel makes it possible to indicate certain of the more important characteristics of the profession. It is noteworthy, for example, that of the 12,143 economists in the Register, approximately 42 per cent held Ph.D. degrees and 35 per cent held Master's degrees, while the remaining 23 per cent, almost all with Bachelor degrees, qualified for inclusion on the basis of their professional experience.

An additional measure of the professional competence of the

individuals included in the Register is revealed by the fact tha they had on the average some 14.5 years of professional exper ence. A more detailed analysis shows that only 16 per cent of th group had less than five years' experience, about 51 per cent ha from 5 to 19 years' experience, while nearly 33 per cent had mor than 20 years' experience.

The principal demographic characteristics of the profession ar indicated by data on the age distribution of the group. Thes show that approximately 10 per cent were between 20 and 2 years old, 63 per cent were in the 30-to-49-year age group, whil the remaining 26 per cent were 50 years of age or older. It may b of further interest to note that of the economists included in th Register there were only 483 women, or about 4 per cent of th total.

The special subjects designated as their fields of greatest profe sional competence give some idea of the various areas of partic lar interest to members of the profession. These included ec nomic theory, economic history and the history of economi thought, economic systems, economic planning and developmen econometrics and economic statistics, international economic business administration, financial marketing and accounting, i dustrial organization and governmental control, land and agr cultural economics, labor economics, and population and welfar economics.

WHAT DO ECONOMISTS DO?

Another important characteristic of the profession is indicate by the distribution of economists included in the Register by typ of employer. In 1964 approximately 45 per cent worked for ed cational institutions, 35 per cent for private industry and bus ness, 11 per cent for the federal government, 4 per cent for no profit organizations, 2.5 per cent for state and local government while just under 2 per cent were self-employed.

The type of work economists do is to a very considerable exter conditioned by the nature of their employment. As might be e pected, those working for educational institutions devote a sul antial portion of their time to teaching. The great majority f college and university faculty members, however, also engage 1 other activities, including research, writing, lecturing to non-cademic audiences, appearing as expert witnesses in court cases r before government committees, and serving as consultants. On 1e other hand, most economists employed by the government are pecialists in fields such as agriculture, labor, business, interna-ional trade, development, and fiscal economics. They may plan nd carry out studies involving the collection of basic data in hese fields, use these data and other information to analyze the eed for changes in government policy, assess the economic condi-ions of the nation, write reports on their findings, and some-mes present these reports before policy-making bodies. Others re employed by the government as statisticians, foreign affairs pecialists, intelligence specialists, and in administrative and ther positions where a background and training in economics re important.

Economists who work for large business firms, including banks nd other financial institutions, are chiefly engaged in research, lthough in many cases they may also have some administrative nd consultative duties. They typically concentrate on problems elating to domestic business conditions, markets and prices of ompany products, government policies affecting business, or in-rnational trade. Their main function is to provide management ith information to be used in making decisions on problems such s the timing of new financing or the advisability of expanding 1e company's business by adding new lines of merchandise or rvices, or by opening branch plants in new areas.

Nonprofit organizations, such as research and development ompanies and research bureaus, commonly hire economists who re specialists in economic analysis and statistics. Other nonprofit rganizations, including foundations interested in the promotion f economic research and plans for economic development, fre-uently employ economic specialists to serve as consultants, or, in ome instances, to administer projects which the foundation is ponsoring or financing. A number of self-employed economists perate their own business concerns; others, probably the ajority, serve as consultants to business firms and governmental gencies.

HOW DO ECONOMISTS MAKE THEIR INFLUENCE FELT

The foregoing description of what economists do suggests th various ways they may make their influence felt on the econom both directly and indirectly. As researchers, for example, they i vestigate the basic problems in economic analysis and formula new ideas and theories to explain the operation of the econom As authors of articles, monographs, and textbooks, or as speake before public audiences, they make the results of their own r search, or that of others, available to a wider audience and ther by contribute to a better understanding of the subject. As co sultants or staff members, they analyze economic problems particular interest to their employers or clients. As teachers, the provide undergraduate students with a knowledge of how th economy functions and with some basis for evaluating policy d cisions that citizens in a democracy are frequently called on make; at the graduate level of instruction they give the specialize training needed for future members of the profession.

All indications point to the fact that the number of economis engaged in these various activities has grown sharply in recer decades. Departments of economics in colleges and universiti have been enlarged, the enrollment of students in econom courses has expanded, new professional societies have been orga ized, funds available for research in the field are more abundan and publications on economic subjects have multiplied.

Insofar as economists are engaged in research, writing, an teaching, however, their influence or impact on the econom tends to be slow and indirect. A better indication of how the direct influence has grown is suggested by the increase in th number of economists employed by government and busine since about 1930—not that prior to that date there were no men bers of the profession working for government and business, b the number so employed was relatively small. This situatio started to change after 1930, when the federal government bega hiring economists to administer and staff the various agencies e tablished under the Roosevelt administration in an attempt t ring about economic recovery. Government economists con-nued to play an important role in mobilizing and directing the se of the nation's manpower and other resources during World Var II. Despite a decline in their numbers immediately after 945, by 1964 approximately one out of every eight members of he profession was a full-time government employee. The most triking development since 1945, however, has been the growing restige of economists in economic policy formation.

Illustrative of this trend was the passage by Congress of the mployment Act of 1946. This legislation, designed to "promote he maximum employment, production, and purchasing power" f the American economy, provided for the appointment of a ouncil of Economic Advisers to assist the President of the Jnited States in implementing the objectives of the Act. The dis-inguished members of the profession who have served on the resident's Council of Economic Advisers have played a key role n the formation of economic policies adopted by the federal gov-rnment. Professional economists currently holding other impor-ant governmental positions include the Director of the Budget, he Under Secretary of the Treasury for Monetary Affairs, the Jnder Secretaries of Agriculture and of Health, Education and Velfare, four members of the Board of Governors of the Federal Reserve System, and several presidents of the Federal Reserve anks.

Meanwhile, the problems encountered in carrying on their perations during World War II and the postwar years prompted usiness and industry to employ economists at an even faster rate han the government. Thus, in 1964, as was also noted earlier, early one-third of the profession was employed by private busi-ess or industrial concerns.

Much of the prestige currently accorded to economists in policy ormation is a reflection of the fact that economics, as a discipline, as developed a set of theories or principles which have proved ighly effective in analyzing and explaining an impressive range f economic phenomena. Moreover, it is a basic part of the train-ng of professional economists to make a systematic evaluation of lternative solutions to particular problems. Their most distinc-ive contribution to policy formation, however, results from a specialized ability to analyze fully the costs and advantages alternative courses of action and, as far as possible, to reduce th net advantages involved to reasonably quantitative terms.

The advantages to policy-makers of having a measure of th costs and advantages of alternative possibilities of achieving particular goal are obvious, be it a choice between generatin electricity by steam or water power, a decision whether or not subsidize public education, or the advisability of changing an ex isting marketing system.

Yet the influence that economists working for government c business have on the formation of policies affecting the America economy should not be exaggerated. Economic principles, lik those of any scientific discipline, hold true only under certai conditions, while not all questions involving policy decisions ca be reduced to quantitative terms. Thus the influence of econo mists on policy decisions tends to be limited or modified whe conditions affecting the economy change or by the extent which it is difficult or impossible to measure precisely such que tions as the costs and benefits of government-supported educa tion, the value of jobs that might result from a cut in taxes, or th net advantages to be gained from the choice of a particular ma keting system. Moreover, not all decisions affecting the econom are made as the result of comparing the relative net cost advan tages involved, even when the latter can be measured.

Finally it should be noted that responsibility for the policy de cisions affecting the American economy is not centralized but widely dispersed, among numerous federal, state, and local gov ernmental agencies as well as among an even greater number c private business and industrial concerns. Not only do these var ous decision-making groups tend to differ in their immediate c long-run policy objectives, but it is not uncommon for the obje tives of one group to be inconsistent with those of another. Fc example, the desire of certain American businessmen to increas their investments outside the United States may run counter t the objective of the United States Treasury of achieving a favo able balance of payments. A government program designed t promote full employment at the risk of inflation may be una ceptable to a Federal Reserve Board committed to maintaining stable price level.

Thus even when economists can quantify the results of their nalysis, their influence on the policies actually adapted may vary ecause of different strategic, welfare, or political considerations : primary interest to their employers or clients.

THE DEMAND AND SUPPLY OF ECONOMISTS

Whatever the limitations on the extent of their direct and inirect influence, all signs indicate that the demand for trained :onomists by government and business as well as by educational nd research institutions in the United States will continue to row.

A small portion of this demand will continue to be filled by idividuals who acquire professional status through their experince and training on the job. The great bulk of future econoists, however, are enrolled as students at one of the 120 or more merican universities which offer graduate programs in econom-s or agricultural economists. To be admitted as candidates for raduate degrees at these universities, students must have at least Bachelor's degree or its equivalent and have achieved a much etter than average grade record for the courses taken as undergraduates. They may also be required to take an examination hich tests their ability to verbalize and think in quantitative rms and in some instances to pass an additional examination hich tests their understanding of economics as a discipline. To n increasing extent, departments emphasize the importance of aining in mathematics, especially for students who plan to do nore advanced work.

The general purpose of these various requirements is to make ire that students are prepared to undertake professional training in the field. At the core of most graduate programs are courses n economic theory, on the assumption that to be an economist a udent must first master a set of abstract principles which make p the basic tools of economic analysis. Equally important, he nust demonstrate his ability to use economic theory and statistial techniques in analyzing economic data. Indeed, training as a pecialist in any of the subfields of economics, such as agricultural conomics, public finance, development, international trade, and the like essentially involves experience in applying econom analysis to specific problem areas.

The types of graduate instruction designed to meet these educational objectives consist principally of lectures, seminars, an research guidance. During the early years of graduate study, fo example, students are typically enrolled in classes which they ar expected to attend and in which they will take examinations. A a more advanced level they frequently meet in smaller groups o in seminars where they prepare papers and participate actively i discussion. At the dissertation or thesis stage of their training the work closely with individual faculty members who advise an guide them in their research.

The amount of time spent in graduate study is closely relate to whether a student elects to work for a Master's or a Ph.D degree. Programs leading to the Master's degree ordinarily tak from one to two years to complete. As a minimum requiremen candidates are expected to maintain a satisfactory grade record i their courses and, in most instances, to prepare a thesis. Program leading to the Ph.D. degree typically require three to five years t complete. As in the case of the Master's degree, Ph.D. candidate must maintain a satisfactory grade record in their courses. In addition, they are expected to pass an oral or written examinatio covering economic theory and certain special subjects, and to prepare a dissertation based on an original piece of research.

The amount of time involved as well as the subjects covere and the method of instruction used suggest the professiona standards that students who receive advanced degrees in economics are expected to meet. In brief, it is assumed that as a result of their training they will have learned to think analyticall and independently, be able to express their ideas clearly, both verbally and in writing, and demonstrate a capacity to do research.

The extent of graduate training in economics in the Unite States is suggested by data for the academic year 1962–1963, whe there were just over 6,400 students enrolled as candidates fo advanced degrees in the field. Because of the time involved i training and because students for various personal, financial, o academic reasons may decide not to continue their studies, th umber of candidates who complete their degrees each year is nly a fraction of the total enrollment of graduate students. Of ,400 registered in 1962–1963, for example, well over half were rst-year students while a substantial proportion of the others vere still taking courses or preparing theses or dissertations. Thus, neasured by the number of graduate degrees actually awarded, he new members added to the profession in 1964 totaled close to ,300. Of this number approximately two-thirds were Master's de-rees and one-third Ph.D. degrees.

As has already been noted, there is nothing in the foreseeable uture to indicate any lack of job opportunities for both new and ld members of the profession. There is also no reason to assume hat the problems that economists will be called on to analyze nd explain will be any less challenging and complex in the fu-ure than they have been in the past. Under these circumstances here is every reason to expect that economics will continue to be ated among the leading scientific professions in the United States.

22 AN ECONOMY STILL ON TRIAL

John R. Coleman

The book concludes with a picking up of loose ends, a sweep ing view of what has gone before, and a hunch that the bes for the American economy is yet to come.

There is a popular American game called "Twenty Questions" i which the interrogator, seeking to uncover some secret, is allowe to pose only those questions that can be answered "yes" or "no." Economists, in their professional lives, could seldom play such game: just about every question that interests them has an answe requiring far more than one word. And few have the patience— or the self-discipline—to answer as many as twenty questions i one half-hour. So I propose, in this the final essay of this book, t play an American economist's version of the game. We'll call i "Ten Questions That Might Be Asked about the American Econ omy and That Cannot Be Answered 'Yes' or 'No' by Its Econo mists."

The questions, I assume, are ones that many non-American might ask about this society. The answers, I hope, are ones tha many American economists might give. But the latter is a hop only. Twenty economists have appeared in this book; they hav twenty (at least) sets of views on the society in which they liv and work. So they are more likely to agree on the worth of th questions and the free-speech rights of the answerer than on th way the answers are worded.

QUESTION: *Let's start with labels. You American economists seem to avoid the issue of what to call your system. Can' you give us a straightforward term for it?*

ANSWER: The charge is a fair one. We've become somewhat defensive about that old favorite "capitalism," and we're unimpressed with the proposal that "people's capitalism" would be better. "Free enterprise" is too simple a term any more, and so is "market economy." "Mixed free enterprise" isn't the kind of term for which one stands up to cheer, but it is perhaps better than any other that has yet been proposed.

There's a temptation to want to dismiss your question and say that labels don't really matter, that it's what is inside the container that really matters. But then we live by labels to some extent. We need shorthand ways of describing complex phenomena. The labels mislead us only when we forget that they do represent shorthand and that they sum up a whole bundle of characteristics, not all of which are neatly compatible with one another.

When we use the shorthand—and not very esthetic—term "mixed free enterprise," we are trying to say something like the following: on any spectrum which arranges the world's economies from free-market-dominated at, say, the left end, to central-government-controlled at the right, the American economy is closer to the free-market end than just about any other economy. That statement doesn't assert that we're making all our decisions through free markets; it doesn't rule out the fact that, on some very specific issues, we might turn out to be further toward the right end of the spectrum than some of the other leading industrial nations; and it doesn't deny constant movement along the spectrum.

So the statement isn't a very precise one. And it resists neat filing of the world's economies into boxes marked simply "capitalism," "socialism," and "communism." But the changing economy we've looked at in these chapters needs something more than a catchy one-word label.

QUESTION: *Your case of the spectrum device reminds me that a Russian economist, Sergei Dalin, has recently written that the free-enterprise economies of the West are slowly transforming themselves into socialism. He spoke of gigantic socialization of production and of capital's ownership in the United States in particular. On the other hand, I've heard some of your econo-*

mists assert that the Communist countries are moving toward capitalism. Without getting us into the label question again, would you say that East and West are going to meet on that spectrum?

ANSWER: It's hard to deny that, in recent years, the American and the Russian economies have come to look more alike in some respects. And this isn't surprising: they're both advanced industrial powers facing some of the same economic issues. Both are oriented toward rapid growth, and the first keys to that growth—better-educated manpower and more capital equipment—apply to them both. They're equally concerned about adjusting to some new international trade patterns. They're both tackling bigger projects—the space race is an example—than man has ever tackled. If the Americans are learning that vast undertakings require more centralizing of decisions than they have been used to in the past, the Russians are learning that vast undertakings cannot be directed wholly from the center. So in this sense there is a movement toward one another on the spectrum.

But that movement shouldn't be the excuse for ignoring the big differences that still persist; the spectrum is a wide one after all, and nations could move toward one another for decades and still be far apart. True, the consumer plays a bigger part in the U.S.S.R. today than he did a decade ago, yet his role is much less than that of the American consumer in deciding what goods are going to be produced. The individual Russian counts for more today than he did under Stalin—or under the Czars, for that matter—yet his freedom remains relatively restricted in comparison with the American's. What freedom? Let one example suffice: the freedom to criticize the way the economy is organized.

With all of the growing similarities, the two nations are unlikely to converge completely in their economic systems within the next decade or two. And after that? Even then it would be surprising if two economies with such different histories, cultures, and resources should ever become indistinguishable. It is a safer bet that the differences will diminish but not disappear as each country follows its own course in pursuit of its own goals. Certainly they don't have to look alike to live together: the facts of military power alone should be enough to persuade us to accept alternative economic systems side by side.

QUESTION: *Turn away now from the U.S.S.R. to the underdeveloped countries. Is the American economic system exportable to them?*

ANSWER: There have been and still are Americans who would give an unqualified "Yes" to that. The fact that the United States has the highest standard of living yet known to man has led some here to say to others, "Go and do thou likewise." But their numbers are small and include only a handful of economists at best. Let there be no mistake about the pride that most Americans have in their own system. We might wish that more of the world saw things our way, but two decades of foreign aid assistance have been enough to deepen our sophistication about the world in which we live. For the most part, we're moving past naïveté and into an awareness that other men are as anxious to choose their own economic paths as we were to choose ours. We're learning the hard lesson that there will be as many paths chosen as there are nations—and we suspect that the Communist nations will learn this too. For just as mixed free enterprise of the American type is unlikely to be the wave of the future for all men, so too, communism is unlikely to be identical from one country to another and is still less likely to appeal to all men.

But to say that most Americans don't expect to export their economic system *in toto* to the rest of the world does not mean that we accept the proposition that we have nothing to offer. On the contrary, there are lessons to be learned from the American experience which, with modifications, can be applied elsewhere. The pursuit of self-interest as a guiding principle for an economy didn't originate with Americans, but it got its biggest push here. That principle has had some harsh overtones, as we have seen; yet men can soften those overtones in their own distinctive ways and still draw most of the driving power from the principle. And there are things to be learned too about pricing systems as allocators of resources. These lessons transcend cultures and times; they are not absolute, but they fit a wide variety of circumstances under which men may try to use their limited resources for maximum progress toward their unlimited goals.

In sum, it's a rare American who expects imitation of this economy in vastly different parts of the world, and yet it's a common —and committed—American who hopes that two centuries of experimenting here with qualified economic freedom will be wort studying elsewhere.

QUESTION: *Let's get back to the American scene. Throughout a of these essays I've noticed a strong concern with th role of the government in the economy. Is that th biggest single issue in the United States economy t day?*

ANSWER: Here we probably ought to give a straight "Yes" answe Certainly the economic stories on the front pages of the new papers in 1966 echo the theme of the critical role of governmer in an essentially private-enterprise society. The biggest nev items concern government's role in heading off inflationar threats in an extraordinarily prosperous year, the federal an local wars on poverty, and the financial crises of more and mor local governmental units faced with bigger demands for service and smaller tax bases to pay for them. We are still quite unce tain as to what and how much government should do.

Today this issue plagues liberals as well as conservatives. Tim was when a fairly sharp line could be drawn between the tw groups, with the expansionists (liberals) on the one side and th contractionists (conservatives) on the other. The line is fuzzie today. Some liberals are less certain that government represents panacea in, say, the anti-poverty campaign and more aware tha private instruments must work in close alliance to achieve desire social ends. Some conservatives are ready now to give governmen certain roles that were more controversial in days gone by; educa tion and the fight against inflation are examples.

But let me add one qualification so that a simple "Yes" doe not ruin the economists' record for "Yes, but—" answers. Whil government's role in the economy is the most debated issue today it doesn't obscure the fact that most economic decisions are sti private decisions. Increasingly tinged with governmental ove tones, yes; but private for all that. And that is the way mos Americans seem to want to keep things. They want a privat economy as the main arbiter of what, how, and for whom good are produced, but they want government to bolster, supplemen and sometimes soften market effects.

There is no doubt about our moving into a very complex time: the survival of most of what we valued in that private society could be threatened by thoughtless, unexamined, and naïve expansion of government. The world will do well to watch us closely to see if we are successful in finding ways to use more government to help us without being engulfed in the process.

QUESTION: *That question on government leads naturally to the next one. Apart from the cant of the Marxists, the most common charge against the American economy has been that it was unstable. Have you licked the problem of depressions yet?*

ANSWER: There's a temptation again to say "Yes" flatly. But I'll resist it by saying that we have licked depressions *if* we have the political good sense to use the economic knowledge now at our disposal. We don't need to—and cannot honestly—argue that our knowledge about recurring cycles in the market economy is anywhere near complete; yet we know enough today, in contrast to what we knew in the 1930's, to say that any future depression would have to be ascribed to political pussyfooting rather than to economic ignorance. Note that these are depressions we're talking about, not minor recessions. We're not yet smart enough—or willing enough—to sacrifice our prized decentralization, to make all recessions a thing of the past.

The political signs are generally optimistic ones on the question of using our know-how to combat depressions if they should loom. Both major political parties are committed to the use of fiscal and monetary powers to achieve reasonable economic stability. One party may be a little faster than the other to see signs of growing unemployment, and the other to see signs of threatened inflation, but these are matters of degree only. Since the stabilizing tax cut of 1964, Congress warrants higher marks for its translation of economic good sense into political profit than it could have earned before. The next—and harder—test will be its handling of the inflationary threats of the future.

QUESTION: *Another charge you often hear is that your economy is a highly materialistic one, that it sacrifices most hu-*

man values other than the wealth and the physic comfort of all but its poorest people. What do you sa to that?

ANSWER: This is one charge which I just don't understand, citizen or as economist. The other side of the charge is, I suppos that some poorer nations are much more concerned with the spi itual than we are. Maybe the late classicist, Edith Hamilton, wa right in suggesting that poor people throughout all ages of histor and places on earth have found some escape from their misery i a mysticism which made this life illusion and only the next on real. In that sense, there's more spiritualism in some places tha one finds in American economic life.

But the goals with which this economy has been concerned— competitive, consumer-oriented economy, stability in emplo ment and prices, a high rate of economic growth, an equitabl income distribution, and an environment of freedom—are mix tures of the material and the spiritual. For some men, the mate rial goods are the ends in themselves. For many others, they ar the means of achieving other goals in self-fulfillment, includin the goal of helping others to achieve their fullest growth. In othe words, there is no necessary incompatibility between living hig in the material sense and living high in the moral or spiritua sense. If the economist doesn't make this point often enough, it i probably because he feels himself beyond his professional limits not because he questions its validity.

Let me offer just one example of the quality of humanity o humaneness built into large parts of the American economy. Th war on poverty with which we are now struggling, ineptly per haps but sincerely, is one that has caught many people's imag ination. We simply do not accept any longer the idea that fre markets by themselves—or even private charity by itself—will pro duce the best of all income distributions. We want these market to do most of the allocating of incomes, but now we're looking fo more satisfactory ways to see that no one is closed out by thes markets from buying a decent share of goods and services. Som say we're moving too slowly on the poverty issue; I agree, but th speed will increase as we learn more about which economic poli cies will make a lasting difference.

QUESTION: *Let me turn that one around on you. Can your economy practice that humaneness and still preserve the hard, driving character that has given it so much past success?*

ANSWER: If by "hard, driving character" you mean that everyone stands on his own feet, then of course we can't preserve that quality and collectively help the poor at the same time. But if your term means preserving the best of the incentive society, then the answer is that we are trying to do just that. Most of the anti-poverty campaign is designed to increase the capacity of the poor to support themselves through income-earning activities. This is certainly in our self-interest—and we think it is in theirs. There will always be some who because of one affliction or another cannot support themselves; the aim must be to reduce that number to the minimum possible.

You know, there is a lot said about how programs to increase economic security will inevitably erode the drive of many, many workers. Well, we have more public and private economic security today than we ever had before; yet I cannot see that general productivity is suffering thereby. Exceptions don't destroy the fact that, for the society as a whole, prosperity, productivity, and security all advanced hand-in-hand in recent years. In this American context at least, where hard work has had an honorable history, most economists believe that we have been able to avoid some of the painful choices between more incentive and more basic security.

QUESTION: *I've noticed that you qualify many of your statements by saying "most economists." Why can't American economists agree on these matters?*

ANSWER: We do of course have a wide spectrum of views on any policy issue. You haven't heard the extremes in this series; some economists will deride the whole bundle of policy views of these twenty economists as being too tame and old-fashioned, and others will say these were the opinions of wild radicals.

But such differences ought not to obscure two facts. One is that on matters of economic principles, as opposed to the economic policies built on those principles, the differences among economists are much less than those among laymen at large. And the second is that, on policy issues, the differences among economists are perfectly natural. Each brings his own value judgments to the policy issues. Hopefully, he keeps his principles straight and uses economic know-how to the utmost, but beyond that he comments on policy issues as an individual who weighs one goal against another in his own highly personal scale of values.

QUESTION: *Could these economists at least agree on a capsule description of the mood of the American economy at this time?*

ANSWER: Probably not. Depending on their special vantage points, they see different aspects of the change that is going on around them. Each will know some part of the change in detail; he may underestimate or exaggerate the changes that are taking place elsewhere.

Yet they might agree on this one statement: whatever else is said about the economy today, it is not in a complacent mood. There were times in the past when self-satisfaction might fairly be said to mark the American economists. Not so today. Perhaps no other period has seen so much introspection and re-examination. Old truths are crumbling and new ones already hardening. The changes are not always dramatic, and certainly they are not uniform. They demand that a man step back every once in a while to see just how much has changed around him. The economy of the mid-1960's is sharply different from that of the 1930's, or even the 1950's. And most economists feel that we have seen nothing yet.

This continued striving within the American society is, I suppose, about as clear proof as we've yet had that man's wants really are unlimited. Here you have an economy that is gigantic by any test you might apply. Its power and the fact that it adds to that power at so rapid a rate are reasons enough for some other nations to fear it—and at the same time to envy it. But those who live in that economy don't see themselves as having reached a plateau; they don't think of the climb as being finished at all. And this is *not* because those people say to themselves, "Look how far ahead of the rest of the world we are in our standard of living. Let's see if we can pull even farther ahead." Except for the paranoiac few who live out their lives comparing their country with some other one in strictly black-and-white terms, international comparisons don't play a very big part in the American growth story.

The economy grows still bigger because we feel that there is still so much to be done. Certainly one impression that a man gets as he travels across this country today is of great wealth. But another equally important impression is of unfinished business. Many Americans still don't have very much; whether they have more than people in the world's poorest lands is almost irrelevant because the driving comparison here is not with men ten thousand miles away but with men ten miles away. The first compelling wants may be for just enough food to guard against hunger and enough shelter to guard against nature. But once these needs are met, another set comes right after them: better food and better shelter. And so it goes, without any seeming end, here or elsewhere either. Economies—and economists—thrive on yearnings.

In fairness, one should add here that there is a small group of men in America who think that we have just about licked the technical problem of meeting all material wants and that the biggest problems for the future are built not on scarcity but on abundance. But solid support for this fear is hard to come by; I have yet to encounter more than a handful of men who felt that they yet had enough. Where these critics may be on more substantial ground is when they argue that this economy still has a long way to go in figuring out how to absorb change as humanely and smoothly as possible.

It is probably also true that there is more concern within the United States today than in the past with the uses to which all of our wealth shall be put. Many of the more persistent questions today, the ones that shattered whatever complacency we had, revolve about that issue. Some of the questions loom in the form of issues about the basis for tomorrow's wealth; this is where problems of conservation of natural resources and long-range building of human resources come into focus. Some of the questions concern that balance between public and private wealth of which we spoke earlier; this is the matter of what to produce and of who shall decide. Some of the questions speak to the issue of distributing the current wealth in such a way that all have a chance to share in it, not equally but at least equitably; this is where you hear the talk about trying to protect those who are victims of change itself. And some of the questions involve the use of American wealth to help other peoples in the world achieve whatever it is that they want; this is where the big achievements and the bigger dilemmas of foreign aid come in. These are not new questions, but we've never asked them so urgently and we've never been so unwilling to settle for simple answers. For now we know that, whenever we find what seem to be answers, new problems arise to take the place of the old ones.

This is the sense, then, in which the American economy continues to be on trial. It is a safe bet that we and the rest of the world are going to judge it not by its past successes, however spectacular they may have been, but by its ability to respond to today's issues and tomorrow's, too. And in that sense the story can't have an ending. It goes on as long as we have to run harder and harder just to keep our institutions and ideas relevant to the times.

QUESTION: *A last question then. Do you personally feel that the economy is changing fast enough to meet the new times at home and abroad?*

ANSWER: That one is easy. Yes and no.

Index